hot &

red hot and sizzling dishes

SPICY

hot &

red hot and sizzling dishes

SPICY

contributing editor:
LINDA FRASER

HERMES
HOUSE

This edition published by Hermes House in 2002

© Anness Publishing Limited 1997, 2000

Hermes House is an imprint of Anness Publishing Limited
Hermes House, 88–89 Blackfriars Road, London SE1 8HA

Published in the USA by Hermes House Publishing Inc.
27 West 20th Street, New York, NY 10011

Hermes House is an imprint of Anness Publishing Inc.

Publisher: Joanna Lorenz
Senior Cookery Editor: Linda Fraser
Project Editor: Anne Hildyard
Designer: Siân Keogh

Photography: William Adams-Lingwood, Karl Adamson, Edward Allwright, David Armstrong, Steve Baxter,
James Duncan, Nelson Hargreaves, Amanda Heywood, Janine Hosegood, David Jordan, Patrick McLeavey,
Michael Michaels and Thomas Odulate
Recipes: Kit Chan, Jacqueline Clark, Roz Denny, Rafi Fernandez, Christine France,
Silvana Franco, Sarah Gates, Deh-Ta Hsiung, Shehzad Husain, Elizabeth Ortiz Lambert, Sallie Morris, Hilaire Walden,
Laura Washburn, Pamela Westland, Steven Wheeler and Judy Williams
Food for Photography: Carla Capalbo, Kit Chan, Jacqueline Clark, Joanne Craig, Rosamund Grant,
Carole Handslip, Jane Hartshorn, Wendy Lee, Lucy McKelvie, Annie Nichols, Jane Stevenson,
Steven Wheeler and Elizabeth Wolf-Cohen
Stylists: Hilary Guy, Clare Hunt, Maria Kelly, Patrick McLeavey, Blake Minton, Thomas Odulate and Kirsty Rawlings

Front cover shows Tex-Mex Baked Potatoes with Chilli. For recipe see page 101.
Previously published as *The Ultimate Hot & Spicy Cookbook*

Printed and bound in Singapore

1 3 5 7 9 10 8 6 4 2

CONTENTS

Introduction 6

Spicy Soups 16

Sizzling Starters and Snacks 36

Fiery Fish and Seafood 64

Scorching Meat and Poultry 96

Hot and Vibrant Vegetables and Salads 132

Flame-filled Rice and Noodles 166

Searing-hot Side Dishes, Salsas and Relishes 202

Sweet and Spicy Desserts and Cakes 222

Spiced Drinks 244

Index 254

INTRODUCTION

IF VARIETY is the spice of life, it certainly must be said that spices give life – or at least food – its variety.

In all their idiosyncratic guises, spices lend richness, heat and complexity to literally every food imaginable, and it is impossible to conceive of a cuisine that does not benefit from unique and distinctive spicing. In fact, from the sun-drenched Caribbean to the deserts of the Middle East, the dense jungles of Vietnam and Indonesia, the bustling sidewalk stalls of Thailand, the great plains of Africa, the crowded streets of Mexico, and the spirited southwestern United States, "hot and spicy" defines good eating for millions of people who would not dream of consuming bland, unseasoned food when piquant delights are available at every turn.

Attention-grabbing spices are nothing if not highly particular, well-defined and capable of transforming dishes with a single pinch. For example, what would a searing Indian vindaloo taste like without its delicately balanced curry? Or a Thai Beef Salad without the powerful punch of chillies? Blackened Chicken Breasts without Cajun seasonings? Jerk Chicken without Habanero chilli peppers? Probably like King Lear's meat without salt – in other words: not much. Indeed, for thousands of years, the right spice, or combination of spices, has actually helped define individual cultures by lending a nation's or a people's cuisine a flavour and a style that is unmistakably its own. Within these pages you will find an exhilarating, mind-expanding, and palate-tingling collection of recipes from every corner of the world.

Archaeological evidence shows that the cultivation of chilli peppers thrived among the Aztecs of South America over 2000 years ago. Among Asian cultures, subtle and varied spicing has been prevalent for years. Some gastronomes hold that spicing first became popular in medieval Europe to enhance the keeping qualities and mask the taste and smell of food that had gone rancid in the days before refrigeration. Whatever their original use, spices became one of the most precious and desired commodities on the market – spices such as pepper and cinnamon from lands as far off as Sumatra and Ceylon were traded for land and even used to pay taxes. What is certain is that whatever the origins of spices, we would live – and eat – in a dull world without them. Surely the sensual pleasure of a well-seasoned meal is reason enough to value the spices that make modern dining such an adventure.

With *The Ultimate Hot and Spicy Cookbook* in hand, mouth-searing, tongue-teasing meals will explode from your kitchen, energizing and inspiring all those who share with you the most exciting dishes around.

HOT AND SPICY INGREDIENTS

ALLSPICE
Available whole or ground, allspice are small, dark brown berries similar in size to large peppercorns. They can be used in sweet or savoury dishes and have a flavour of nutmeg, cinnamon and clove, hence the name.

CARDAMOM
These pods are green, black and creamy beige, green being the most common. Whole pods are used in rice and meat dishes to add flavour and should not be eaten. Black seeds are used in desserts.

CHILLIES
Chillies are available from greengrocers and supermarkets. They are grown on a dwarf bush with small dense green leaves, white flowers and red or green finger shaped fruit. In general, the green chilli is less hot and has a rather earthy heat; the red is usually hotter and is often very fiery.

To prepare chillies, remove the cap from the stalk end and slit it from top to bottom with a small knife. Under running water, scoop out the seeds with the knife point. The fire comes from the seeds so leave them if you like food to be fiercely hot. Chillies contain volatile oil that can irritate the skin and

Clockwise from left: fresh turmeric roots before being ground to a fine powder, cut to show their vivid golden colour, creamy coloured fresh galangal roots, showing typical rings on the skin and pink nodules, and a large piece of unpeeled fresh ginger root showing the characteristic silvery brown skin.

From left: fresh, glossy lime leaves, lemon grass and fresh coriander leaves and root.

sting the eyes, so it is best to use rubber gloves when preparing chillies, or wash hands afterwards with soap and water.

There are many different varieties of chillies. The small red and green fresh chillies are known as Thai or bird's eye chillies and are extremely hot. One of the hottest varieties is the fat and fiery Scotch Bonnet or *habanero*. It has a spicy smell and flavour and can be red, green, yellow or brown. There are innumerable types of chillies that are indigenous to Mexico. The most commonly used fresh green chillies are *serrano*, *jalapeño* and *poblano*. These varieties are all very hot.

Dried chillies are very popular and

In the spice chest (top right), from the left: cayenne pepper, fennel seeds and ground turmeric. On the table: fresh red and green chillies. In the large bowl: a selection of ingredients for an Indian vegetarian curry: red chillies, aubergines, okra, bitter gourds, bay leaves, red peppers; and in the small bowl: dried coriander seeds.

there are numerous varieties available. The most commonly used dried chillies are *ancho*, which is full-flavoured and mild; *chipotle*, a very hot variety; *mulato*, which is pungent, and the hot *pasilla*.

CHILLI PRODUCTS

Cayenne pepper is a pungent spicy powder made from a blend of small ripe red chillies.

Chilli powder is made from dried, ground chillies and is often mixed with other spices and herbs.

Chilli flakes are made from dried, crushed chillies and are used in pickles and sauces.

Chilli oil is widely used in Chinese cooking. Dried red chillies are heated with vegetable oil to make this hot, pungent condiment.

Chilli paste is a convenient way of adding fiery heat to sauces.

Hot pepper sauce is made from red chillies and vinegar and is used to sprinkle over many dishes.

CINNAMON

Available as bark or in the ground form, cinnamon has a woody aroma with a fragrant and warm flavour. The powdered form is widely used in the Middle East, especially in Khoresh.

Cinnamon is a versatile spice and is good in lamb dishes as well as in spiced drinks, fruit compotes, chocolate cakes and desserts.

CLOVES

Cloves are used in spice mixtures such as garam masala and in many meat and rice dishes. They can also be used to add spicy flavour to fruit and desserts.

CORIANDER

This spice is used throughout the world. It is available as either whole seeds or ground powder. The ripe seeds have a sweet, spicy aroma with a hint of orange flavour. Coriander can be used in both sweet and savoury dishes and is one of the essential ingredients in curry powder. The flavour of coriander can be accentuated by dry-frying.

The leaves are essential in the cooking of South-East Asia and India and the root is often used in Thai cooking.

CUMIN

Cumin is available as small brown ridged seeds or in the ground form. Both types have a characteristic pungent, warm flavour. Cumin is also often dry-roasted to bring out the flavour. This spice is popular in the Middle East; it is used in spice mixtures such as garam masala and is added to pickles and salads. Cumin is one of the main ingredients of curry powder.

CURRY PASTE

Curry pastes are made by pounding spices with red or green chillies. They are ferociously hot and will keep for about 1 month in the fridge.

FISH SAUCE

Known as *nam pla,* this is a commonly used flavouring in Thai dishes in the same way that soy sauce is used in Chinese cooking. Fish sauce is made from salted anchovies and although not a spice, it contributes a depth of

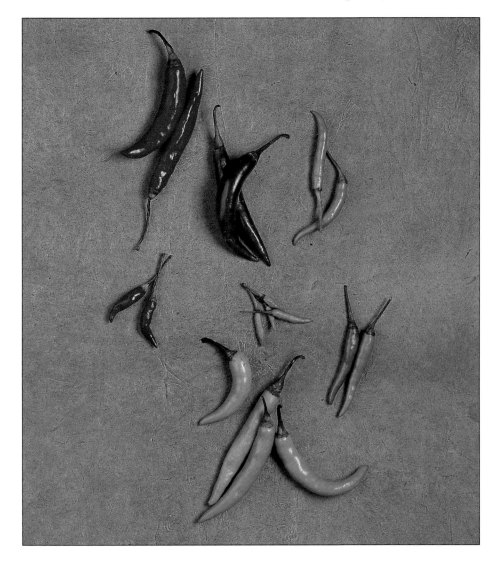

Clockwise from top left: red chillies, mild, glossy green Kenyan chillies, hot green chillies, green chillies, orange Thai chillies, red birdseye chillies and green birdseye chillies.

Clockwise from top left: green jalapeño chillies, large green anaheim chillies, small green chillies, chipotle (smoked dried jalapeño chillies), dried mulato chillies, dried habanero chillies, dried pasilla chillies, green peppers, and (centre top left) yellow and red Scotch Bonnet chillies, (centre right) fresh red chillies.

pungent salty flavour to any dish.

FIVE-SPICE POWDER

This reddish brown powder is a combination of five ground spices – star anise seed, fennel, clove, cinnamon and Szechuan pepper. Used sparingly, it has a wonderful flavour, but it can be dominant if too much is added.

GALANGAL

This is a member of the ginger family and looks rather similar to fresh root ginger. The root is creamy coloured, with a translucent skin that has rings, and may have pink nodules rather like young ginger. It has a refreshing sharp, lemony taste and is best used fresh, although it is available in dried or powder form. If you cannot find fresh galangal, use about 5ml/1tsp of the dried powder to replace each 2.5cm/1in fresh galangal.

To prepare, cut a piece of the required size. Trim off any knobbly bits, then peel carefully, as the tough skin has an unpleasant taste. Slice to use in a paste and use up as soon as possible after peeling, to prevent loss of flavour. The flesh is much more woody and fibrous than ginger and has a distinctive, pine-like smell. Store galangal wrapped, in the salad drawer of the fridge.

GARAM MASALA

This spice mixture is made from a variety of spices and can be a simple blend, consisting of two or three spices

Overleaf: Hot and Spicy ingredients from left to right, from top row:

Whole cloves, dried ground ginger, fresh root ginger and green cardamoms.

Tamarind pulp, whole cumin seeds, garam masala, saffron, garlic, bay leaves and fresh coriander.

Whole black mustard seeds, ground cumin, whole nutmeg, black peppercorns, fennel seeds, whole cinnamon sticks and paprika.

Curry leaves, ground turmeric, fresh mint leaves, fenugreek seeds and ground coriander.

Curry powder, sesame seeds, chilli powder, dried red chillies and coriander seeds.

Opposite page: A selection of spices, left to right from top row: paprika, whole green cardamoms, cumin seeds, saffron strands, ground turmeric, whole nutmeg and mace, ground sumac, cinnamon sticks and ground nutmeg.

and herbs, or a more complex masala, made from twelve or more different spices. The dry spices and seeds are often dry-roasted first and sometimes whole spices are used. Garam masala may be added to the dish at different cooking stages.

GINGER
A root of Chinese and Indian origin with a silvery brown skin, ginger is best used fresh, and should be peeled and chopped or crushed before cooking. It is available in supermarkets – look for shiny smooth fat roots. Store in the salad drawer of the fridge, wrapped in kitchen paper. Ginger is a good alternative to galangal in Thai cooking.

LEMON GRASS
This tropical grass has a fresh, highly aromatic lemony taste and is a vital ingredient in South-East Asian cooking. It combines well with garlic and chillies and is pounded to a paste then added to curries. Unless it is finely chopped, lemon grass is usually removed before serving as it has a very fibrous texture.

LIME LEAVES
These glossy, dark green leaves come from the kaffir lime tree. They have a pleasing, distinctive smell and can be torn or left whole. Lime leaves can be frozen and used straight from the freezer in curries and sauces.

NUTMEG
Whole nutmegs are the hard aromatic seeds of an evergreen tree. The spice, which has a sweet, nutty flavour, is widely used all over the world. Whole nutmegs can be grated for cooking, but the ground spice is often used, particularly in the Middle East. Nutmeg can be used in both savoury and sweet dishes.

PAPRIKA
This is made from a mixture of ground dried red peppers. Both mild and hot peppers are used, but paprika is always milder than cayenne pepper. It is widely used in the Middle East in soups, meat dishes, salad dressings and as a garnish.

PEPPERCORNS
White, green and black peppercorns are berries from the same plant, picked at different stages of maturity, and are used whole and ground. Pepper has a pungent flavour and can be used in either savoury or sweet dishes. Peppercorns can be used whole, crushed or ground.

Szechuan pepper is also known as anise pepper. The berries are red-brown in colour and are prickly. They are spicy with a rather numbing taste.

SAFFRON
Made from the dried stamens of a type of crocus, saffron has a superb aroma and flavour. It also adds a delicate yellow colour to food. For the best results it should be ground to a powder and diluted in a small amount of boiling water.

TAMARIND
An acidic-tasting tropical fruit that resembles a bean pod. It is added to curries to give a sharp flavour. Tamarind is usually sold dried or pulped. To make tamarind juice, soak a piece of tamarind pulp in warm water for about 10 minutes. Squeeze out as much tamarind juice as possible by pressing all the liquid through a sieve.

TURMERIC
Turmeric is another member of the ginger family. When the whole spice is peeled or scraped, a rich golden root is revealed. Turmeric adds a distinctive flavour and rich yellow colour to meat and rice dishes. It is widely used throughout the Middle East and India. Because of its strong, bitter flavour, turmeric should be used sparingly.

ZERESHK
This is a small sour berry that comes from Iran. It is traditionally served with Persian rice dishes.

SPICY SOUPS

Soups are always satisfying and warming, and these soups certainly fill the bill. Drawn from Thailand, Africa, India and the Middle East, where chillies and spices are everyday foods, the recipes are a rich mixture of flavourful ingredients, enlivened by the addition of hot pickles, peppers and chillies, as well as aromatic spices. Hot and Spicy Seafood Soup and Mulligatawny Soup are sure to stimulate the appetite.

Tortilla Soup

INGREDIENTS

Serves 4–6

15ml/1 tbsp vegetable oil
1 onion, chopped
1 large garlic clove, minced
2 tomatoes, peeled, seeded
  and chopped
2.5ml/½ tsp salt
2.4 litres/4 pints/10 cups chicken stock
1 carrot, diced
1 small courgette, diced
1 skinless boneless chicken breast,
  cooked and shredded
6 canned green chillies, chopped

To garnish

4 corn tortillas
oil, for frying
1 small ripe avocado
2 spring onions, chopped
chopped fresh coriander

1 Heat the oil in a saucepan. Add the onion and garlic and cook over a medium heat for 5–8 minutes, until just softened. Add the tomatoes and salt and cook for another 5 minutes.

2 Stir in the chicken stock. Bring the liquid to the boil, covered, then lower the heat and simmer for about 15 minutes.

3 Meanwhile, for the garnish, trim the tortillas into squares, then cut them into strips.

4 Put a 1cm/½in layer of oil in a frying pan and heat until hot but not smoking. Add the tortilla strips, in batches, and fry until just beginning to brown, turning occasionally. Remove with a slotted spoon and drain on kitchen paper.

5 Add the carrot to the soup. Cook, covered, for 10 minutes. Add the courgette, chicken and chillies and continue cooking, uncovered, for about 5 minutes, until the vegetables are just tender.

6 Meanwhile, peel and stone the avocado. Chop into fine dice.

7 Divide the tortilla strips among four soup bowls and sprinkle each one with the avocado. Ladle in the soup, then scatter the onions and coriander on top. Serve immediately.

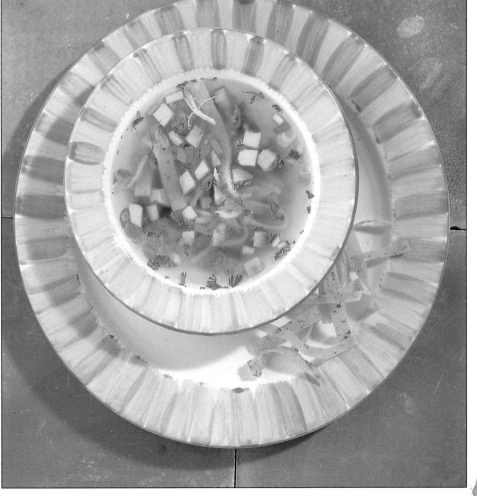

Tamarind Soup with Peanuts and Vegetables

Sayur Asam is a colourful and refreshing soup from Jakarta with more than a hint of sharpness.

INGREDIENTS

Serves 4 or 8 as part of a buffet
For the spice paste
5 shallots or 1 medium red
    onion, sliced
3 garlic cloves, crushed
2.5cm/1in *lengkuas*, peeled and sliced
1–2 fresh red chillies, seeded and sliced
25g/1oz raw peanuts
1cm/½in cube *terasi*, prepared
1.2 litres/2 pints/5 cups well-
    flavoured stock
50–75g/2–3oz salted peanuts,
    lightly crushed
15–30ml/1–2 tbsp dark brown sugar
5ml/1 tsp tamarind pulp, soaked in
    75ml/5 tbsp warm water for
    15 minutes
salt

For the vegetables
1 chayote, thinly peeled, seeds
    removed, flesh finely sliced
115g/4oz French beans, trimmed and
    finely sliced
50g/2oz sweetcorn kernels (optional)
handful green leaves, such as
    watercress, rocket or Chinese leaves,
    finely shredded
1 fresh green chilli, sliced, to garnish

1 Prepare the spice paste by grinding the shallots or onion, garlic, *lengkuas*, chillies, raw peanuts and *terasi* to a paste in a food processor or with a pestle and mortar.

2 Pour in some of the stock to moisten and then pour this mixture into a pan or wok, adding the rest of the stock. Cook for 15 minutes with the lightly crushed peanuts and sugar.

3 Strain the tamarind, discarding the seeds, and reserve the juice.

4 About 5 minutes before serving, add the chayote slices, beans and sweetcorn, if using, to the soup and cook fairly rapidly. At the last minute, add the green leaves and salt to taste.

5 Add the tamarind juice and taste for seasoning. Serve, garnished with slices of green chilli.

Pumpkin and Chilli Soup

INGREDIENTS

Serves 4–6

2 garlic cloves, crushed
4 shallots, finely chopped
2.5ml/½ tsp shrimp paste
15ml/1 tbsp dried shrimps soaked for
  10 minutes and drained
1 stalk lemon grass, chopped
2 green chillies, seeded
salt, to taste
600ml/1 pint/2½ cups chicken stock
450g/1lb pumpkin, cut into 2cm/¾in
  thick chunks
600ml/1 pint/2½ cups coconut cream
30ml/2 tbsp fish sauce
5ml/1 tsp granulated sugar
115g/4oz small cooked shelled prawns
freshly ground black pepper
2 red chillies, seeded and finely sliced,
  to garnish
10–12 basil leaves, to garnish

1 Grind the garlic, shallots, shrimp paste, dried shrimps, lemon grass, green chillies and salt into a paste.

2 In a large saucepan, bring the chicken stock to the boil, add the ground paste and stir to dissolve.

3 Add the pumpkin and simmer for about 10–15 minutes or until the pumpkin is tender.

4 Stir in the coconut cream, then bring back to a simmer. Add the fish sauce, sugar and ground black pepper to taste

5 Add the prawns and cook until they are heated through. Serve garnished with the sliced red chillies and basil leaves.

COOK'S TIP

Shrimp paste, which is made from ground shrimps fermented in brine, is used to give food a savoury flavour.

Spicy Vegetable Soup

INGREDIENTS

Serves 4

½ red onion
175g/6oz each, turnip, sweet potato
  and pumpkin
30ml/2 tbsp butter or margarine
5ml/1 tsp dried marjoram
2.5ml/½ tsp ground ginger
1.5ml/¼ tsp ground cinnamon
15ml/1 tbsp chopped spring onion
1 litre/1¾ pint/4 cups well-flavoured
  vegetable stock
30ml/2 tbsp flaked almonds
1 fresh chilli, seeded and chopped
5ml/1 tsp sugar
25g/1oz creamed coconut
salt and freshly ground black pepper
chopped coriander, to garnish

1 Finely chop the onion, then peel the turnip, sweet potato and pumpkin and chop into medium-size dice.

2 Melt the butter or margarine in a large non-stick saucepan. Fry the onion for 4–5 minutes. Add the diced vegetables and fry for 3–4 minutes.

3 Add the marjoram, ginger, cinnamon, spring onion, salt and pepper. Fry over a low heat for about 10 minutes, stirring frequently.

4 Add the vegetable stock, flaked almonds, chopped chilli and sugar and stir well to mix, then cover and simmer gently for 10–15 minutes until the vegetables are just tender.

5 Grate the creamed coconut into the soup and stir to mix. Sprinkle with chopped coriander, if liked, spoon into warmed bowls and serve.

Plantain Soup with Corn and Chilli

INGREDIENTS

Serves 4

25g/1oz/2 tbsp butter or margarine
1 onion, finely chopped
1 garlic clove, crushed
275g/10oz yellow plantains, peeled
and sliced
1 large tomato, peeled and chopped
175g/6oz/1 cup sweetcorn
5ml/1 tsp dried tarragon, crushed
900ml/1½ pints/3¾ cups vegetable or
chicken stock
1 green chilli, seeded and chopped
pinch of grated nutmeg
salt and freshly ground black pepper

1 Melt the butter or margarine in a
saucepan over a moderate heat, add
the onion and garlic and fry for a few
minutes until the onion is soft.

2 Add the plantain, tomato and
sweetcorn and cook for 5 minutes.

3 Add the tarragon, vegetable stock,
chilli and salt and pepper and
simmer for 10 minutes or until the
plantain is tender. Stir in the nutmeg
and serve at once.

Spicy Groundnut Soup

This soup is widely eaten in
Africa. Groundnuts (or peanuts)
are spiced with a mixture of fresh
ginger and chilli powder with
herbs added for extra flavour.
The amount of chilli powder can
be varied according to taste, add
more for a fiery hot soup.

INGREDIENTS

Serves 4

45ml/3 tbsp pure groundnut paste
or peanut butter
1.5 litres/2½ pints/6¼ cups stock
or water
30ml/2 tbsp tomato purée
1 onion, chopped
2 slices fresh root ginger
1.5ml/¼ tsp dried thyme
1 bay leaf
salt and chilli powder
225g/8oz white yam, diced
10 small okras, trimmed (optional)

1 Place the groundnut paste or
peanut butter in a bowl, add
300ml/½ pint/1¼ cups of the stock or
water and the tomato purée and blend
together to make a smooth paste.

2 Spoon the nut mixture into a
saucepan and add the onion,
ginger, thyme, bay leaf, salt, chilli and
the remaining stock.

3 Heat gently until simmering, then
cook for 1 hour, stirring from time to
time to prevent the nut mixture sticking.

4 Add the white yam, cook for a
further 10 minutes, and then add
the okra, if using, and simmer until
both are tender. Serve at once.

Beef and Turmeric Soup

The addition of turmeric and saffron colours this satisfying soup a deep, vibrant yellow. It is a popular dish in Iran.

INGREDIENTS

Serves 6
2 large onions
30ml/2 tbsp oil
15ml/1 tbsp ground turmeric
100g/3½ oz/½ cup yellow split peas
1.2 litres/2 pints/5 cups water
225g/8oz minced beef
200g/7oz/1 cup rice
45ml/3 tbsp each fresh chopped
   parsley, coriander and chives
15g/½ oz/1 tbsp butter
1 large garlic clove, finely chopped
60ml/4 tbsp chopped mint
2–3 saffron strands dissolved in
   15ml/1 tbsp boiling water (optional)
salt and freshly ground black pepper
yogurt and naan bread, to serve

1 Chop one of the onions then heat the oil in a large saucepan and fry the onion until golden brown. Add the turmeric, split peas and water, bring to the boil, then reduce the heat and simmer for 20 minutes.

2 Grate the other onion into a bowl, add the minced beef and seasoning and mix well. Using your hands, form the mixture into small balls, about the size of walnuts. Carefully add to the pan and simmer for 10 minutes.

— COOK'S TIP —

Fresh spinach is also delicious in this soup. Add 50g/2oz finely chopped spinach leaves to the soup with the parsley, coriander and chives.

3 Add the rice, then stir in the parsley, coriander, and chives and simmer for about 30 minutes, until the rice is tender, stirring frequently.

4 Melt the butter in a small pan and gently fry the garlic. Add the mint, stir briefly and sprinkle over the soup with the saffron, if using.

5 Spoon the soup into warmed serving dishes and serve with yogurt and naan bread.

Mulligatawny Soup

Mulligatawny (which means "pepper water") was introduced into England in the late eighteenth century by members of the army and colonial service returning home from India.

INGREDIENTS

Serves 4

50g/2oz/4 tbsp butter or
   60ml/4 tbsp oil
2 large chicken joints, about
   350g/12oz each
1 onion, chopped
1 carrot, chopped
1 small turnip, chopped
about 15ml/1 tbsp curry powder,
   to taste
4 cloves
6 black peppercorns, lightly crushed
50g/2oz/¼ cup lentils
900ml/1½ pints/3¾ cups
   chicken stock
40g/1½oz/¼ cup sultanas
salt and ground black pepper

1 Melt the butter or heat the oil in a large saucepan, then brown the chicken over a brisk heat. Transfer the chicken to a plate.

2 Add the chopped onion, carrot and turnip to the saucepan and cook, stirring occasionally, until they are lightly coloured. Stir in the curry powder, cloves and black peppercorns and cook for 1–2 minutes more before adding the lentils.

3 Pour the stock into the pan, bring to the boil, then add the sultanas and chicken and any juices from the plate. Cover and simmer gently for about 1¼ hours.

4 Remove the chicken from the pan and discard the skin and bones. Chop the flesh, return to the soup and reheat. Check the seasoning before serving the soup piping hot.

COOK'S TIP

Choose red split lentils for the best colour, although either green or brown lentils could also be used.

Spicy Yogurt Soup

INGREDIENTS

Serves 4–6

450ml/³/₄ pint/1¹/₂ cups natural
    yogurt, beaten
60ml/4 tbsp gram flour
2.5ml/¹/₂ tsp chilli powder
2.5ml/¹/₂ tsp turmeric
salt, to taste
2–3 green chillies, finely chopped
60ml/4 tbsp vegetable oil
4 whole dried red chillies
5ml/1 tsp cumin seeds
3–4 curry leaves
3 garlic cloves, crushed
5cm/2in piece of fresh root
    ginger, crushed
fresh coriander leaves, chopped,
    to garnish

1 Mix together the yogurt, gram flour, chilli powder, turmeric and salt and strain them into a saucepan. Add the green chillies and cook gently for about 10 minutes, stirring occasionally. Be careful not to let the soup boil over.

2 Heat the oil in a frying pan and fry the remaining spices, crushed garlic and fresh ginger until the dried chillies turn black.

3 Pour the oil and the spices over the yogurt soup, cover the pan and leave to rest for 5 minutes off the heat. Mix well and gently reheat for a further 5 minutes. Serve hot, garnished with the coriander leaves.

--- VARIATION ---

Sugar can be added to this soup to bring out the full flavour. For an extra creamy soup, use Greek-style yogurt instead of natural yogurt. Adjust the amount of chillies according to how hot you want the soup to be.

Hot and Spicy Seafood Soup

For a special occasion serve creamy rice noodles in a spicy coconut-flavoured soup, topped with seafood. There is a fair amount of work involved in the preparation but you can make the soup base ahead.

INGREDIENTS

Serves 4

4 red chillies, seeded and
   roughly chopped
1 onion, roughly chopped
1 piece *blacan*, the size of a stock cube
1 lemon grass stalk, chopped
1 small piece fresh root ginger,
   roughly chopped
6 macadamia nuts or almonds
60ml/4 tbsp vegetable oil
5ml/1 tsp paprika
5ml/1 tsp ground turmeric
475ml/16fl oz/2 cups stock or water
600ml/1 pint/2½ cups coconut milk
fish sauce (see method)
12 king prawns, peeled and deveined
8 scallops
225g/8oz prepared squid, cut
   into rings
350g/12oz rice vermicelli or rice
   noodles, soaked in warm water
   until soft
salt and freshly ground black pepper
lime halves, to serve

For the garnish

¼ cucumber, cut into matchsticks
2 red chillies, seeded and finely sliced
30ml/2 tbsp mint leaves
30ml/2 tbsp fried shallots or onions

1 In a blender or food processor, process the chillies, onion, *blacan*, lemon grass, ginger and nuts until smooth in texture.

COOK'S TIP

Blacan is dried shrimp or prawn paste. It is sold in small blocks and you will find it in oriental supermarkets.

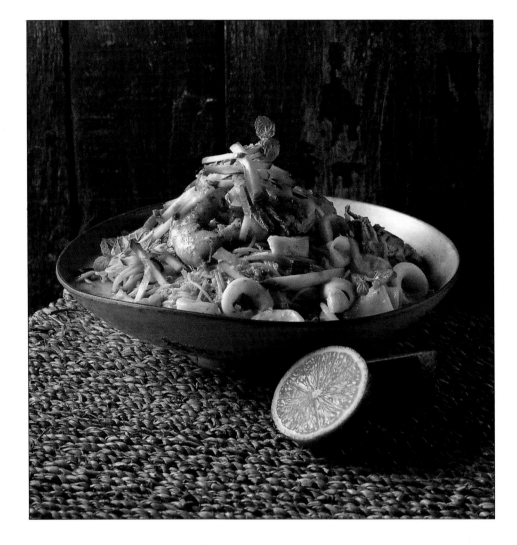

2 Heat 45ml/3 tbsp of the oil in a large saucepan. Add the chilli paste and fry for 6 minutes. Stir in the paprika and turmeric and fry for about 2 minutes more.

3 Add the stock or water and the coconut milk to the pan. Bring to the boil, reduce the heat and simmer gently for 15–20 minutes. Season to taste with fish sauce.

4 Season the seafood with salt and pepper. Heat the remaining oil in a frying pan, add the seafood and fry quickly for 2–3 minutes until cooked.

5 Add the noodles to the soup and heat through. Divide among individual serving bowls. Place the fried seafood on top, then garnish with the cucumber, chillies, mint and fried shallots or onions. Serve with the limes.

Ginger, Chicken and Coconut Soup

This aromatic soup is rich with coconut milk and intensely flavoured with galangal, lemon grass and kaffir lime leaves.

INGREDIENTS

Serves 4–6
750ml/1¼ pints/3 cups coconut milk
475ml/16fl oz/2 cups chicken stock
4 stalks lemon grass, bruised
  and chopped
2.5cm/1in piece galangal, thinly sliced
10 black peppercorns, crushed
10 kaffir lime leaves, torn
300g/11oz boneless chicken, cut
  into thin strips
115g/4oz button mushrooms
50g/2oz baby sweetcorn
60ml/4 tbsp lime juice
45ml/3 tbsp fish sauce
2 red chillies, chopped, to garnish
chopped spring onions, to garnish
coriander leaves, to garnish

1 Bring the coconut milk and chicken stock to the boil. Add the lemon grass, galangal, peppercorns and half the kaffir lime leaves, reduce the heat and simmer gently for 10 minutes.

2 Strain the stock into a clean pan. Return to the heat, then add the chicken, button mushrooms and baby sweetcorn. Cook for about 5–7 minutes or until the chicken is cooked.

3 Stir in the lime juice, fish sauce to taste and the rest of the lime leaves. Serve hot, garnished with red chillies, spring onions and coriander.

Hot and Sour Prawn Soup with Lemon Grass

This is a classic Thai seafood soup – *Tom Yam Goong* – and is probably the most popular and well known soup from Thailand.

INGREDIENTS

Serves 4–6
450g/1lb king prawns
1 litre/1¾ pints/4 cups chicken stock
  or water
3 stalks lemon grass
10 kaffir lime leaves, torn in half
225g/8oz can straw mushrooms,
  drained
45ml/3 tbsp fish sauce
50ml/2fl oz/¼ cup lime juice
30ml/2 tbsp chopped spring onion
15ml/1 tbsp coriander leaves
4 red chillies, seeded and chopped
2 spring onions, finely chopped

1 Shell and devein the prawns and set aside. Rinse the prawn shells and place in a large saucepan with the stock or water and bring to the boil.

2 Bruise the lemon grass stalks with the blunt edge of a chopping knife and add them to the stock together with half of the lime leaves. Simmer gently for 5–6 minutes, until the stalks change colour and the stock is fragrant.

3 Strain the stock and return to the saucepan and reheat. Add the mushrooms and prawns, then cook until the prawns turn pink.

4 Stir in the fish sauce, lime juice, spring onions, coriander, red chillies and the rest of the lime leaves. Taste and adjust the seasoning. It should be sour, salty, spicy and hot.

Spiced Lamb Soup

INGREDIENTS

Serves 4

115g/4oz split black-eyed beans,
  soaked for 1–2 hours, or overnight
675g/1½lb neck of lamb, cut into
  medium-size chunks
5ml/1 tsp chopped fresh thyme, or
  2.5ml/½ tsp dried
2 bay leaves
1.2 litres/2 pints/5 cups stock or water
1 onion, sliced
225g/8oz pumpkin, diced
2 black cardamom pods
7.5ml/1½ tsp ground turmeric
15ml/1 tbsp chopped fresh coriander
2.5ml/½ tsp caraway seeds
1 fresh green chilli, seeded and chopped
2 green bananas
1 carrot
salt and freshly ground black pepper

1 Drain the black-eyed beans, place them in a saucepan and cover with fresh cold water.

2 Bring the beans to the boil, boil rapidly for 10 minutes and then reduce the heat and simmer, covered for 40–50 minutes until tender, adding more water if necessary. Remove from the heat and set aside to cool.

3 Meanwhile, put the lamb in a large saucepan, add the thyme, bay leaves and stock or water and bring to the boil. Cover and simmer over a moderate heat for 1 hour, until tender.

4 Add the onion, pumpkin, cardamoms, turmeric, coriander, caraway, chilli and seasoning and stir. Bring back to a simmer and then cook, uncovered, for 15 minutes until the pumpkin is tender, stirring occasionally.

5 When the beans are cool, spoon into a blender or food processor with their liquid and blend to a smooth purée.

6 Cut the bananas into medium slices and the carrot into thin slices. Stir into the soup with the beans and cook for 10–12 minutes, until the vegetables are tender. Adjust seasoning and serve.

Spicy Pepper Soup

This is a highly soothing broth for winter evenings, also known as Mulla-ga-tani. Serve with the whole spices, or strain and reheat if you so wish. The lemon juice may be adjusted to taste, but this dish should be distinctly sour.

INGREDIENTS

Serves 4–6

30ml/2 tbsp vegetable oil
2.5ml/½ tsp freshly ground
 black pepper
5ml/1 tsp cumin seeds
2.5ml/½ tsp mustard seeds
1.5ml/¼ tsp asafoetida
2 whole dried red chillies
4–6 curry leaves
2.5ml/½ tsp turmeric
2 garlic cloves, crushed
300ml/½ pint/1¼ cups tomato juice
juice of 2 lemons
120ml/4fl oz/½ cup water
salt, to taste
coriander leaves, chopped, to garnish

VARIATION

If you prefer, use lime juice instead of lemon juice. Add 5ml/1 tsp tamarind paste for extra sourness.

1 In a large saucepan, heat the oil and fry the pepper, cumin and mustard seeds, asafoetida, red chillies, curry leaves, turmeric and garlic until the chillies are nearly black and the garlic is golden brown.

2 Lower the heat and add the tomato juice, lemon juice, water and salt. Bring the soup to the boil, then simmer gently for about 10 minutes. Pour the soup into bowls, garnish with the chopped coriander and serve.

Noodle Soup with Pork and Szechuan Pickle

INGREDIENTS

Serves 4

1 litre/1³/₄ pints/4 cups chicken stock
350g/12oz egg noodles
15ml/1 tbsp dried shrimps, soaked
　in water
30ml/2 tbsp vegetable oil
225g/8oz lean pork,
　finely shredded
15ml/1 tbsp yellow bean paste
15ml/1 tbsp soy sauce
115g/4oz Szechuan hot pickle, rinsed,
　drained and shredded
pinch of sugar
salt and freshly ground black pepper
2 spring onions, finely sliced,
　to garnish

1 Bring the stock to the boil in a large saucepan. Add the noodles and cook until almost tender. Drain the dried shrimps, rinse them under cold water, drain again and add to the stock. Lower the heat and simmer for a further 2 minutes. Keep hot. Heat the oil in a frying pan or wok. Add the pork and stir-fry over a high heat for about 3 minutes.

2 Add the bean paste and soy sauce to the pork; stir-fry for 1 minute more. Add the hot pickle with a pinch of sugar. Stir-fry for 1 minute more.

3 Divide the noodles and soup among individual serving bowls. Spoon the pork mixture on top, then sprinkle with the spring onions and serve at once.

Snapper, Tomato and Tamarind Noodle Soup

Tamarind gives this light, fragrant noodle soup a slightly sour taste.

INGREDIENTS

Serves 4

2 litres/3¹/₂ pints/8 cups water
1kg/2¹/₄lb red snapper (or other red
　fish such as mullet)
1 onion, sliced
50g/2oz tamarind pods
15ml/1 tbsp fish sauce
15ml/1 tbsp sugar
30ml/2 tbsp vegetable oil
2 garlic cloves, finely chopped
2 lemon grass stalks, very
　finely chopped
4 ripe tomatoes, roughly chopped
30ml/2 tbsp yellow bean paste
225g/8oz rice vermicelli, soaked in
　warm water until soft
115g/4oz beansprouts
8–10 basil or mint sprigs
25g/1oz roasted peanuts, ground
salt and freshly ground black pepper

1 Bring the water to the boil in a saucepan. Lower the heat and add the fish and onion, with 2.5ml/¹/₂ tsp salt. Simmer gently until the fish is cooked through.

2 Remove the fish from the stock; set aside. Add the tamarind, fish sauce and sugar to the stock. Cook for 5 minutes, then strain the stock into a large jug or bowl. Carefully remove all of the bones from the fish, keeping the flesh in big pieces.

3 Heat the oil in a large frying pan. Add the garlic and lemon grass and fry for a few seconds. Stir in the tomatoes and bean paste. Cook gently for 5–7 minutes, until the tomatoes are soft. Add the stock, bring back to a simmer and adjust the seasoning.

4 Drain the vermicelli. Plunge it into a saucepan of boiling water for a few minutes, drain and divide among individual serving bowls. Add the beansprouts, fish, basil or mint, and sprinkle the ground peanuts on top. Top up each bowl with the hot soup.

Chicken Mulligatawny

INGREDIENTS

Serves 4–6

900g/2lb chicken, boned and skinned
600ml/1 pint/2½ cups water
6 green cardamom pods
5cm/2in piece of cinnamon stick
4–6 curry leaves
15ml/1 tbsp ground coriander
5ml/1 tsp ground cumin
2.5ml/½ tsp turmeric
3 garlic cloves, crushed
12 whole peppercorns
4 cloves
1 onion, finely chopped
115g/4oz coconut cream
salt, to taste
juice of 2 lemons
deep-fried onions, to garnish
coriander leaves, chopped, to garnish

1 Cut the chicken into pieces, then place it in a large saucepan with the water and cook until the chicken is tender. Skim the surface, then strain, reserving the stock and keeping the chicken pieces warm.

2 Return the chicken stock to the saucepan and reheat. Add the cardamom pods, cinnamon stick, curry leaves, coriander, cumin, turmeric, garlic, peppercorns, cloves, chopped onion, coconut cream, salt and lemon juice to the saucepan. Simmer for 10–15 minutes, then strain to remove the whole spices and return the chicken to the soup. Reheat the soup, garnish with deep-fried onions and chopped coriander and serve.

COOK'S TIP

For a fast version of this soup, use ready-cooked chicken. Remove any skin and bone and chop into cubes. Add to the soup just before serving, then reheat.

Curried Noodle and Chicken Soup

Hot red curry paste, coconut milk, lime and red chillies are used to flavour this deliciously hot and spicy chicken soup, which originated in Burma.

INGREDIENTS

Serves 4–6

600ml/1 pint/2½ cups coconut milk
30ml/2 tbsp red curry paste
5ml/1 tsp ground turmeric
450g/1lb chicken thighs, boned and
    cut into bite-size chunks
600ml/1 pint/2½ cups chicken stock
60ml/4 tbsp fish sauce
15ml/1 tbsp dark soy sauce
salt and freshly ground black pepper
juice of ½–1 lime
450g/1lb fresh egg noodles, blanched
    briefly in boiling water

For the garnish

3 spring onions, chopped
4 red chillies, chopped
4 shallots, chopped
60ml/4 tbsp sliced pickled mustard
    leaves, rinsed
30ml/2 tbsp fried sliced garlic
coriander leaves
4 fried noodle nests (optional)

1 In a large saucepan, add about one third of the coconut milk and bring to the boil, stirring often with a wooden spoon until it separates.

2 Add the curry paste and ground turmeric, stir to mix completely and cook until fragrant.

3 Add the chicken and stir-fry for about 2 minutes, ensuring that all the chunks are coated with the paste.

4 Add the remaining coconut milk, chicken stock, fish sauce and soy sauce. Season with salt and freshly ground black pepper to taste. Simmer gently for 7–10 minutes. Remove from the heat and stir in the lime juice.

5 Reheat the noodles in boiling water, drain and divide between individual bowls. Divide the chicken between the bowls and ladle in the hot soup. Top each serving with a few of each of the garnishes.

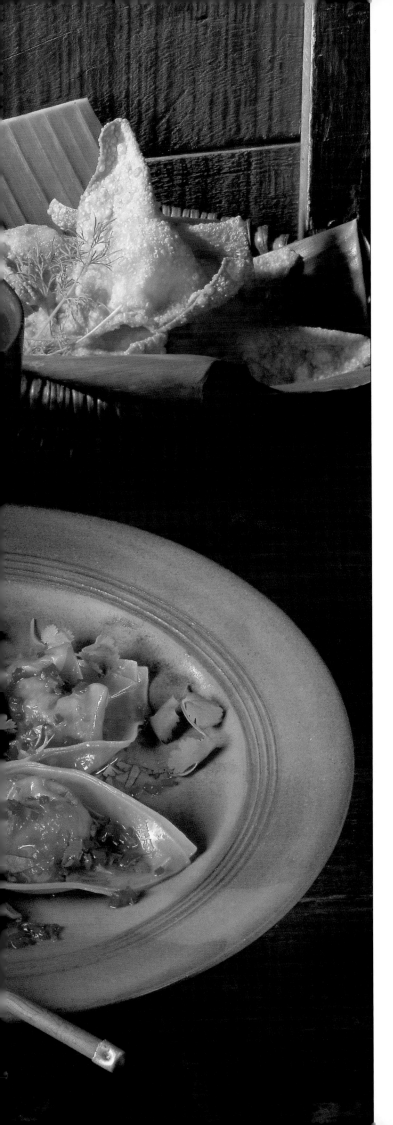

SIZZLING STARTERS AND SNACKS

*Starters and snacks offer lots of highly spiced,
mouth-watering morsels and searingly hot bites.
Spicy Kebabs set the taste buds tingling, while
Samosas and Seafood Wontons with Spicy
Dressing are perfect to hand round at a drinks
party for a quick spicy appetizer. Start off a meal
in lively style with Chillied Monkfish Parcels.*

Butterflied Prawns in Chilli Chocolate

Although the combination of hot and sweet flavours may seem odd, this is a delicious starter. The use of bitter chocolate adds richness without increasing the sweetness.

INGREDIENTS

Serves 4

8 large raw prawns, in the shell
15ml/1 tbsp seasoned flour
15ml/1 tbsp dry sherry
juice of 4 clementines or 1 large orange
15g/½oz unsweetened dark
   chocolate, chopped
30ml/2 tbsp olive oil
2 garlic cloves, finely chopped
2.5cm/1in piece fresh root ginger,
   finely chopped
1 small red chilli, seeded and chopped
salt and freshly ground black pepper

1 Peel the prawns, leaving just the tail sections intact. Make a shallow cut down the back of each prawn and carefully pull out and discard the dark intestinal tract. Turn over the prawns so that the undersides are uppermost, then carefully split them open from tail to top, using a small sharp knife, cutting almost, but not quite, through to the back.

2 Press the prawns down firmly to flatten them out. Coat with the seasoned flour and set aside.

3 Gently heat the sherry and clementine or orange juice in a small saucepan. When warm, remove from the heat and stir in the chopped chocolate until melted.

4 Heat the olive oil in a frying pan. Fry the garlic, ginger and chilli over a moderate heat for 2 minutes until golden. Remove with a slotted spoon and reserve. Add the prawns, cut-side down, to the pan; cook for 2 – 3 minutes until golden brown with pink edges. Turn and cook for a further 2 minutes.

5 Return the garlic mixture to the pan and pour over the chocolate sauce. Cook for 1 minute, turning the prawns to coat them in the glossy sauce. Season to taste and serve hot.

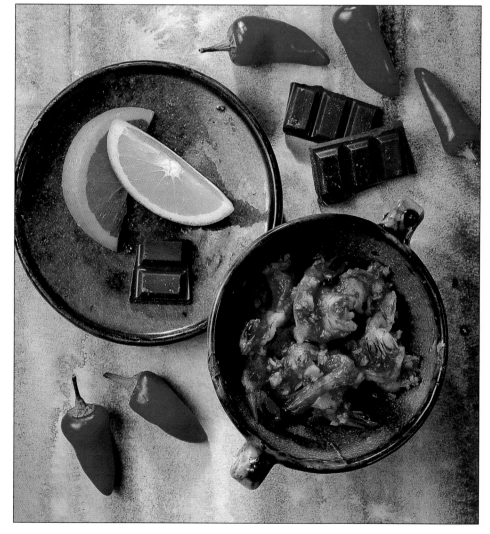

Spicy Potatoes

Spicy potatoes, *patatas picantes*, are among the most popular tapas dishes in Spain, where they are sometimes described as *patatas bravas* (wild potatoes). There are many variations of this classic: boiled new potatoes or large wedges of fried potato may be used, but they are perhaps best simply roasted as in this recipe.

INGREDIENTS

Serves 2 – 4
225g/8oz small new potatoes
15ml/1 tbsp olive oil
5ml/1 tsp paprika
5ml/1 tsp chilli powder
2.5ml/½ tsp ground cumin
2.5ml/½ tsp salt
flat leaf parsley, to garnish

1 Preheat the oven to 200°C/400°F/ Gas 6. Prick the skin of each potato in several places with a fork, then place them in a bowl.

2 Add the olive oil, paprika, chilli, cumin and salt and toss well.

3 Transfer the potatoes to a roasting tin and bake for 40 minutes.

—————— COOK'S TIP ——————

This dish is delicious served with tomato sauce or Fiery Salsa – provide small forks for dipping.

4 During cooking, remove the potatoes from the oven and turn occasionally, until tender. Serve hot, garnished with flat leaf parsley.

Falafel

These tasty deep fried patties are one of the national dishes of Egypt. They make an excellent starter or else can be served as a buffet dish.

INGREDIENTS

Serves 6
450g/1lb/2½ cups dried white beans
2 red onions, chopped
2 large garlic cloves, crushed
45ml/3 tbsp finely chopped fresh
   parsley
5ml/1 tsp ground coriander
5ml/1 tsp ground cumin
7.5ml/1½ tsp baking powder
oil, for deep frying
salt and freshly ground black pepper
tomato salad, to serve

1 Soak the white beans overnight in water. Remove the skins and process in a blender or food processor. Add the chopped onions, garlic, parsley, coriander, cumin, baking powder and seasoning and blend again to make a very smooth paste. Allow the mixture to stand at room temperature for at least 30 minutes.

2 Take walnut-sized pieces of mixture and flatten into small patties. Set aside again for about 15 minutes.

3 Heat the oil until it's very hot and then fry the patties in batches until golden brown. Drain on kitchen paper and then serve with a tomato salad.

Hummus

This popular Middle Eastern dip is widely available in supermarkets, but nothing compares with the delicious home-made variety.

INGREDIENTS

Serves 4–6
175g/6oz/1 cup cooked chick-peas
120ml/4fl oz/½ cup tahini paste
3 garlic cloves
juice of 2 lemons
45–60ml/3–4 tbsp water
salt and freshly ground black pepper
fresh radishes, to serve

For the garnish
15ml/1 tbsp olive oil
15ml/1 tbsp finely chopped fresh
   parsley
2.5ml/½ tsp cayenne pepper
4 black olives

1 Place the chick-peas, tahini paste, garlic, lemon juice, seasoning and a little of the water in a blender or food processor. Process until smooth adding a little more water, if necessary.

2 Alternatively if you don't have a blender or food processor, mix the ingredients together in a small bowl until smooth in consistency.

3 Spoon the mixture into a shallow dish. Make a dent in the middle and pour the olive oil into it. Garnish with parsley, cayenne and olives and serve with the radishes.

--- COOK'S TIP ---

Canned chick-peas can be used for hummus. Drain and rinse under cold water before processing.

San Francisco Chicken Wings

INGREDIENTS

Serves 4

75ml/5 tbsp soy sauce
15ml/1 tbsp light brown sugar
15ml/1 tbsp rice vinegar
30ml/2 tbsp dry sherry
juice of 1 orange
5cm/2in strip of orange peel
1 star anise
5ml/1 tsp cornflour
50ml/2fl oz/¼ cup water
15ml/1 tbsp chopped fresh
    root ginger
5ml/1 tsp chilli-garlic sauce, to taste
1.5kg/3–3½lb chicken wings,
    tips removed

1 Preheat the oven to 200°C/400°F/ Gas 6. Mix the soy sauce, sugar, vinegar, sherry, orange juice and peel and anise in a pan. Bring to the boil.

2 Combine the cornflour and water in a small bowl and stir until blended. Add to the boiling soy sauce mixture, stirring well. Boil for another minute, stirring constantly.

3 Remove the soy sauce mixture from the heat and stir in the ginger and chilli-garlic sauce.

4 Arrange the chicken wings, in one layer, in a large baking dish. Pour over the soy sauce mixture and stir to coat the wings evenly.

5 Bake in the centre of the oven for 30–40 minutes until the chicken wings are tender and browned, basting occasionally. Serve the chicken wings either hot or warm.

Cajun "Popcorn"

Cornmeal-coated spicy seafood resembles popcorn when made, hence the name for this tasty Cajun snack served with a delicious basil mayonnaise.

INGREDIENTS

Serves 8
900g/2lb raw crayfish tails, peeled, or
 small prawns, peeled and deveined
2 eggs
250ml/8fl oz/1 cup dry white wine
50g/2oz/½ cup fine cornmeal (or
 plain flour, if not available)
50g/2oz/½ cup plain flour
15ml/1 tbsp snipped fresh chives
1 garlic clove, crushed
2.5ml/½ tsp fresh thyme leaves
1.5ml/¼ tsp salt
1.5ml/¼ tsp cayenne pepper
1.5ml/¼ tsp ground black pepper
oil, for deep-frying

For the mayonnaise
1 egg yolk
10ml/2 tsp Dijon mustard
15ml/1 tbsp white wine vinegar
250ml/8fl oz/1 cup olive or
 vegetable oil
15g/½oz/½ cup fresh basil leaves,
 chopped
salt and ground black pepper

1 Rinse the crayfish tails or prawns in cold water. Drain well and set aside in a cool place.

2 Mix together the eggs and wine in a small bowl.

3 In a mixing bowl, combine the cornmeal and/or flour, chives, garlic, thyme, salt, cayenne and pepper. Gradually whisk in the egg mixture, blending well. Cover the batter and stand for 1 hour at room temperature.

4 For the mayonnaise, combine the egg yolk, mustard and vinegar in a mixing bowl and add salt and pepper to taste. Add the oil in a thin stream, beating vigorously with a wire whisk. When the mixture is thick and smooth, stir in the basil. Cover and chill until ready to serve.

5 Heat 7.5cm/3in of oil in a large frying pan or deep-fryer to a temperature of 180°C/350°F. Dip the seafood into the batter and fry in small batches for 2–3 minutes, until golden brown. Turn as necessary for even colouring. Remove with a slotted spoon and drain on kitchen paper. Serve hot, with the basil mayonnaise.

Mixed Tostadas

Like little edible plates, these fried tortillas can support anything that is not too juicy.

INGREDIENTS

Makes 14
oil, for shallow frying
14 freshly prepared unbaked
    corn tortillas
225g/8oz/1 cup mashed red kidney or
    pinto beans
1 iceberg lettuce, shredded
oil and vinegar dressing (optional)
2 cooked chicken breasts, skinned and
    thinly sliced
225g/8oz Guacamole
115g/4oz/1 cup coarsely grated
    Cheddar cheese
pickled *jalapeño* chillies, seeded and
    sliced, to taste

1 Heat the oil in a frying pan and fry the tortillas until golden brown on both sides and crisp but not hard.

2 Spread each tortilla with a layer of beans. Put a layer of shredded lettuce (which can be left plain or lightly tossed with a little dressing) over the beans.

3 Arrange pieces of chicken in a layer on top of the lettuce. Carefully spread over a layer of the Guacamole and finally sprinkle over a layer of the grated cheese.

4 Arrange the mixed tostadas on a large platter. Serve on individual plates but eat using your hands.

Quesadillas

These delicious filled and deep-fried tortilla turnovers make a popular snack and smaller versions make excellent canapés.

INGREDIENTS

Makes 14
14 freshly prepared unbaked tortillas

For the filling
225g/8oz/1 cup finely chopped or
    grated Cheddar cheese
3 *jalapeño* chillies, seeded and cut
    into strips
salt
oil, for shallow frying

1 Have the tortillas ready, covered with a clean cloth. Combine the grated cheese and chilli strips in a bowl. Season with salt. Set aside.

2 Heat the oil in a frying pan, then holding an unbaked tortilla on your palm, put a spoonful of filling along the centre, avoiding the edges.

COOK'S TIP

For other stuffing ideas try leftover beans with chillies, or chopped chorizo sausage fried with a little chopped onion.

---

3 Fold the tortilla and seal the edges by pressing or crimping well together. Fry in hot oil, on both sides, until golden brown and crisp.

4 Using a fish slice, lift out the quesadilla and drain it on kitchen paper. Transfer to a plate and keep warm while frying the remaining quesadillas. Serve hot.

Chillied Monkfish Parcels

Hot red chilli, garlic and lemon rind add tangy flavour to monkfish in these tasty little parcels.

INGREDIENTS

Serves 4

175g/6oz/1½ cups strong plain flour
2 eggs
115g/4oz skinless monkfish fillet, diced
grated rind of 1 lemon
1 garlic clove, chopped
1 small red chilli, seeded and sliced
45ml/3 tbsp chopped fresh parsley
30ml/2 tbsp single cream

For the tomato oil

2 tomatoes, peeled, seeded and
  finely diced
45ml/3 tbsp extra virgin olive oil
30ml/1 tbsp fresh lemon juice
salt and freshly ground black pepper

1 Place the flour, eggs and 2.5ml/½ tsp salt in a food processor; pulse until the mixture forms a soft dough. Knead for 2–3 minutes then wrap in clear film. Chill for 20 minutes.

2 Place the monkfish, lemon rind, garlic, chilli and parsley in the clean food processor; process until very finely chopped. Add the cream, with plenty of salt and pepper and whizz again to form a very thick purée.

3 Make the tomato oil by stirring the diced tomato with the olive oil and lemon juice in a bowl. Add salt to taste. Cover and chill.

4 Roll out the dough on a lightly floured surface and cut out 32 rounds, using a 4cm/1½in plain cutter. Divide the filling among half the rounds, then cover with the remaining rounds. Pinch the edges tightly to seal, trying to exclude as much air as possible.

5 Bring a large saucepan of water to simmering point and poach the parcels, in batches, for 2–3 minutes or until they rise to the surface. Drain and serve hot, drizzled with the tomato oil.

Samosas

A selection of highly spiced vegetables in a pastry casing makes these samosas a delicious snack at any time of the day.

INGREDIENTS

Makes 30

1 packet spring roll pastry, thawed and
   wrapped in a damp towel
vegetable oil, for deep-frying

For the filling

3 large potatoes, boiled and
   coarsely mashed
75g/3oz/³/₄ cup frozen peas, thawed
50g/2oz/¹/₃ cup canned
   sweetcorn, drained
5ml/1 tsp ground coriander
5ml/1 tsp ground cumin
5ml/1 tsp amchur (dry mango powder)
1 small onion, finely chopped
2 green chillies, finely chopped
30ml/2 tbsp coriander leaves, chopped
30ml/2 tbsp mint leaves, chopped
juice of 1 lemon
salt, to taste
chilli sauce, to serve

1 Toss all the filling ingredients together in a large mixing bowl until they are all well blended. Adjust the seasoning with salt and lemon juice, if necessary.

2 Using one strip of pastry at a time, place 15ml/1 tbsp of the filling mixture at one end of the strip and diagonally fold the pastry up to form a triangle shape.

3 Heat enough oil for deep-frying and fry the samosas in small batches until they are golden brown. Keep them hot while frying the rest. Serve hot with chilli sauce.

Guacamole

This popular Mexican dip can be served with tortilla chips, or used as a dip with fresh vegetables.

INGREDIENTS

Makes 475ml/16fl oz/2 cups

3 large ripe avocados
3 spring onions, minced
1 garlic clove, crushed
15ml/1 tbsp olive oil
15ml/1 tbsp soured cream
2.5ml/½ tsp salt
30ml/2 tbsp fresh lemon or lime juice
2.5ml/½ tsp cayenne pepper

--- COOK'S TIP ---

Guacamole does not keep well, but, if necessary, it can be stored in the fridge for a few hours. Cover the surface with clear film to prevent discolouring.

1 Halve the avocados and remove the stones. Peel the halves. Put the avocado flesh in a large bowl.

2 With a fork, mash the avocado flesh coarsely.

3 Add the spring onions, garlic, olive oil, cream, salt and lemon or lime juice. Mash until well blended, but do not overwork the mixture. Small chunks of avocado should still remain. Adjust the seasoning, if necessary, with salt or lemon or lime juice. Transfer the mixture to a serving bowl. Serve the dip immediately, sprinkled with the cayenne pepper.

Tomato Salsa

INGREDIENTS

Makes 900ml/1½ pints/3¾ cups

1 fresh hot green chilli pepper, seeded and chopped
1 garlic clove
½ red onion, coarsely chopped
3 spring onions, chopped
15g/½oz/½ cup fresh coriander leaves
675g/1½lb ripe tomatoes, seeded and roughly chopped
1–3 canned green chillies
15ml/1 tbsp olive oil
30ml/2 tbsp fresh lime or lemon juice
2.5ml/½ tsp salt, to taste
45ml/3 tbsp tomato juice or cold water

1 In a food processor or blender, combine the fresh green chilli, garlic clove, chopped red onion, spring onions and fresh coriander leaves. Process together until everything is finely chopped.

2 Add the tomatoes, canned chillies, olive oil, lime or lemon juice, salt and tomato juice or water. Pulse on and off until chopped; the tomato salsa should be chunky.

3 Transfer to a bowl and taste for seasoning. Leave to stand for at least 30 minutes before serving. This salsa is best served the day it is made.

--- COOK'S TIP ---

For less heat, remove the seeds from both fresh and canned chillies.

Seafood Wontons with Spicy Dressing

These tasty prawn and crabmeat wontons are spiced with chilli and ginger, and served with a spicy sauce.

INGREDIENTS

Serves 4

225g/8oz raw prawns, peeled
   and deveined
115g/4oz white crabmeat, picked over
4 canned water chestnuts, finely diced
1 spring onion, finely chopped
1 small green chilli, seeded and
   finely chopped
1.25ml/½ tsp grated fresh root ginger
20–24 wonton wrappers
1 egg, separated
salt and freshly ground black pepper
coriander leaves, to garnish

For the spicy dressing

30ml/2 tbsp rice vinegar
15ml/1 tbsp chopped pickled ginger
90ml/6 tbsp olive oil
15ml/1 tbsp soy sauce
45ml/3 tbsp chopped coriander
30ml/2 tbsp finely diced red pepper

1 Finely dice the prawns and place them in a bowl. Add the crabmeat, water chestnuts, spring onion, chilli, ginger and egg white. Season with salt and pepper and stir well.

2 Place a wonton wrapper on a board. Put about 5ml/1 tsp of the filling just above the centre of the wrapper. With a pastry brush, moisten the edges of the wrapper with a little of the egg yolk. Bring the bottom of the wrapper up over the filling. Press gently to expel any air, then seal the wrapper neatly in a triangle.

3 For a more elaborate shape, bring the two side points up over the filling, overlap the points and pinch the ends firmly together. Space the filled wontons on a large baking sheet lined with greaseproof paper, so that they do not stick together.

4 Half fill a large saucepan with water. Bring to simmering point. Add the filled wontons, a few at a time, and simmer for 2–3 minutes. The wontons will float to the surface. When ready the wrappers will be translucent and the filling should be cooked. Remove the wontons with a large slotted spoon, drain them briefly, then spread them on trays. Keep warm while cooking the remaining wontons.

5 Make the coriander dressing by whisking all the ingredients together in a bowl. Divide the wontons among serving dishes, drizzle with the dressing and serve garnished with a handful of coriander leaves.

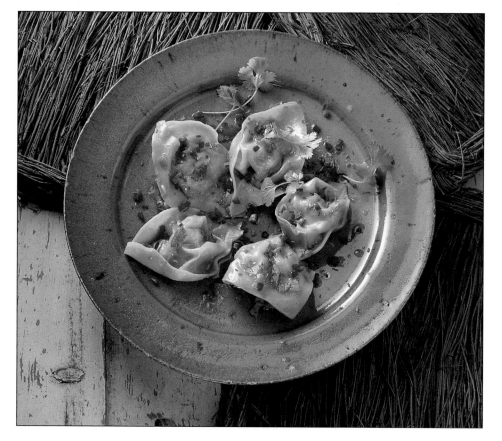

Devilled Kidneys

"Devilled" dishes are always hot and spicy. If you have time, mix the spicy ingredients together in advance to give the flavours time to mingle and mature.

INGREDIENTS

Serves 4
10ml/2 tsp Worcestershire sauce
15ml/1 tbsp prepared English mustard
15ml/1 tbsp lemon juice
15ml/1 tbsp tomato purée
pinch of cayenne pepper
40g/1½oz/3 tbsp butter
1 shallot, finely chopped
8 lamb's kidneys, skinned,
    halved and cored
salt and ground black pepper
15ml/1 tbsp chopped fresh parsley,
    to garnish

1 Mix the Worcestershire sauce, mustard, lemon juice, tomato purée, cayenne pepper and salt together to make a sauce.

2 Melt the butter in a frying pan, add the chopped shallot and cook, stirring occasionally, until it is softened but not coloured.

3 Stir the kidney halves into the shallot in the pan and cook over a medium-high heat for about 3 minutes on each side.

4 Pour the sauce over the kidneys and quickly stir so that they become evenly coated. Serve the dish immediately, sprinkled with fresh chopped parsley.

----- COOK'S TIP -----

To remove the cores from the lamb's kidneys, use sharp kitchen scissors, rather than a knife – you will find that it is much easier to do so.

Desert Nachos

Tortilla chips are livened up with jalapeños in this quick-and-easy snack. Served with a variety of spicy Mexican dips, this always proves to be a popular dish.

INGREDIENTS

Serves 2

450g/1lb blue corn tortilla chips or ordinary tortilla chips
45ml/3 tbsp chopped pickled jalapeños, according to taste
12 black olives, sliced
225g/8oz/2 cups grated Cheddar cheese

To serve
guacamole
tomato salsa
soured cream

1 Preheat the oven to 180°C/350°F/ Gas 4. Put the tortilla chips in a 23 x 33cm/9 x 13in baking dish and spread them out evenly. Sprinkle the jalapeños, olives and cheese evenly over the tortilla chips.

2 Place the prepared tortilla chips in the top of the oven and bake for 10–15 minutes until the cheese melts. Serve the nachos at once, with the guacamole, tomato salsa and soured cream for dipping.

Huevos Rancheros

INGREDIENTS

Serves 4

450g/1lb can refried beans
300ml/½ pint/1¼ cups enchilada sauce
oil, for frying
4 corn tortillas
4 eggs
150g/5oz/1¼ cups grated Cheddar cheese
salt and ground black pepper

1 Heat the refried beans in a saucepan. Cover and set aside.

2 Heat the enchilada sauce in a small saucepan. Cover and set aside.

COOK'S TIP

For a simple enchilada sauce, blend a can of tomatoes with 3 garlic cloves, 1 chopped onion, 45ml/3 tbsp chilli powder, 5ml/1 tsp each cayenne and cumin, and 2.5ml/½ tsp each dried oregano and salt.

---

3 Preheat the oven to 110°C/225°F/ Gas ¼. Put a 5mm/¼in layer of oil in a small non-stick frying pan and heat carefully. When the oil is hot, add the tortillas, one at a time, and fry for about 30 seconds on each side, until just crisp. Remove and drain the tortillas on kitchen paper and keep them warm on a baking sheet in the oven. Discard the oil used for frying. Let the pan cool slightly, then wipe it with kitchen paper to remove all but a film of oil.

4 Heat the frying pan over a low heat. Break in two eggs and cook until the whites are just set. Season with salt and pepper, then transfer to the oven to keep warm. Repeat to cook the remaining eggs.

5 To serve, place a tortilla on each of four plates. Spread a layer of refried beans over each tortilla, then top each with an egg. Spoon over the warm enchilada sauce, then sprinkle with the cheese. Serve hot.

Spicy Meat-filled Parcels

In Indonesia the finest gossamer dough is made for *Martabak*. You can achieve equally good results using ready-made filo pastry or spring roll wrappers.

INGREDIENTS

Makes 16

450g/1lb lean minced beef
2 small onions, finely chopped
2 small leeks, very
    finely chopped
2 garlic cloves, crushed
10ml/2 tsp coriander seeds, dry-fried
    and ground
5ml/1 tsp cumin seeds, dry-fried
    and ground
5–10ml/1–2 tsp mild curry powder
2 eggs, beaten
400g/14oz packet filo pastry
45–60ml/3–4 tbsp sunflower oil
salt and freshly ground black pepper
light soy sauce, to serve

1 To make the filling, mix the meat with the onions, leeks, garlic, coriander, cumin, curry powder and seasoning. Turn into a heated wok, without oil, and stir all the time, until the meat has changed colour and looks cooked, about 5 minutes.

2 Allow to cool and then mix in enough beaten egg to bind to a soft consistency. Any leftover egg can be used to seal the edges of the dough; otherwise, use milk.

3 Brush a sheet of filo with oil and lay another sheet on top. Cut the sheets in half. Place a large spoonful of the filling on each double piece of filo. Fold the sides to the middle so that the edges just overlap. Brush these edges with either beaten egg or milk and fold the other two sides to the middle in the same way, so that you now have a square parcel shape. Make sure that the parcel is as flat as possible, to speed cooking. Repeat with the remaining fifteen parcels and place on a floured tray in the fridge.

4 Heat the remaining oil in a shallow pan and cook several parcels at a time, depending on the size of the pan. Cook for 3 minutes on the first side and then turn them over and cook for a further 2 minutes, or until heated through. Cook the remaining parcels in the same way and serve hot, sprinkled with light soy sauce.

5 If preferred, these spicy parcels can be cooked in a hot oven at 200°C/400°F/Gas 6 for 20 minutes. Glaze with more beaten egg before baking for a rich, golden colour.

Welsh Rabbit

This delicious supper dish is made from toast and a flavourful cheese sauce spiked with hot mustard and Worcestershire sauce. It doesn't, as the name might suggest, contain any meat. It is also called "Welsh Rarebit", although "rabbit" seems to have been the original name.

INGREDIENTS

Serves 4

4 thick slices of bread, crusts removed
25g/1oz/2 tbsp butter
225g/8oz/2 cups grated mature
 Cheddar cheese
5ml/1 tsp English mustard powder
few drops Worcestershire sauce
60ml/4 tbsp brown ale, beer or milk

COOK'S TIP

Use a strong-tasting cheese so the topping has plenty of flavour.

1 Preheat the grill. Toast the bread until golden, then place in a single layer in a wide, shallow baking dish. Keep warm.

2 Slowly melt the butter in a small to medium, heavy-based, preferably non-stick saucepan over a very low heat, or in a bowl placed over a saucepan of hot water. Stir it constantly as it melts, then remove from the heat.

3 Stir the cheese, mustard powder and Worcestershire sauce into the melted butter, then slowly pour in the ale, beer or milk in a steady stream, stirring the cheese mixture all the time until very well blended.

4 Preheat the grill. Spoon the Cheddar cheese mixture on to the toast in the baking dish, then place it under the hot grill until it is bubbling hot and golden brown in colour. Serve immediately.

Chicken Naan Pockets

This quick-and-easy dish is ideal for a snack lunch or supper.

INGREDIENTS

Serves 4

4 naan
45ml/3 tbsp natural yogurt
7.5ml/1½ tsp garam masala
5ml/1 tsp chilli powder
5ml/1 tsp salt
45ml/3 tbsp lemon juice
15ml/1 tbsp chopped fresh coriander
1 fresh green chilli, chopped
450g/1lb/3¼ cups chicken, skinned, boned and cubed
15ml/1 tbsp vegetable oil
8 onion rings
2 tomatoes, quartered
½ white cabbage, shredded
lemon wedges, 2 small tomatoes, halved, mixed salad leaves and fresh coriander, to garnish

1 Using a small, sharp knife, carefully cut into the middle of each naan to make a pocket, then set them aside until needed.

2 In a bowl, mix together the natural yogurt, garam masala, chilli powder, salt, lemon juice, fresh coriander and chopped fresh green chilli. Pour this marinade over the chicken pieces and leave to marinate for about 1 hour.

3 After 1 hour preheat the grill to very hot, then lower the heat to medium. Place the marinated chicken pieces in a flameproof dish and grill for about 15–20 minutes, until they are tender and cooked through, turning the chicken pieces at least twice. Baste with the vegetable oil occasionally while cooking.

4 Remove the dish from the heat and fill each naan with the chicken and then with the onion rings, tomatoes and shredded cabbage. Serve garnished with lemon, tomatoes, salad leaves and coriander.

Chicken Tikka

A mixture of ginger, garlic and chilli powder adds a characteristic spicy taste to this popular Indian starter which is quick and easy to cook.

INGREDIENTS

Serves 6

450g/1lb/3¼ cups chicken, skinned, boned and cubed
5ml/1 tsp ginger pulp
5ml/1 tsp garlic pulp
5ml/1 tsp chilli powder
1.5ml/¼ tsp turmeric
5ml/1 tsp salt
150ml/¼ pint/⅔ cup natural yogurt
60ml/4 tbsp lemon juice
15ml/1 tbsp chopped fresh coriander
15ml/1 tbsp vegetable oil
1 small onion, cut into rings, lime wedges, mixed salad and fresh coriander, to garnish

1 In a medium mixing bowl, combine the chicken pieces, ginger and garlic pulp, chilli powder, turmeric, salt, yogurt, lemon juice and fresh coriander and leave to marinate for at least 2 hours.

2 Place the marinated chicken on a grill tray or in a flameproof dish lined with foil and baste with the vegetable oil.

3 Preheat the grill to medium. Grill the chicken for 15–20 minutes until cooked, turning and basting 2–3 times. Serve garnished with onion, lime, salad and coriander.

—— COOK'S TIP ——

Chicken Tikka can be served with naan or chapatis, pickles and salad as a main dish for four people.

Spicy Kebabs

INGREDIENTS

Makes 18–20 balls

450g/1lb minced beef
1 egg
3 garlic cloves, crushed
½ onion, finely chopped
2.5ml/½ tsp freshly ground black
    pepper
7.5ml/1½ tsp ground cumin
7.5ml/1½ tsp dhania (ground
    coriander)
5ml/1 tsp ground ginger
10ml/2 tsp garam masala
15ml/1 tbsp lemon juice
50–75g/2–3oz/1–1½ cups fresh white
    breadcrumbs
1 small chilli, seeded and chopped
salt
oil, for deep frying

1 Place the minced beef in a large bowl and add the egg, garlic, onion, spices, seasoning, lemon juice, about 50g/1oz/1 cup of the breadcrumbs and the chilli.

2 Using your hands or a wooden spoon, mix the ingredients together until the mixture is firm. If it feels sticky, add more of the breadcrumbs and mix again until firm.

3 Heat the oil in a large heavy pan or deep-fat fryer. Shape the mixture into balls or fingers and fry, a few at a time, for 5 minutes or until well browned all over.

4 Using a slotted spoon, drain the kebabs and then transfer to a plate lined with kitchen paper. Cook the remaining kebabs in the same way and then serve, if you like, with Kachumbali or a spicy dip.

Cod with Chilli and Mustard Seeds

INGREDIENTS

Serves 4

30ml/2 tbsp olive oil
5ml/1 tsp mustard seeds
1 large potato, cubed
2 slices of serrano ham, shredded
1 onion, thinly sliced
2 garlic cloves, thinly sliced
1 red chilli, seeded and sliced
115g/4oz skinless, boneless cod, cubed
120ml/4fl oz/½ cup vegetable stock
50g/2oz/½ cup grated tasty cheese,
    such as Manchego or Cheddar
salt and freshly ground black pepper

———— COOK'S TIP ————

For a crisp topping, substitute half the
cheese with wholemeal breadcrumbs.

1 Heat the oil in a heavy-based
frying pan. Add the mustard seeds.
Cook for a minute or two until the
seeds begin to pop and splutter, then
add the potato, ham and onion.

2 Cook, stirring regularly for about
10–15 minutes, until the potatoes
are brown and almost tender.

3 Add the garlic and chilli and cook
for 2 minutes more.

4 Stir in the cod cubes and cook for
2–3 minutes until white, then add
the stock and plenty of salt and pepper.
Cover the pan and cook for 5 minutes,
until the fish is just cooked and the
potatoes are tender.

5 Transfer the mixture to a flameproof dish. Sprinkle over the
grated cheese and place under a hot
grill for about 2–3 minutes until the
cheese is golden and bubbling.

Fried Dough Balls with Fiery Salsa

These crunchy dough balls are accompanied by a hot and spicy tomato salsa. Serve them with a juicy tomato salad, if you prefer.

INGREDIENTS

Serves 10

450g/1lb/4 cups strong white flour
5ml/1 tsp easy-blend dried yeast
5ml/1 tsp salt
30ml/2 tbsp chopped fresh parsley
2 garlic cloves, finely chopped
30ml/2 tbsp olive oil, plus extra
  for greasing
vegetable oil, for frying

For the salsa

6 hot red chillies, seeded and
  roughly chopped
1 onion, roughly chopped
2 garlic cloves, quartered
2.5cm/1in piece of root ginger,
  roughly chopped
450g/1lb tomatoes, roughly chopped
30ml/2 tbsp olive oil
pinch of sugar
salt and freshly ground black pepper

1 Sift the flour into a large bowl. Stir in the yeast and salt and make a well in the centre. Add the parsley, garlic, olive oil and enough warm water to make a firm dough.

2 Gather the dough in the bowl together then tip out on to a lightly floured surface or board. Knead for about 10 minutes, until the dough feels very smooth and elastic.

3 Rub a little oil into the surface of the dough. Return it to the clean bowl, cover with clear film or a clean dish towel and leave in a warm place to rise for about 1 hour, or until doubled in bulk.

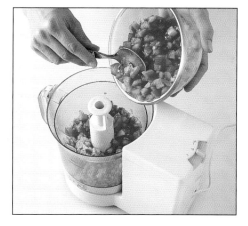

4 Meanwhile, make the salsa. Combine the chillies, onion, garlic and ginger in a food processor and whizz together until very finely chopped. Add the tomatoes and olive oil and process until smooth.

5 Sieve the mixture into a saucepan. Add sugar, salt and pepper to taste and simmer gently for 15 minutes. Do not allow the salsa to boil.

6 Roll the dough into about 40 balls. Shallow fry in batches in hot oil for 4–5 minutes until crisp and golden. Drain on kitchen paper and serve hot, with the fiery salsa in a separate bowl for dipping.

COOK'S TIP

These dough balls can be deep-fried for 3–4 minutes or baked at 200°C/400°F/ Gas 6 for 15–20 minutes.

Cheese Fritters

These crisp fritters owe their inspiration to Italy. A note of caution – do be careful not to burn your mouth when you take your first bite, as the soft, rich cheese filling will be very hot.

Ingredients

Makes 15–16

115g/4oz ricotta cheese
50g/2oz fontina cheese, grated
25g/1oz Parmesan cheese, finely grated
2.5ml/½ tsp cayenne pepper
1 egg, beaten, plus a little extra to seal
   the wontons
15–16 wonton wrappers
oil for deep frying

1 Line a large baking sheet with greaseproof paper or sprinkle it lightly with flour. Set aside. Combine the cheeses in a bowl, then add the cayenne and beaten egg and mix well.

2 Place one wonton wrapper at a time on a board. Brush the edges with egg. Spoon a little filling in the centre; pull the top corner down to the bottom corner, to make a triangle.

3 Transfer the filled wontons to the prepared baking sheet.

4 Heat the oil in a deep-fryer or large saucepan. Slip in as many wontons at one time as can be accommodated without overcrowding. Fry them for 2–3 minutes on each side or until the fritters are golden. Remove with a slotted spoon. Drain on kitchen paper and serve at once.

Chilled Soba Noodles with Nori

Ingredients

Serves 4

350g/12oz dried soba noodles
1 sheet nori seaweed

For the dipping sauce

300ml/½ pint/1¼ cups fish stock
120ml/4fl oz/½ cup dark soy sauce
60ml/4 tbsp mirin
5ml/1 tsp sugar
15ml/1 tbsp fish sauce

Flavourings

4 spring onions, finely chopped
30ml/2 tbsp grated daikon
wasabi paste
4 egg yolks (optional)

— Cook's Tip —

Daikon is a slim white vegetable, sometimes also known as mooli.

---

1 Make the dipping sauce. Combine the stock, soy sauce, mirin and sugar in a saucepan. Bring rapidly to the boil, add the fish sauce, then remove from the heat. When cool, strain the sauce into a bowl and cover. This can be done in advance and the sauce kept chilled for up to a week.

2 Cook the soba noodles in a saucepan of lightly salted boiling water for 6–7 minutes or until just tender, following the manufacturer's directions on the packet.

3 Drain and rinse the noodles under cold running water, agitating them gently to remove the excess starch. Drain well.

4 Toast the nori over a high gas flame or under a hot grill, then crumble into thin strips. Divide the noodles among four serving dishes and top with the nori. Serve each portion with an individual bowl of dipping sauce and offer the flavourings separately.

FIERY FISH AND SEAFOOD

Fresh fish is popular all over the world and there are hundreds of ways of adding spicy flavour; fish can be fired up with hot red chillies or chilli paste, pickled with jalapeño chillies or made into a curry with aromatic warm spices and spiked with hot chilli powder. Steamed Fish with Chilli Sauce is a delicious dish – the fish is cooked to perfection, with all the moistness and flavour retained.

Steamed Fish with Chilli Sauce

In this red-hot dish from Thailand, whole fish is cooked with red chillies, ginger and lemon grass, then served with a mouth-tingling chilli sauce.

INGREDIENTS

Serves 4

1 large or 2 medium firm fish like bass or grouper, scaled and cleaned
1 fresh banana leaf
30ml/2 tbsp rice wine
3 red chillies, seeded and finely sliced
2 garlic cloves, finely chopped
2cm/³/₄in piece fresh root ginger, finely shredded
2 stalks lemon grass, crushed and finely chopped
2 spring onions, chopped
30ml/2 tbsp fish sauce
juice of 1 lime

For the chilli sauce

10 red chillies, seeded and chopped
4 garlic cloves, chopped
60 ml/4 tbsp fish sauce
15ml/1 tbsp sugar
75ml/5 tbsp lime juice

1 Rinse the fish under cold running water. Pat dry with kitchen paper. With a sharp knife, slash the skin of the fish a few times on both sides.

2 Place the fish on a banana leaf. Mix together all the remaining ingredients and spread over the fish.

3 Place a small upturned plate in the bottom of a wok and add 5cm/2in boiling water; place a banana leaf on top. Lift the banana leaf, together with the fish, and place on the plate or rack. Cover with a lid and steam for about 10–15 minutes or until the fish is cooked.

4 Place all the chilli sauce ingredients in a food processor and process until smooth. You may need to add a little cold water.

5 Serve the fish hot, on the banana leaf if liked, with the sweet chilli sauce to spoon over the top.

Fried Catfish Fillets with Piquant Sauce

Spicy fillets of catfish are fried in a herby batter and served with a wonderfully tasty sauce to create this excellent supper dish.

INGREDIENTS

Serves 4

1 egg
50ml/2fl oz/¼ cup olive oil
squeeze of lemon juice
2.5ml/½ tsp chopped fresh dill
4 catfish fillets
50g/2oz/½ cup flour
25g/1oz/2 tbsp butter or margarine
salt and ground black pepper

For the sauce

1 egg yolk
30ml/2 tbsp Dijon mustard
30ml/2 tbsp white wine vinegar
10ml/2 tsp paprika
300ml/½ pint/1¼ cups olive or
    vegetable oil
30ml/2 tbsp prepared horseradish
2.5ml/½ tsp chopped garlic
1 celery stick, chopped
30ml/2 tbsp tomato ketchup
2.5ml/½ tsp ground black pepper
2.5ml/½ tsp salt

1 For the sauce, combine the egg yolk, mustard, vinegar and paprika in a mixing bowl. Add the oil in a thin stream, beating vigorously with a wire whisk to blend it in.

2 When the mixture is smooth and thick, beat in all the other sauce ingredients. Cover and chill until ready to serve.

3 Combine the egg, 15ml/1 tbsp olive oil, the lemon juice, dill and a little salt and pepper in a shallow dish. Beat until well combined.

4 Dip both sides of each catfish fillet in the egg and herb mixture, then coat lightly with flour, shaking off any excess from it.

5 Heat the butter or margarine with the remaining olive oil in a large heavy-based frying pan. Add the fish fillets and fry until they are golden brown on both sides and cooked, for about 8–10 minutes. To test they are done, insert the point of a sharp knife into the fish: the flesh should be opaque in the centre.

6 Serve the fried catfish fillets hot, accompanied by the piquant sauce in a dish.

COOK'S TIP

If you can't find catfish, use any firm fish fillets instead. Cod or haddock fillets would both make good substitutes.

Pickled Fish

INGREDIENTS

Serves 4

900g/2lb white fish fillets
60ml/4 tbsp freshly squeezed lime or
  lemon juice
300ml/½ pint/1¼ cups olive or corn oil
2 whole cloves
6 peppercorns
2 garlic cloves
2.5ml/½ tsp ground cumin
2.5ml/½ tsp dried oregano
2 bay leaves
1 drained canned *jalapeño* chilli, seeded,
  and cut into strips
1 onion, thinly sliced
250ml/8fl oz/1 cup white wine vinegar
250ml/8fl oz/1 cup olive or corn oil
salt

For the garnish

lettuce leaves
green olives

1 Cut the fish fillets into eight pieces and arrange them in a single layer in a shallow dish. Drizzle with the lime or lemon juice. Cover and marinate for 15 minutes, turning the fillets once.

2 Lift out the fillets with a fish slice, pat them dry with kitchen paper and season with salt. Heat 60ml/4 tbsp of the oil in a frying pan and sauté the fish until lightly golden brown. Transfer to a platter and set aside.

3 Combine the cloves, peppercorns, garlic, cumin, oregano, bay leaves, chilli and vinegar in a pan. Bring to the boil, then simmer for 3–4 minutes.

4 Add the remaining oil, and bring to a simmer. Pour over the fish. Cool, cover and chill for 24 hours. To serve, lift out the fillets with a fish slice and arrange on a serving dish. Garnish with lettuce and olives.

—— COOK'S TIP ——

To make the dish special, add an elaborate garnish of radishes, capers and chilli strips.

Red Snapper, Veracruz-style

This is Mexico's best-known fish dish. In Veracruz red snapper is always used but fillets of any firm-fleshed white fish can be substituted successfully.

INGREDIENTS

Serves 4

4 large red snapper fillets
30ml/2 tbsp freshly squeezed lime or lemon juice
120ml/4fl oz/½ cup olive oil
1 onion, finely chopped
2 garlic cloves, chopped
675g/1½lb tomatoes, peeled and chopped
1 bay leaf, plus a few sprigs to garnish
1.5ml/¼ tsp dried oregano
30ml/2 tbsp large capers, plus extra to serve (optional)
16 stoned green olives, halved
2 drained canned *jalapeño* chillies, seeded and cut into strips
butter, for frying
3 slices firm white bread, cut into triangles
salt and freshly ground black pepper

1 Arrange the fish fillets in a single layer in a shallow dish. Season with salt and pepper, drizzle with the lime or lemon juice and set aside.

2 Heat the oil in a large frying pan and sauté the onion and garlic until the onion is soft. Add the tomatoes and cook for about 10 minutes until the mixture is thick and flavoursome. Stir the mixture from time to time.

3 Stir in the bay leaf, oregano, capers, olives and chillies. Add the fish and cook over a very low heat for about 10 minutes or until tender.

--- COOK'S TIP ---

This dish can also be made with a whole fish, weighing about 1.5kg/3–3½lb. Bake together with the sauce, in a preheated oven at 160°C/325°F/Gas 3. Allow 10 minutes cooking time for every 2.5cm/1in thickness of the fish.

4 While the fish is cooking, heat the butter in a small frying pan and sauté the bread triangles until they are golden brown on both sides.

5 Transfer the fish to a heated platter, pour over the sauce and surround with the fried bread triangles. Garnish with bay leaves and serve with extra capers, if you like.

Prawns with Chayote in Turmeric Sauce

Galangal, red chillies and turmeric add distinctive hot and spicy flavour to this tasty Indonesian dish.

INGREDIENTS

Serves 4

1–2 chayotes or 2–3 courgettes
2 fresh red chillies, seeded
1 onion, quartered
5mm/¼in fresh galangal, peeled
1 lemon grass stem, lower 5cm/2in
   sliced, top bruised
2.5cm/1in fresh turmeric, peeled
200ml/7fl oz/scant 1 cup water
lemon juice
400ml/14fl oz can coconut milk
450g/1lb cooked, peeled prawns
salt
red chilli shreds, to garnish (optional)
boiled rice, to serve

1 Peel the chayotes, remove the seeds and cut into strips. If using courgettes, cut into 5cm/2in strips.

2 Grind the fresh red chillies, onion, sliced galangal, sliced lemon grass and the fresh turmeric to a paste in a food processor or with a pestle and mortar. Add the water to the paste mixture, with a squeeze of lemon juice and salt to taste.

3 Pour into a pan. Add the top of the lemon grass stem. Bring to the boil and cook for 1–2 minutes. Add the chayote or courgette pieces and cook for 2 minutes. Stir in the coconut milk. Taste and adjust the seasoning.

4 Stir in the prawns and cook gently for 2–3 minutes. Remove the lemon grass stem. Garnish with shreds of chilli, if using, and serve with rice.

Indonesian Spicy Fish

Fish is given a hot, piquant twist in this flavourful dish.

INGREDIENTS

Serves 6–8

1kg/2¼lb fresh mackerel
   fillets, skinned
30ml/2 tbsp tamarind pulp, soaked in
   200ml/7fl oz/scant 1 cup water
1 onion
1cm/½in fresh galangal, peeled
2 garlic cloves
1–2 fresh red chillies, seeded, or 5ml/
   1 tsp chilli powder
5ml/1 tsp ground coriander
5ml/1 tsp ground turmeric
2.5ml/½ tsp ground fennel seeds
15ml/1 tbsp dark brown sugar
90–105ml/6–7 tbsp oil
200ml/7fl oz/scant 1 cup
   coconut cream
salt and freshly ground black pepper
fresh chilli shreds, to garnish

1 Rinse the fish fillets in cold water and dry them well on kitchen paper. Put into a shallow dish and sprinkle with a little salt. Strain the tamarind and pour the juice over the fish fillets. Leave for 30 minutes.

2 Quarter the onion, peel and slice the galangal and peel the garlic. Grind the onion, galangal, garlic and chillies or chilli powder to a paste in a food processor or with a pestle and mortar. Add the ground coriander, turmeric, fennel seeds and sugar.

3 Heat half of the oil in a frying pan. Drain the fish fillets and fry for 5 minutes, or until cooked. Set aside.

4 Wipe out the pan and heat the remaining oil. Fry the spice paste, stirring all the time, until it gives off a spicy aroma. Do not let it brown. Add the coconut cream and simmer gently for a few minutes. Add the fish fillets and gently heat through.

5 Taste for seasoning and serve scattered with shredded chilli.

Braised Fish in Chilli and Garlic Sauce

INGREDIENTS

Serves 4–6

1 bream or trout, 675g/1½lb, gutted
15ml/1 tbsp light soy sauce
15ml/1 tbsp Chinese rice wine
vegetable oil, for deep-frying

For the sauce

2 garlic cloves, finely chopped
2–3 spring onions, finely chopped
5ml/1 tsp chopped fresh root ginger
30ml/2 tbsp chilli bean sauce
15ml/1 tbsp tomato purée
10ml/2 tsp light brown sugar
15ml/1 tbsp rice vinegar
about 120ml/4fl oz/½ cup fish stock
15ml/1 tbsp cornflour paste
few drops sesame oil

1 Rinse and dry the fish well. Using a sharp knife, score both sides of the fish as far down as the bone with diagonal cuts about 2.5cm/1in apart. Rub the whole fish with soy sauce and wine on both sides, then leave to marinate for 10–15 minutes.

2 In a wok, deep-fry the fish in hot oil for about 3–4 minutes on both sides until golden brown.

3 Pour off the excess oil, leaving a thin layer in the wok. Push the fish to one side of the wok and add the garlic, the white part of the spring onions, fresh ginger, chilli bean sauce, tomato purée, brown sugar, rice vinegar and stock. Bring to the boil and braise the fish in the sauce for about 4–5 minutes, turning it over once. Add the green part of the chopped spring onions. Thicken the sauce with the cornflour paste, sprinkle with the sesame oil and place on a dish to serve immediately.

--- VARIATION ---

Any whole fish is suitable for this dish; try sea bass, grouper or grey mullet, if you like. Also, if you can't find Chinese wine, use dry sherry instead.

Salt Cod in Mild Chilli Sauce

INGREDIENTS

Serves 6
900g/2lb dried salt cod
1 onion, chopped
2 garlic cloves, chopped

For the sauce
6 dried *ancho* chillies
1 onion, chopped
2.5ml/½ tsp dried oregano
2.5ml/½ tsp ground coriander
1 *serrano* chilli, seeded and chopped
45ml/3 tbsp corn oil
750ml/1¼ pints/3 cups fish or
 chicken stock
salt

For the garnish
1 fresh green chilli, sliced

COOK'S TIP

Dried salt cod is a great favourite in Spain and Portugal and throughout Latin America. Look for it in Spanish and Portuguese markets.

1 Soak the cod in cold water for several hours, depending on how hard and salty it is. Change the water once or twice during soaking.

2 Drain the fish and transfer it to a saucepan. Pour in water to cover. Bring to a gentle simmer and cook for about 15 minutes until the fish is tender. Drain, reserving the stock. Remove any skin or bones from the fish and cut it into 4cm/1½in pieces.

3 Make the sauce. Remove the stems and shake out the seeds from the *ancho* chillies. Tear the pods into pieces, put in a bowl of warm water and soak until they are soft.

4 Drain the soaked chillies and put them into a food processor with the onion, oregano, coriander and *serrano* chilli. Process to a purée.

5 Heat the oil in a frying pan and cook the purée, stirring, for about 5 minutes. Stir in the fish or chicken stock and simmer for 3–4 minutes.

6 Add the prepared cod and simmer for a few minutes longer to heat the fish through and blend the flavours. Serve garnished with the sliced chilli.

Baked or Grilled Spiced Whole Fish

INGREDIENTS

Serves 6

1kg/2¼lb bream, carp or pomfret,
    cleaned and scaled if necessary
1 fresh red chilli, seeded and ground,
    or 5ml/1 tsp chopped chilli
    from a jar
4 garlic cloves, crushed
2.5cm/1in fresh root ginger, peeled
    and sliced
4 spring onions, chopped
juice of ½ lemon
30ml/2 tbsp sunflower oil
salt

1 Rinse the fish and dry it well inside
and out with absorbent kitchen
paper. Slash two or three times through
the fleshy part on each side of the fish.

2 Place the chilli, garlic, ginger and
spring onions in a food processor
and blend to a paste, or grind the
mixture together with a pestle and
mortar. Add the lemon juice and salt,
then stir in the oil.

3 Spoon a little of the mixture inside
the fish and pour the rest over the
top. Turn the fish to coat it completely
in the spice mixture and leave to
marinate for at least an hour.

4 Preheat the grill. Place a long strip
of double foil under the fish to
support it and to make turning it over
easier. Put on a rack in a grill pan and
cook under the hot grill for 5 minutes
on one side and 8 minutes on the
second side, basting with the marinade
during cooking. Serve with boiled rice.

Vinegar Chilli Fish

INGREDIENTS

Serves 2–3

2–3 mackerel, filleted
2–3 fresh red chillies, seeded
4 macadamia nuts or 8 almonds
1 red onion, quartered
2 garlic cloves, crushed
1cm/½in fresh root ginger, peeled
    and sliced
5ml/1 tsp ground turmeric
45ml/3 tbsp coconut or vegetable oil
45ml/3 tbsp wine vinegar
150ml/¼ pint/⅔ cup water
salt
Deep-fried Onions, to garnish
finely chopped fresh chilli, to garnish

1 Rinse the fish fillets in cold water
and then dry them well on kitchen
paper. Set aside.

2 Grind the chillies, nuts, onion,
garlic, ginger, turmeric and 15ml/
1 tbsp of the oil to a paste in a food
processor or with a pestle and mortar.
Heat the remaining oil in a frying pan
and cook the paste for 1–2 minutes,
without browning. Stir in the vinegar
and water. Add salt to taste. Bring to
the boil, then reduce to a simmer.

3 Place the fish fillets in the sauce.
Cover and cook for 6–8 minutes,
or until the fish is tender.

4 Lift the fish on to a plate and keep
warm. Reduce the sauce by
boiling rapidly for 1 minute. Pour over
the fish and serve. Garnish with Deep-
fried Onions and chopped chilli.

Mexican Spicy Fish

This is a typical Mexican dish.

INGREDIENTS

Serves 6

1.5kg/3 – 3½lb striped bass or any non-
  oily white fish, cut into 6 steaks
120ml/4fl oz/½ cup corn oil
1 large onion, thinly sliced
2 garlic cloves, chopped
350g/12oz tomatoes, sliced
2 drained canned *jalapeño* chillies,
  rinsed and sliced

For the marinade

4 garlic cloves, crushed
5ml/1 tsp black peppercorns
5ml/1 tsp dried oregano
2.5ml/½ tsp ground cumin
5ml/1 tsp ground *achiote* (annatto)
2.5ml/½ tsp ground cinnamon
120ml/4fl oz/½ cup mild white vinegar
salt
flat leaf parsley, to garnish

1 Arrange the fish steaks in a single
layer in a shallow dish. Make the
marinade. Using a pestle, grind the
garlic and black peppercorns in a
mortar. Add the dried oregano, cumin,
achiote (annatto) and cinnamon and mix
to a paste with the vinegar. Add salt to
taste and spread the marinade on both
sides of each of the fish steaks. Cover
and leave in a cool place for 1 hour.

2 Select a flameproof dish large
enough to hold the fish in a single
layer and pour in enough of the oil to
coat the bottom. Arrange the fish in
the dish with any remaining marinade.

3 Top the fish with the onion, garlic,
tomatoes and chillies and pour the
rest of the oil over the top.

4 Cover the dish and cook over a
low heat on top of the stove for
15 – 20 minutes, or until the fish is no
longer translucent. Serve at once
garnished with flat leaf parsley.

Citrus Fish with Chillies

INGREDIENTS

Serves 4

4 halibut or cod steaks or cutlets, about
    175g/6oz each
juice of 1 lemon
5ml/1 tsp garlic granules
5ml/1 tsp paprika
5ml/1 tsp ground cumin
4ml/¾ tsp dried tarragon
about 60ml/4 tbsp olive oil
flour, for dusting
300ml/½ pint/1¼ cups fish stock
2 red chillies, seeded and finely
    chopped
30ml/2 tbsp chopped fresh coriander
1 red onion, cut into rings
salt and freshly ground black pepper

1 Place the fish in a shallow bowl and
    mix together the lemon juice,
garlic, paprika, cumin, tarragon and a
little salt and pepper. Spoon over the
lemon mixture, cover loosely with
clear film and allow to marinate for a
few hours or overnight in the fridge.

2 Gently heat all of the oil in a large
    non-stick frying pan, dust the fish
with flour and then fry the fish for a
few minutes each side, until golden
brown all over.

3 Pour the fish stock around the fish,
    and simmer, covered for about
5 minutes until the fish is thoroughly
cooked through.

4 Add the chopped red chillies and
    15ml/1 tbsp of the coriander to the
pan. Simmer for 5 minutes.

5 Transfer the fish and sauce to a
    serving plate and keep warm.

6 Wipe the pan, heat some olive oil
    and stir fry the onion rings until
speckled brown. Scatter over the fish
with the remaining chopped coriander
and serve at once.

Saffron Fish

INGREDIENTS

Serves 4

2–3 saffron strands
2 egg yolks
1 garlic clove, crushed
4 salmon trout steaks
oil for deep frying
salt and ground black pepper
green salad, to serve

1 Soak the saffron in 15ml/1 tbsp boiling water and then beat the mixture into the egg yolks. Season with garlic, salt and pepper.

COOK'S TIP

Any type of fish can be used in this recipe. Try a combination of plain and smoked for a delicious change, such as smoked and unsmoked cod or haddock.

---

2 Place the fish steaks in a shallow dish and coat with the egg mixture. Cover with clear film and marinate for up to 1 hour.

3 Heat the oil in a deep fryer until it is very hot then fry the fish, one steak at a time, for about 10 minutes until golden brown. Drain each steak on kitchen paper. Serve with a green salad.

Pan-fried Spicy Sardines

This delicious fish recipe is a favourite in many Arab countries.

INGREDIENTS

Serves 4

10g/¼oz fresh parsley
3–4 garlic cloves, crushed
8–12 sardines, prepared
30ml/2 tbsp lemon juice
50g/2oz/½ cup plain flour
2.5ml/½ tsp ground cumin
60ml/4 tbsp vegetable oil
salt and freshly ground black pepper
naan bread and salad, to serve

COOK'S TIP

If you don't have a garlic crusher, crush the garlic using the flat side of a large knife blade instead.

---

1 Finely chop the parsley and mix in a small bowl with the garlic.

2 Pat the parsley and garlic mixture all over the outsides and insides of the sardines. Sprinkle them with the lemon juice and set aside, covered, in a cool place for about 2 hours to absorb the flavours.

3 Place the flour on a large plate and season with cumin, salt and pepper. Roll the sardines in the flour, taking care to coat each fish thoroughly.

4 Heat the oil in a large frying pan and fry the fish in batches for 5 minutes on each side until crisp. Keep warm in the oven while cooking the remaining fish and then serve with naan bread and salad.

Whole Fish with Sweet and Sour Sauce

Ingredients

Serves 4

1 whole fish, such as red snapper or
  carp, about 1kg/2¼lb
30–45ml/2–3 tbsp cornflour
oil for frying
salt and freshly ground black pepper
boiled rice, to serve

For the spice paste

2 garlic cloves
2 lemon grass stems
2.5cm/1in fresh galangal, peeled
2.5cm/1in fresh root ginger
2cm/¾in fresh turmeric or 2.5ml/
  ½ tsp ground turmeric
5 macadamia nuts or 10 almonds

For the sauce

15ml/1 tbsp brown sugar
45ml/3 tbsp cider vinegar
about 350ml/12fl oz/1½ cups water
2 lime leaves, torn
4 shallots, quartered
3 tomatoes, skinned and cut in wedges
3 spring onions, finely shredded
1 fresh red chilli, seeded and shredded

1 Ask the fishmonger to gut and scale the fish, leaving on the head and tail, or you may do this yourself. Wash and dry the fish thoroughly and then sprinkle it inside and out with salt. Set aside for 15 minutes, while preparing the other ingredients.

2 Peel and crush the garlic cloves. Use only the lower white part of the lemon grass stems and slice thinly. Peel and slice the fresh galangal, the fresh root ginger and fresh turmeric and grind to a fine paste in a food processor or with a pestle and mortar.

3 Scrape the paste into a bowl. Stir in the brown sugar, cider vinegar, seasoning to taste and the water. Add the lime leaves.

4 Dust the fish with the cornflour and fry on both sides in hot oil for about 8–9 minutes or until almost cooked through. Drain the fish on kitchen paper and transfer to a serving dish. Keep warm.

5 Pour off most of the oil and then pour in the spicy liquid and allow to come to the boil. Reduce the heat and cook for 3–4 minutes. Add the shallots and tomatoes, followed a minute later by the spring onions and chilli. Taste and adjust the seasoning.

6 Pour the sauce over the fish. Serve at once, with plenty of rice.

Turkish Cold Fish

Green chilli, garlic and paprika add subtle spicing to this delicious fish dish. Cold fish is enjoyed in many parts of the Middle East – this particular version is from Turkey.

INGREDIENTS

Serves 4

60ml/4 tbsp olive oil
900g/2lb red mullet or snapper
2 onions, sliced
1 green chilli, seeded and chopped
1 each red and green pepper, sliced
3 garlic cloves, crushed
15ml/1 tbsp tomato purée
50ml/2fl oz/¼ cup fish stock
   or water
5–6 tomatoes, peeled and sliced or
   400g/14oz can tomatoes
30ml/2 tbsp chopped fresh parsley
30ml/2 tbsp lemon juice
5ml/1 tsp paprika
15–20 green and black olives
salt and freshly ground black pepper
bread and salad, to serve

1 Heat 30ml/2 tbsp of the oil in a large roasting tin or frying pan and fry the fish on both sides until golden brown. Remove from the tin or pan, cover and keep warm.

COOK'S TIP

One large fish looks spectacular, but it is tricky to both cook and serve. If you prefer, buy four smaller fish and cook for a shorter time, until just tender and cooked through but not overdone.

2 Heat the remaining oil in the tin or pan and fry the onions for 2–3 minutes until slightly softened. Add the chilli and red and green peppers and continue cooking for 3–4 minutes, stirring occasionally, then add the garlic and stir-fry for a further minute.

3 Blend the tomato purée with the fish stock or water and stir into the pan with the tomatoes, parsley, lemon juice, paprika and seasoning. Simmer gently without boiling for 15 minutes, stirring occasionally.

4 Return the fish to the tin or pan and cover with the sauce. Cook for 10 minutes then add the olives and cook for a further 5 minutes or until just cooked through.

5 Transfer the fish to a serving dish and pour the sauce over the top. Allow to cool, then cover and chill until completely cold. Serve cold with bread and salad.

King Prawns in Curry Sauce

INGREDIENTS

Serves 4

450g/1lb raw king prawns
600ml/1 pint/2½ cups water
3 thin slices fresh root ginger
10ml/2 tsp curry powder
2 garlic cloves, crushed
15g/½ oz/1 tbsp butter or margarine
60ml/4 tbsp ground almonds
1 green chilli, seeded and finely
    chopped
45ml/3 tbsp single cream
salt and freshly ground black pepper

For the vegetables

15ml/1 tbsp mustard oil
15ml/1 tbsp vegetable oil
1 onion, sliced
½ red pepper, seeded and thinly sliced
½ green pepper, seeded and thinly
    sliced
1 christophene, peeled, stoned and cut
    into strips
salt and freshly ground black pepper

1 Shell the prawns and place shells in a saucepan with the water and ginger. Simmer, uncovered, for 15 minutes until reduced by half. Strain into a jug and discard the shells.

2 Devein the prawns, place in a bowl and season with the curry powder, garlic and salt and pepper and set aside.

3 Heat the mustard and vegetable oils in a large frying pan, add all the vegetables and stir fry for 5 minutes. Season with salt and pepper, spoon into a serving dish and keep warm.

4 Wipe out the frying pan, then melt the butter or margarine and sauté the prawns for about 5 minutes until pink. Spoon over the bed of vegetables, cover and keep warm.

5 Add the ground almonds and chilli to the pan, stir fry for a few seconds and then add the reserved stock and bring to the boil. Reduce the heat, stir in the cream and simmer for a few minutes, without boiling.

6 Pour the sauce over the vegetables and prawns before serving.

Fried Fish in Green Chilli Sauce

INGREDIENTS

Serves 4

4 medium pomfret
juice of 1 lemon
5ml/1 tsp garlic granules
salt and freshly ground black pepper
vegetable oil, for shallow frying

For the coconut sauce

450ml/¾ pint/1⅞ cups water
2 thin slices fresh root ginger
25–40g/1–1½ oz creamed coconut
30ml/2 tbsp vegetable oil
1 red onion, sliced
2 garlic cloves, crushed
1 green chilli, seeded and thinly sliced
15ml/1 tbsp chopped fresh coriander
salt and freshly ground black pepper

1 Cut the fish in half and sprinkle inside and out with the lemon juice. Season with the garlic granules and salt and pepper and set aside to marinate for a few hours.

2 Heat a little oil in a large frying pan. Pat away the excess lemon juice from the fish, fry in the oil for 10 minutes, turning once. Set aside.

3 To make the sauce, place the water in a saucepan with the slices of ginger, bring to the boil and simmer until the liquid is reduced to just over 300ml/½ pint/1¼ cups. Take out the ginger and reserve, then add the creamed coconut to the pan and stir until the coconut has melted.

4 Heat the oil in a wok or large pan and fry the onion and garlic for 2–3 minutes. Add the reserved ginger and coconut stock, the chilli and coriander, stir well and then gently add the fish. Simmer for 10 minutes, until the fish is cooked through. Transfer the fish to a warmed serving plate, adjust the seasoning for the sauce and pour over the fish. Serve immediately.

Chilli Crabs

There are variations on this recipe all over Asia, but all are hot and spicy. This delicious dish owes its spiciness and flavour to chillies, ginger and shrimp paste.

INGREDIENTS

Serves 4

2 cooked crabs, about 675g/1½ lb
1cm/½ in cube shrimp paste
2 garlic cloves
2 fresh red chillies, seeded, or 5ml/
  1 tsp chopped chilli from a jar
1cm/½ in fresh root ginger, peeled
  and sliced
60ml/4 tbsp sunflower oil
300ml/½ pint/1¼ cups tomato ketchup
15ml/1 tbsp dark brown sugar
150ml/¼ pint/⅔ cup warm water
4 spring onions, chopped, to garnish
cucumber chunks and hot toast,
  to serve (optional)

1 Remove the large claws of one crab and turn on to its back, with the head facing away from you. Use your thumbs to push the body up from the main shell. Discard the stomach sac and "dead men's fingers", i.e. lungs and any green matter. Leave the creamy brown meat in the shell and cut the shell in half, with a cleaver or strong knife. Cut the body section in half and crack the claws with a sharp blow from a hammer or cleaver. Avoid splintering the claws. Repeat with the other crab.

2 Grind the shrimp paste, garlic, chillies and ginger to a paste with a pestle and mortar.

3 Heat a wok and add the oil. Fry the spice paste, stirring it all the time, without browning.

4 Stir in the tomato ketchup, sugar and water and mix the sauce well. When just boiling, add all the crab pieces and toss in the sauce until well-coated and hot. Serve in a large bowl, sprinkled with the spring onions. Place in the centre of the table for everyone to help themselves. Accompany this finger-licking dish with cool cucumber chunks and hot toast for mopping up the sauce, if you like.

Caribbean Spiced Fish

This dish is of Spanish origin and is very popular throughout the Caribbean. There are as many variations of the name of the dish as there are ways of preparing it.

INGREDIENTS

Serves 4–6
900g/2lb cod fillet
½ lemon
15ml/1 tbsp spice seasoning
flour, for dusting
oil, for frying
lemon wedges, to garnish

For the sauce
30ml/2 tbsp vegetable oil
1 onion, sliced
½ red pepper, sliced
½ christophene, peeled and seeded, cut
  into small pieces
2 garlic cloves, crushed
120ml/4fl oz/½ cup malt vinegar
75ml/5 tbsp water
2.5ml/½ tsp ground allspice
1 bay leaf
1 small Scotch Bonnet pepper, chopped
15ml/1 tbsp soft brown sugar
salt and freshly ground black pepper

1 Place the fish in a shallow dish, squeeze over the lemon, then sprinkle with the spice seasoning and pat into the fish. Leave to marinate in a cool place for at least 1 hour.

2 Cut the fish into 7.5cm/3in pieces and dust with a little flour, shaking off the excess.

3 Heat the oil in a heavy frying pan and fry the fish pieces for 2–3 minutes until golden brown and crisp, turning occasionally. To make the sauce, heat the oil in a heavy frying pan and fry the onion until soft.

4 Add the pepper, christophene and garlic and stir-fry for 2 minutes. Pour in the vinegar, then add the remaining ingredients and simmer gently for 5 minutes. Leave to stand for 10 minutes, then pour over the fish. Serve hot, garnished with lemon wedges.

--- COOK'S TIP ---

In the Caribbean, whole red snapper or red mullet are used for this dish.

Prawns in Spicy Tomato Sauce

Cumin and cinnamon add subtle spiciness to this delicious, simple-to-make prawn recipe, which comes from the Middle East.

INGREDIENTS

Serves 4

30ml/2 tbsp oil
2 onions, finely chopped
2–3 garlic cloves, crushed
5–6 tomatoes, peeled and chopped
30ml/2 tbsp tomato purée
120ml/4fl oz/½ cup fish stock
   or water
2.5ml/½ tsp ground cumin
2.5ml/½ tsp ground cinnamon
450g/1lb raw, peeled Mediterranean
   prawns
juice of 1 lemon
salt and freshly ground black pepper
fresh parsley, to garnish
rice, to serve

1 Heat the oil in a large frying pan or saucepan and fry the onions for 3–4 minutes until golden. Add the garlic, fry for about 1 minute, and then stir in the tomatoes.

2 Blend the tomato purée with the stock or water and stir into the pan with the cumin, cinnamon and seasoning. Simmer, covered, over a low heat for 15 minutes, stirring occasionally. Do not allow to boil.

3 Add the prawns and lemon juice and simmer the sauce for a further 10–15 minutes over a low to moderate heat until the prawns are cooked and the stock is reduced by about half.

4 Serve with plain rice or in a decorative ring of Persian Rice, garnished with parsley.

Spiced Fish Kebabs

Marinating adds spicy flavour to these delicious kebabs.

Serves 4–6

900g/2lb swordfish steaks
45ml/3 tbsp olive oil
juice of ½ lemon
1 garlic clove, crushed
5ml/1 tsp cayenne pepper
3 tomatoes, quartered
2 onions, cut into wedges
salt and freshly ground black pepper
salad and pitta bread, to serve

--- COOK'S TIP ---

Almost any type of firm white fish can be used for this recipe.

1 Cut the fish into large cubes and place in a dish.

2 Blend together the oil, lemon juice, garlic, paprika and seasoning in a small mixing bowl and pour over the fish. Cover loosely with clear film and leave to marinate in a cool place for up to 2 hours.

3 Thread the fish cubes on to skewers alternating with pieces of tomato and onion.

4 Grill the kebabs over hot charcoal for 5–10 minutes, basting frequently with the remaining marinade and turning occasionally. Serve with salad and pitta bread.

Prawns in Spiced Coconut Sauce

Spices, chillies and herbs make a fragrant sauce for this dish.

INGREDIENTS

Serves 4
24–30 large raw prawns
spice seasoning, for dusting
juice of 1 lemon
30ml/2 tbsp butter or margarine
1 onion, chopped
2 garlic cloves, crushed
30ml/2 tbsp tomato purée
2.5ml/½ tsp dried thyme
2.5ml/½ tsp ground cinnamon
15ml/1 tbsp chopped fresh coriander
½ hot chilli pepper, chopped
175g/6oz frozen or canned sweetcorn
300ml/½ pint/1¼ cups coconut milk
chopped fresh coriander, to garnish

1 Sprinkle the prawns with spice seasoning and lemon juice and marinate in a cool place for an hour.

2 Melt the butter or margarine in a saucepan, fry the onion and garlic for 5 minutes, until slightly softened. Add the prawns and cook for a few minutes, stirring occasionally until cooked through and pink.

3 Transfer the prawns, onion and garlic to a bowl, leaving behind some of the buttery liquid. Add the tomato purée to the pan and cook over a low heat, stirring thoroughly. Add the thyme, cinnamon, coriander and hot pepper and stir well.

4 Blend the sweetcorn (reserving 15ml/1 tbsp) in a blender or food processor with the coconut milk. Add to the pan and simmer until reduced. Add the prawns and reserved corn, and simmer for 5 minutes. Serve hot, garnished with coriander.

COOK'S TIP

If you use raw king prawns, make a stock from the shells and use in place of some of the coconut milk.

Curried Prawns and Saltfish

Shrimp paste and spices add tasty flavour to this fish dish.

INGREDIENTS

Serves 4
450g/1lb raw prawns, peeled
15ml/1 tbsp spice seasoning
25g/1oz/2 tbsp butter or margarine
15ml/1 tbsp olive oil
2 shallots, finely chopped
1 garlic clove, crushed
350g/12oz okra, topped, tailed and cut
  into 2.5cm/1in lengths
5ml/1 tsp curry powder
10ml/2 tsp shrimp paste
15ml/1 tbsp chopped fresh coriander
15ml/1 tbsp lemon juice
175g/6oz prepared saltfish (see Cook's
  Tip), shredded

1 Season the prawns with the spice seasoning and leave to marinate in a cool place for about 1 hour.

2 Heat the butter or margarine and olive oil in a large frying pan or wok over a moderate heat and stir-fry the shallots and garlic for 5 minutes. Add the okra, curry powder and shrimp paste, stir well and cook for about 10 minutes, until the okra is tender.

3 Add 30ml/2 tbsp water, coriander, lemon juice, prawns and saltfish, and cook gently for 5–10 minutes. Adjust the seasoning and serve hot.

COOK'S TIP

Soak the saltfish for 12 hours, changing the water two or three times. Rinse, bring to the boil in fresh water, then cool.

Lemon Grass Prawns on Crisp Noodle Cake

INGREDIENTS

Serves 4

300g/11oz thin egg noodles
60ml/4 tbsp vegetable oil
500g/1¼lb medium raw king prawns,
    peeled and deveined
2.5ml/½ tsp ground coriander
15ml/1 tbsp ground turmeric
2 garlic cloves, finely chopped
2 slices fresh root ginger,
    finely chopped
2 lemon grass stalks, finely chopped
2 shallots, finely chopped
15ml/1 tbsp tomato purée
250ml/8fl oz/1 cup coconut cream
4–6 kaffir lime leaves (optional)
15–30ml/1–2 tbsp fresh lime juice
15–30ml/1–2 tbsp fish sauce
1 cucumber, peeled, seeded and cut
    into 5cm/2in batons
1 tomato, seeded and cut into strips
2 red chillies, seeded and
    finely sliced
salt and freshly ground black pepper
2 spring onions, finely sliced, and
    a few coriander sprigs, to garnish

1 Cook the egg noodles in a saucepan of boiling water until just tender. Drain, rinse under cold running water and drain well.

2 Heat 15ml/1 tbsp of the oil in a large frying pan. Add the noodles, distributing them evenly, and fry for 4–5 minutes until crisp and golden. Turn the noodle cake over and fry the other side. Alternatively, make four individual cakes. Keep hot.

3 In a bowl, toss the prawns with the ground coriander, turmeric, garlic, ginger and lemon grass. Add salt and pepper to taste.

4 Heat the remaining oil in a large frying pan. Add the shallots, fry for 1 minute, then add the prawns and fry for 2 minutes more. Using a slotted spoon remove the prawns.

5 Stir the tomato purée and coconut cream into the mixture remaining in the pan. Stir in lime juice to taste and season with the fish sauce. Bring the sauce to a simmer, return the prawns to the sauce, then add the kaffir lime leaves, if using, and the cucumber. Simmer gently until the prawns are cooked and the sauce is reduced to a nice coating consistency.

6 Add the tomato, stir until just warmed through, then add the chillies. Serve on top of the crisp noodle cake(s), garnished with sliced spring onions and coriander sprigs.

Stir-fried Prawns with Tamarind

The sour, tangy flavour that is characteristic of many Thai dishes comes from tamarind. Fresh tamarind pods from the tamarind tree can sometimes be bought, but preparing them for cooking is a laborious process. The Thais, however, usually prefer to use compressed blocks of tamarind paste, which is simply soaked in warm water and then strained.

INGREDIENTS

Serves 4–6

50g/2oz tamarind paste
150ml/¼ pint/⅔ cup boiling water
30ml/2 tbsp vegetable oil
30ml/2 tbsp chopped onion
30ml/2 tbsp palm sugar
30ml/2 tbsp chicken stock or water
15ml/1 tbsp fish sauce
6 dried red chillies, fried
450g/1lb uncooked shelled prawns
15ml/1 tbsp fried chopped garlic
30ml/2 tbsp fried sliced shallots
2 spring onions, chopped, to garnish

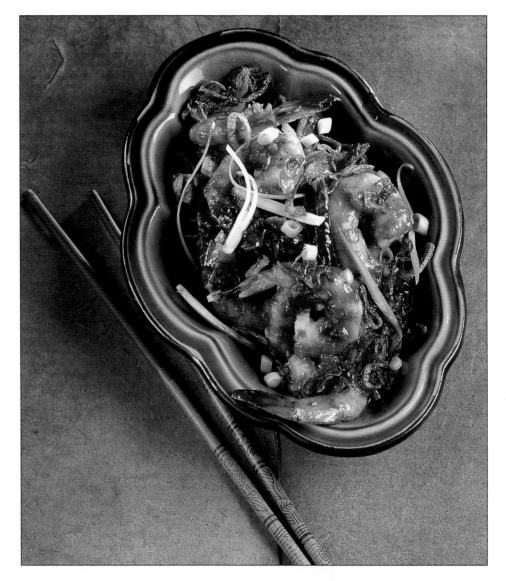

1 Put the tamarind paste in a small bowl, pour over the boiling water and stir well to break up any lumps. Leave for 30 minutes. Strain, pushing as much of the juice through as possible. Measure 90ml/6 tbsp of the juice, the amount needed, and store the remainder in the fridge. Heat the oil in a wok. Add the chopped onion and fry until golden brown.

2 Add the sugar, stock, fish sauce, dried chillies and the tamarind juice, stirring well until the sugar dissolves. Bring to the boil.

3 Add the prawns, garlic and shallots. Stir-fry until the prawns are cooked, about 3–4 minutes. Garnish with the spring onions.

Spicy Prawns with Okra

INGREDIENTS

Serves 4–6

60–90ml/4–6 tbsp oil
225g/8oz okra, washed, dried and
   left whole
4 garlic cloves, crushed
5cm/2in piece of fresh root
   ginger, chopped
4–6 green chillies, cut diagonally
2.5ml/½ tsp turmeric
4–6 curry leaves
5ml/1 tsp cumin seeds
450g/1lb fresh king prawns, peeled
   and deveined
10ml/2 tsp brown sugar
juice of 2 lemons
salt, to taste

1 Heat the oil in a frying pan and fry the okra on a fairly high heat until they are slightly crisp and browned on all sides. Remove from the oil and keep aside on a piece of kitchen paper.

2 In the same oil, gently fry the garlic, ginger, chillies, turmeric, curry leaves and cumin seeds for 2–3 minutes. Add the prawns and mix well. Cook until the prawns are tender.

3 Add the salt, sugar, lemon juice and fried okra. Increase the heat and quickly fry for a further 5 minutes, stirring gently to prevent the okra from breaking. Adjust the seasoning, if necessary. Serve hot.

COOK'S TIP

Okra should be cooked rapidly to prevent the pods from breaking up and releasing their distinctive thick, sticky liquid.

Spicy Prawns with Cornmeal

These crispy fried prawns with a cornmeal coating and a cheesy topping are truly delicious when served with a spicy tomato salsa and lime wedges to ease the heat.

INGREDIENTS

Serves 4

115g/4oz/³⁄₄ cup cornmeal
5–10ml/1–2 tsp cayenne pepper
2.5ml/½ tsp ground cumin
5ml/1 tsp salt
30ml/2 tbsp chopped fresh coriander
    or parsley
900g/2lb large raw prawns, peeled and
    deveined
flour, for dredging
¼ cup vegetable oil
115g/4oz/1 cup grated
    Cheddar cheese

To serve
lime wedges
tomato salsa

1 Preheat the grill. In a mixing bowl, combine the cornmeal, cayenne, cumin, salt and coriander or parsley.

2 Coat the prawns lightly in flour, then dip them in water and roll them in the cornmeal mixture to coat.

3 Heat the oil in a non-stick frying pan. When hot, add the prawns, in batches if necessary. Cook them until they are opaque throughout, for about 2–3 minutes on each side. Drain on kitchen paper.

4 Place the prawns in a large baking dish, or in individual dishes. Sprinkle the cheese evenly over the top. Grill about 8cm/3in from the heat until the cheese melts, for about 2–3 minutes. Serve immediately, with lime wedges and tomato salsa.

Pineapple Curry with Prawns and Mussels

The delicate sweet and sour flavour of this curry comes from the pineapple and although it seems an odd combination, it is rather delicious. Use the freshest shellfish that you can find.

INGREDIENTS

Serves 4–6

600ml/1 pint/2½ cups coconut milk
30ml/2 tbsp red curry paste
30ml/2 tbsp fish sauce
15ml/1 tbsp granulated sugar
225g/8oz king prawns, shelled
    and deveined
450g/1lb mussels, cleaned and
    beards removed
175g/6oz fresh pineapple, finely
    crushed or chopped
5 kaffir lime leaves, torn
2 red chillies, chopped, to garnish
coriander leaves, to garnish

1 In a large saucepan, bring half the coconut milk to the boil and heat, stirring, until it separates.

2 Add the red curry paste and cook until fragrant. Add the fish sauce and sugar and continue to cook for a few moments.

3 Stir in the rest of the coconut milk and bring back to the boil. Add the king prawns, mussels, pineapple and kaffir lime leaves.

4 Reheat until boiling and then simmer for 3–5 minutes, until the prawns are cooked and the mussels have opened. Remove any mussels that have not opened and discard. Serve garnished with chopped red chillies and coriander leaves.

Curried Prawns in Coconut Milk

A curry-like dish where the prawns are cooked in a spicy coconut gravy.

INGREDIENTS

Serves 4–6

600ml/1 pint/2½ cups coconut milk
30ml/2 tbsp yellow curry paste (see
    Cook's Tip)
15ml/1 tbsp fish sauce
2.5ml/½ tsp salt
5ml/1 tsp granulated sugar
450g/1lb king prawns, shelled, tails left
    intact and deveined
225g/8oz cherry tomatoes
juice of ½ lime, to serve
2 red chillies, cut into strips, to garnish
coriander leaves, to garnish

1 Put half the coconut milk into a pan or wok and bring to the boil.

2 Add the yellow curry paste to the coconut milk, stir until it disperses, then simmer for about 10 minutes.

3 Add the fish sauce, salt, sugar and remaining coconut milk. Simmer for another 5 minutes.

4 Add the prawns and cherry tomatoes. Simmer very gently for about 5 minutes until the prawns are pink and tender.

5 Serve sprinkled with lime juice and garnish with chillies and coriander.

COOK'S TIP

To make yellow curry paste, process together 6–8 yellow chillies, 1 chopped lemon grass stalk, 4 peeled shallots, 4 garlic cloves, 15ml/1 tbsp peeled chopped fresh root ginger, 5ml/1 tsp coriander seeds, 5ml/1 tsp mustard powder, 5ml/1 tsp salt, 2.5ml/½ tsp ground cinnamon, 15ml/1 tbsp light brown sugar and 30ml/2 tbsp oil in a blender or food procesor. When a paste has formed, transfer to a glass jar and keep in the fridge.

SCORCHING MEAT AND POULTRY

Meat and poultry dishes cooked with chillies and spices are universally popular, but recipe variations are endless and each country adds its own twist and unique mixture of spices; Blackened Hot Chicken Breasts from the deep South, Caribbean Barbecued Jerk Chicken, Beef Enchiladas from Mexico and Spicy Meat Fritters from Indonesia are just a few of the fiery dishes on offer.

Spicy Meat Fritters

INGREDIENTS

Makes 30

450g/1lb potatoes, boiled and drained
450g/1lb lean minced beef
1 onion, quartered
1 bunch spring onions, chopped
3 garlic cloves, crushed
5ml/1 tsp ground nutmeg
15ml/1 tbsp coriander seeds, dry-fried
   and ground
10ml/2 tsp cumin seeds, dry-fried
   and ground
4 eggs, beaten
oil for shallow-frying
salt and freshly ground black pepper

1 While the potatoes are still warm, mash them in the pan until they are well broken up. Add to the minced beef and mix well together.

2 Finely chop the onion, spring onions and garlic. Add to the meat with the ground nutmeg, coriander and cumin. Stir in enough beaten egg to give a soft consistency which can be formed into fritters. Season to taste.

3 Heat the oil in a large frying pan. Using a dessertspoon, scoop out 6–8 oval-shaped fritters and drop them into the hot oil. Allow to set, so that they keep their shape (this will take about 3 minutes) and then turn over and cook for a further minute.

4 Drain well on kitchen paper and keep warm while cooking the remaining fritters.

Barbecued Pork Spareribs

INGREDIENTS

Serves 4

1kg/2¼lb pork spareribs
1 onion
2 garlic cloves
2.5cm/1in fresh root ginger
75ml/3fl oz/⅓ cup dark soy sauce
1–2 fresh red chillies, seeded
   and chopped
5ml/1 tsp tamarind pulp, soaked in
   75ml/3fl oz/⅓ cup water
15–30ml/1–2 tbsp dark brown sugar
30ml/2 tbsp groundnut oil
salt and freshly ground black pepper

1 Wipe the pork ribs and place them in a wok, wide frying pan or large flameproof casserole.

2 Finely chop the onion, crush the garlic and peel and slice the ginger. Blend the soy sauce, onion, garlic, ginger and chopped chillies together to a paste in a food processor or with a pestle and mortar. Strain the tamarind and reserve the juice. Add the tamarind juice, brown sugar, oil and seasoning to taste to the onion mixture and mix well together.

3 Pour the sauce over the ribs and toss well to coat. Bring to the boil and then simmer, uncovered and stirring frequently, for 30 minutes. Add extra water if necessary.

4 Put the ribs on a rack in a roasting tin, place under a preheated grill, on a barbecue or in the oven at 200°C/400°F/Gas 6 and continue cooking until the ribs are tender, about 20 minutes, depending on the thickness of the ribs. Baste the ribs with the sauce and turn them over from time to time.

Beef with Cactus Pieces

Nopalitos – chunks of an edible cactus – are used as a vegetable in Mexico, and are the basis of several salads, soups and bakes.

INGREDIENTS

Serves 6
900g/2lb braising beef, cut into
    5cm/2in cubes
30ml/2 tbsp corn oil
1 onion, finely chopped
2 garlic cloves, chopped
1 or 2 *jalapeño* chillies, seeded and
    chopped
115g/4oz can *nopalitos* (cactus pieces),
    rinsed and drained
2 x 275g/10oz tomatillos (Mexican
    green tomatoes)
50g/2oz/½ cup fresh chopped
    coriander
beef stock (optional)
salt and freshly ground black pepper
chopped fresh coriander, to garnish

1 Pat the beef cubes dry with kitchen paper. Heat the oil in a frying pan and sauté the beef cubes a few at a time, until browned all over. Using a slotted spoon, transfer the beef cubes to a flameproof casserole or pan.

2 Add the onion and garlic to the oil remaining in the frying pan and sauté until the onion is tender. Add more oil if necesssary. Add the onions and garlic to the casserole or pan together with the chillies.

3 Add the *nopalitos* and tomatillos, with the can juices, to the casserole. Stir in the coriander until well mixed. If more liquid is needed to cover the beef, stir in as much stock as needed. Season with salt and pepper.

4 Bring to a slow simmer, cover and cook over a low heat for about 2½ hours or until the beef is very tender. Serve sprinkled with the chopped coriander.

COOK'S TIP

Tomatillos (Mexican green tomatoes) are not to be confused with ordinary green unripe tomatoes. Look for them, canned, in speciality markets and food shops.

Tex-Mex Baked Potatoes with Chilli

INGREDIENTS

Serves 4

2 large potatoes
15ml/1 tbsp oil
1 garlic clove, crushed
1 small onion, chopped
½ red pepper, seeded and chopped
225g/8oz lean minced beef
½ fresh red chilli, seeded and chopped
5ml/1 tsp ground cumin
pinch of cayenne pepper
200g/7oz can chopped tomatoes
30ml/2 tbsp tomato purée
2.5ml/½ tsp dried oregano
2.5ml/½ tsp dried marjoram
200g/7oz can red kidney beans
15ml/1 tbsp chopped fresh coriander
60ml/4 tbsp soured cream
salt and ground black pepper
chopped fresh parsley, to garnish

1 Preheat the oven to 220°C/425°F/ Gas 7. Oil the potatoes and pierce with skewers. Bake for 30 minutes.

2 Heat the oil in a pan and add the garlic, onion and pepper. Fry gently for 4–5 minutes until softened.

3 Add the minced beef and fry until it is browned all over, then stir in the chopped chilli, ground cumin, cayenne pepper, tomatoes, tomato purée, 60ml/4 tbsp water and the herbs. Cover and simmer for about 25 minutes, stirring occasionally.

VARIATION

For a lower fat topping, use natural yogurt instead of soured cream.

4 Drain the kidney beans and add to the pan. Cook for 5 minutes, turn off the heat and stir in the chopped coriander. Season well and set aside.

5 Cut the baked potatoes in half and place one half in each of four serving bowls. Top them with the chilli beef mixture and a dollop of soured cream and garnish with plenty of chopped fresh parsley.

Beef Enchiladas

INGREDIENTS

Serves 4

900g/2lb chuck steak
15ml/1 tbsp vegetable oil, plus extra
   for frying
5ml/1 tsp salt
5ml/1 tsp dried oregano
2.5ml/½ tsp ground cumin
1 onion, quartered
2 garlic cloves, crushed
1 litre/1¾ pints/4 cups enchilada sauce
12 corn tortillas
115g/4oz/1 cup grated cheese
chopped spring onions, to garnish
soured cream, to serve

1 Preheat the oven to 160°C/325°F/ Gas 3. Place the meat on a sheet of foil and rub it all over with the oil. Sprinkle both sides with the salt, oregano and cumin and rub in well. Add the onion and garlic. Top with another sheet of foil and roll up to seal the edges, leaving room for some steam expansion during cooking.

2 Place in a baking dish and bake for 3 hours, until the meat is tender enough to shred. Remove from the foil and shred the meat using two forks.

3 Stir 120ml/4fl oz/½ cup of the enchilada sauce into the beef. Spoon a thin layer of enchilada sauce on the bottom of a rectangular baking dish, or in four individual dishes.

4 Place the remaining sauce in a frying pan and warm gently.

5 Put a 1cm/½in layer of vegetable oil in a second frying pan and heat until hot but not smoking. With tongs, lower a tortilla into the oil; the temperature is correct if it just sizzles. Cook for 2 seconds, then turn and cook the other side for 2 seconds. Lift out, drain over the pan, and then transfer to the pan with the sauce. Dip in the sauce just to coat both sides.

6 Transfer the softened tortilla immediately to a plate. Spread about 2–3 spoonfuls of the beef mixture down the centre of the tortilla. Roll it up and place the filled tortilla seam-side down in the prepared dish. Repeat this process for all the remaining tortillas.

7 Spoon the remaining sauce from the frying pan over the beef enchiladas, spreading it right down to the ends. Sprinkle the grated cheese down the centre.

8 Bake the enchiladas until the cheese topping just melts, for about 10–15 minutes. Sprinkle with chopped spring onions and serve at once, with soured cream on the side.

COOK'S TIP

For a quicker recipe, use minced beef. Fry in a little oil with chopped onion and garlic, until browned all over. Continue the recipe from step 3.

Red Enchiladas

INGREDIENTS

Serves 6

4 dried *ancho* chillies
450g/1lb tomatoes, peeled, seeded
   and chopped
1 onion, finely chopped
1 garlic clove, chopped
15ml/1 tbsp chopped fresh coriander
lard or corn oil for frying
250ml/8fl oz/1 cup soured cream
4 chorizo sausages, skinned
   and chopped
18 freshly prepared unbaked
   corn tortillas
50g/2oz/2½ cups freshly grated
   Parmesan cheese
salt and freshly ground black pepper

1 Roast the *ancho* chillies in a dry frying pan over moderate heat for 1–2 minutes, shaking the pan frequently. When cool, carefully slit the chillies, remove the stems and seeds, and tear the pods into pieces. Put in a bowl, add warm water to just cover, and soak for 20 minutes.

2 Tip the chillies, with a little of the soaking water, into a food processor. Add the tomatoes, onion, garlic and coriander; purée.

--- COOK'S TIP ---

The method of dipping the tortillas first in sauce, then quickly cooking them in lard or oil gives the best flavour. If you prefer, fry the plain tortillas very quickly, then dip them in the sauce, stuff and roll. There is not a great loss of flavour, and no spatter.

3 Heat 15ml/1 tbsp lard or oil in a saucepan. Add the purée and cook gently over a moderate heat, stirring, for 3–4 minutes. Season to taste with salt and pepper and then stir in the soured cream. Remove the pan from the heat and set it aside.

4 Heat a further 15ml/1 tbsp lard or oil in a small frying pan; sauté the chorizo for a few minutes until lightly browned. Moisten with a little of the sauce and set the pan aside.

5 Preheat the oven to 180°C/350°F/ Gas 4. Heat 30ml/2 tbsp lard or oil in a frying pan. Dip a tortilla in the sauce and add to the pan. Cook for a few seconds, shaking the pan gently, turn over and briefly fry the other side.

6 Slide the tortilla on to a plate, top with some of the sausage mixture, and roll up. Pack the prepared tortillas in a single layer in a baking dish. Pour the sauce over, sprinkle with Parmesan and bake for about 20 minutes.

Caribbean Lamb Curry

This popular national dish of Jamaica is known as Curry Goat although goat meat or lamb can be used to make it.

INGREDIENTS

Serves 4–6

2 pounds boned leg of lamb
4 tablespoons curry powder
3 garlic cloves, crushed
1 large onion, chopped
4 thyme sprigs or 1 teaspoon dried thyme
3 bay leaves
1 teaspoon ground allspice
2 tablespoons vegetable oil
4 tablespoons butter or margarine
3³/₄ cups stock or water
1 fresh hot chili pepper, chopped
cooked rice, to serve
cilantro sprigs, to garnish

1 Cut the meat into 2-inch cubes, discarding any excess fat and gristle.

2 Place the lamb, curry powder, garlic, onion, thyme, bay leaves, allspice and oil in a large bowl and mix. Marinate in the fridge for at least 3 hours or overnight.

3 Melt the butter or margarine in a large heavy saucepan, add the seasoned lamb and fry over a moderate heat for about 10 minutes, turning the meat frequently.

4 Stir in the stock and chili pepper and bring to a boil. Reduce the heat, cover the pan and simmer for 1½ hours, or until the meat is tender. Serve with rice, garnish with cilantro.

—— COOK'S TIP ——

Try goat, or mutton, if you can and enjoy a robust curry.

Lamb Stew

This stew is known as *Estofado de Carnero* in Mexico. The recipe for this dish has an interesting mix of chillies – the mild, full-flavoured *ancho,* and the piquant *jalapeño* which gives extra "bite". The heat of the chillies is mellowed by the addition of ground cinnamon and cloves. Boneless neck fillet is very good for this dish; it is lean, tender, flavoursome and inexpensive.

INGREDIENTS

Serves 4
3 dried *ancho* chillies
30ml/2 tbsp olive oil
1 *jalapeño* chilli, seeded and
   chopped
1 onion, finely chopped
2 garlic cloves, chopped
450g/1lb tomatoes, peeled
   and chopped
50g/2oz/⅓ cup seedless raisins
1.5ml/¼ tsp ground cinnamon
1.5ml/¼ tsp ground cloves
900g/2lb boneless lamb, cut into
   5cm/2in cubes
250ml/8fl oz/1 cup lamb stock
   or water
salt and freshly ground black pepper
a few sprigs of fresh coriander,
   to garnish
coriander rice, to serve

1 Roast the *ancho* chillies lightly in a dry frying pan over gentle heat to bring out the flavour.

2 Remove the stems, shake out the seeds and tear the pods into pieces, then put them into a bowl. Pour in enough warm water to just cover. Leave to soak for 30 minutes.

3 Heat the olive oil in a frying pan and sauté the *jalapeño* chilli together with the onion and garlic until the onion is tender.

4 Add the chopped tomatoes to the pan and cook until the mixture is thick and well blended. Stir in the raisins, ground cinnamon and cloves, and season to taste with salt and ground black pepper. Transfer the mixture to a flameproof casserole.

5 Tip the *ancho* chillies and their soaking water into a food processor and process to a smooth purée. Add the chilli purée to the tomato mixture in the casserole.

6 Add the lamb cubes to the casserole, stir to mix and pour in enough of the lamb stock or water to just cover the meat.

7 Bring to a simmer, then cover the casserole and cook over a low heat for about 2 hours or until the lamb is tender. Garnish with fresh coriander and serve with coriander rice.

--- COOK'S TIP ---

To make coriander rice, simply heat 30ml/2 tbsp corn oil in a large frying pan and gently cook 1 finely chopped onion for about 8 minutes or until soft but not brown. Stir in enough cooked, long grain rice for four and stir gently over a very moderate heat until heated through. Sprinkle over 30–45ml/2–3 tbsp chopped fresh coriander and stir in thoroughly.

Sweet and Sour Pork

INGREDIENTS

Serves 4

350g/12oz lean pork
1.5ml/¼ tsp salt and 2.5ml/½ tsp
 ground Szechuan peppercorns
15ml/1 tbsp Chinese rice wine
115g/4oz bamboo shoots
30ml/2 tbsp plain flour
1 egg, lightly beaten
vegetable oil, for frying
15ml/1 tbsp vegetable oil
1 garlic clove, finely chopped
1 spring onion, cut into short sections
1 small green pepper, diced finely
1 fresh red chilli, seeded
 and shredded
15ml/1 tbsp light soy sauce
30ml/2 tbsp light brown sugar
45ml/3 tbsp rice vinegar
15ml/1 tbsp tomato purée
about 120ml/4fl oz/½ cup stock

1 Using a sharp knife, cut the lean pork into small bite-size cubes. Marinate with the salt, ground peppercorns and Chinese wine for about 15–20 minutes.

2 Cut the bamboo shoots into small cubes about the same size as the pork pieces.

3 Dust the pork with flour, dip in the beaten egg, and coat with more flour. Deep-fry in moderately hot oil for 3–4 minutes, stirring to separate the pieces. Remove.

4 Reheat the oil, add the pork and bamboo shoots and fry for 1 minute, or until golden. Drain.

5 Heat 15ml/1 tbsp oil and add the garlic, spring onion, pepper and chilli. Stir-fry for 30–40 seconds, then add the seasonings with the stock. Bring to the boil, then add the pork and bamboo shoots.

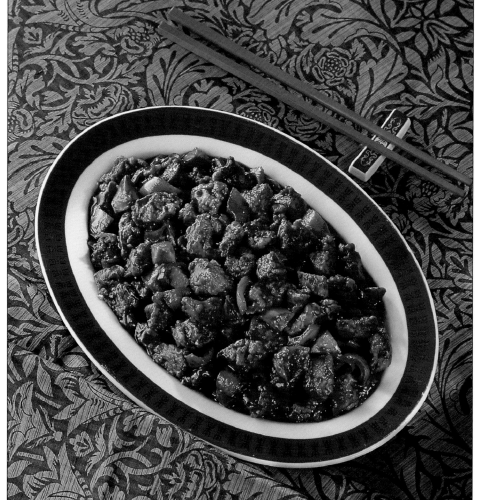

Lamb Tagine with Coriander and Spices

This is a version of a Moroccan-style tagine in which chops or cutlets are sprinkled with spices and either marinated for a few hours or cooked straightaway.

INGREDIENTS

Serves 4

4 lamb chump chops
2 garlic cloves, crushed
pinch of saffron strands
2.5ml/½ tsp ground cinnamon, plus
   extra to garnish
2.5ml/½ tsp ground ginger
15ml/1 tbsp chopped fresh coriander
15ml/1 tbsp chopped fresh parsley
1 onion, finely chopped
45ml/3 tbsp olive oil
300ml/½ pint/1¼ cups lamb stock
50g/2oz/½ cup blanched almonds,
   to garnish
5ml/1 tsp sugar
salt and freshly ground black pepper

1 Season the lamb with the garlic, saffron, cinnamon, ginger and a little salt and black pepper. Place on a large plate and sprinkle with the coriander, parsley and onion. Cover loosely and set aside in the fridge for a few hours to marinate.

2 Heat the oil in a large frying pan, over a moderate heat. Add the marinated lamb and all the herbs and onion from the dish.

3 Fry for 1–2 minutes, turning once, then add the stock, bring to the boil and simmer gently for 30 minutes, turning the chops once.

4 Meanwhile, heat a small frying pan over a moderate heat, add the almonds and dry fry until golden, shaking the pan occasionally to ensure they colour evenly. Transfer to a bowl and set aside.

5 Transfer the chops to a serving plate and keep warm. Increase the heat under the pan and boil the sauce until reduced by about half. Stir in the sugar. Pour the sauce over the chops and sprinkle with the fried almonds and a little extra ground cinnamon.

COOK'S TIP

Lamb tagine is a fragrant dish, originating in North Africa. It is traditionally made in a cooking dish, known as a tagine, from where it takes its name. This dish consists of a plate with a tall lid with sloping sides. It has a narrow opening to let steam escape, while retaining the flavour.

Khara Masala Lamb

Whole spices are used in this curry so you should warn the diners of their presence in advance! It is delicious when served with freshly baked naan bread or a rice accompaniment. This dish is best made with good-quality spring lamb.

INGREDIENTS

Serves 4
75ml/5 tbsp corn oil
2 onions, chopped
5ml/1 tsp shredded ginger
5ml/1 tsp sliced garlic
6 whole dried red chillies
3 cardamom pods
2 cinnamon sticks
6 black peppercorns
3 cloves
2.5ml/½ tsp salt
450g/1lb boned leg of lamb, cubed
600ml/1 pint/2½ cups water
2 fresh green chillies, sliced
30ml/2 tbsp chopped fresh coriander

1 Heat the oil in a large saucepan. Lower the heat slightly and fry the onions until they are lightly browned.

2 Add half the ginger and half the garlic and stir well.

3 Throw in half the red chillies, the cardamoms, cinnamon, peppercorns, cloves and salt.

4 Add the lamb and fry over a medium heat. Stir continuously with a semi-circular movement, using a wooden spoon to scrape the bottom of the pan. Continue in this way for about 5 minutes.

5 Pour in the water, cover with a lid and cook over a medium-low heat for 35–40 minutes, or until the water has evaporated and the meat is tender.

6 Add the rest of the shredded ginger, sliced garlic and the whole dried red chillies, along with the sliced fresh green chillies and the fresh chopped coriander.

COOK'S TIP

The action of stirring the meat and spices together using a semi-circular motion, as described in step 4, is called bhoono-ing. It ensures that the meat becomes well-coated and combined with the spice mixture before the cooking liquid is added.

---

7 Continue to stir over the heat until you see some free oil on the sides of the pan. Transfer to a serving dish and serve immediately.

Deep-fried Spareribs with Spicy Salt and Pepper

If you want these spareribs to be hotter, just increase the amount of chilli sauce.

INGREDIENTS

Serves 4–6

10–12 finger ribs, in total about 675g/1½lb, with excess fat and gristle trimmed
about 30–45ml/2–3 tbsp flour
vegetable oil, for deep-frying

For the marinade

1 garlic clove, crushed and chopped
15ml/1 tbsp light brown sugar
15ml/1 tbsp dark soy sauce
30ml/2 tbsp Chinese rice wine or dry sherry
2.5ml/½ tsp chilli sauce
few drops sesame oil

1 Chop each rib into 3–4 pieces. Combine all the marinade ingredients in a bowl, add the spareribs and leave to marinate for at least 2–3 hours.

2 Coat the spareribs with flour and deep-fry them in medium-hot oil for 4–5 minutes, stirring to separate. Remove and drain.

3 Heat the oil to high and deep-fry the spareribs once more for about 1 minute, or until the colour is an even dark brown. Remove and drain, then serve hot.

SPICY SALT AND PEPPER

To make Spicy Salt and Pepper, mix 15ml/1 tbsp salt with 10ml/2 tsp ground Szechuan peppercorns and 5ml/1 tsp five-spice powder. Heat together in a preheated dry pan for about 2 minutes over a low heat, stirring constantly. This quantity is sufficient for at least six servings.

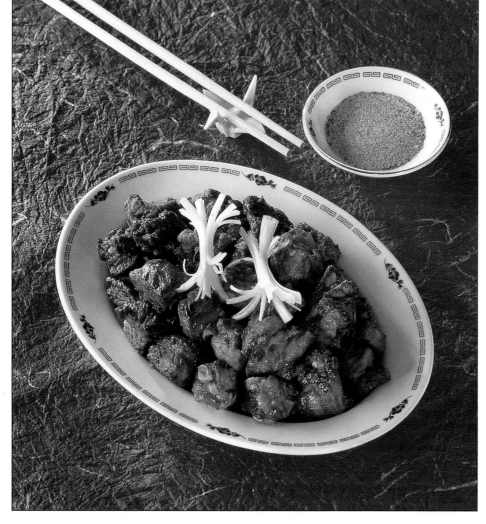

Pork with Chillies and Pineapple

INGREDIENTS

Serves 6

30ml/2 tbsp corn oil
900g/2lb boneless pork shoulder or
   loin, cut into 5cm/2in cubes
1 onion, finely chopped
1 large red pepper, seeded and
   finely chopped
1 or more *jalapeño* chillies, seeded and
   finely chopped
450g/1lb fresh pineapple chunks
8 fresh mint leaves, chopped
250ml/8fl oz/1 cup chicken stock
salt and freshly ground black pepper
fresh mint sprig, to garnish
rice, to serve

1 Heat the oil in a large frying pan and sauté the pork in batches until the cubes are lightly coloured. Transfer the pork to a flameproof casserole, leaving the oil behind in the pan.

2 Add the finely chopped onion, finely chopped red pepper and the chilli(es) to the oil remaining in the pan. Sauté until the onion is tender, then add to the casserole with the pineapple. Stir to mix.

3 Add the mint, then cover and simmer gently for about 2 hours, or until the pork is tender. Garnish with fresh mint and serve with rice.

— COOK'S TIP —

If fresh pineapple is not available, use pineapple canned in its own juice.

Mole Poblano de Guajolote

Mole Poblano de Guajolote is *the* great festive dish of Mexico. It is served at any special occasion, be it a birthday, wedding, or family get-together. Rice, beans, tortillas and Guacamole are the traditional accompaniments

INGREDIENTS

Serves 6–8
2.75–3.6kg/6–8lb turkey, cut into
   serving pieces
1 onion, chopped
1 garlic clove, chopped
salt
90ml/6 tbsp lard or corn oil
fresh coriander and 30ml/2 tbsp toasted
   sesame seeds, to garnish

For the sauce
6 dried *ancho* chillies
4 dried *pasilla* chillies
4 dried *mulato* chillies
1 drained canned *chipotle* chilli, seeded
   and chopped (optional)
2 onions, chopped
2 garlic cloves, chopped
450g/1lb tomatoes, peeled
   and chopped
1 stale tortilla, torn into pieces
50g/2oz/⅓ cup seedless raisins
115g/4oz/1 cup ground almonds
45ml/3 tbsp sesame seeds, ground
2.5ml/½ tsp coriander seeds, ground
5ml/1 tsp ground cinnamon
2.5ml/½ tsp ground anise
1.5ml/¼ tsp ground black peppercorns
60ml/4 tbsp lard or corn oil
40g/1½oz unsweetened (bitter)
   chocolate, broken into squares
15ml/1 tbsp sugar
salt and freshly ground pepper

COOK'S TIP

Roasting the dried chillies lightly, taking care not to burn them, brings out the flavour and is worth the extra effort.

---

1 Put the turkey pieces into a saucepan or flameproof casserole large enough to hold them in one layer comfortably. Add the onion and garlic, and enough cold water to cover. Season with salt, bring to a gentle simmer, cover and cook for about 1 hour or until the turkey is tender.

2 Meanwhile, put the *ancho, pasilla* and *mulato* chillies in a dry frying pan over gentle heat and roast them for a few minutes, shaking the pan frequently. Remove the stems and shake out the seeds. Tear the pods into pieces and put these into a small bowl. Add sufficient warm water to just cover and soak, turning from time to time, for 30 minutes until soft.

3 Lift out the turkey pieces and pat them dry with kitchen paper. Reserve the stock in a measuring jug. Heat the lard or oil in a large frying pan and sauté the turkey pieces until lightly browned all over. Transfer to a plate and set aside. Reserve the oil that is left in the frying pan.

4 Tip the chillies, with the water in which they have been soaked, into a food processor. Add the *chipotle* chilli, if using, with the onions, garlic, tomatoes, tortilla, raisins, ground almonds and spices. Process to a purée. Do this in batches if necessary.

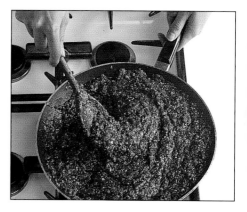

5 Add the lard or oil to the fat remaining in the frying pan used for sautéing the turkey. Heat the mixture, then add the chilli and spice paste. Cook, stirring, for 5 minutes.

6 Transfer the mixture to the pan or casserole in which the turkey was originally cooked. Stir in 475ml/ 16fl oz/2 cups of the turkey stock (make it up with water if necessary). Add the chocolate and season with salt and pepper. Cook over a low heat until the chocolate has melted. Stir in the sugar. Add the turkey and more stock if needed. Cover the pan and simmer very gently for 30 minutes. Serve, garnished with fresh coriander and sprinkled with the sesame seeds.

Spicy Meatballs

Serve these Indonesian meatballs with a sambal or a spicy sauce.

INGREDIENTS

Makes 24

1 large onion, roughly chopped
1–2 fresh red chillies, seeded
  and chopped
2 garlic cloves, crushed
1cm/½in cube shrimp paste
15ml/1 tbsp coriander seeds
5ml/1 tsp cumin seeds
450g/1lb lean minced beef
10ml/2 tsp dark soy sauce
5ml/1 tsp dark brown sugar
juice of ½ lemon
a little beaten egg
oil for shallow-frying
salt and freshly ground black pepper
fresh coriander sprigs, to garnish

1 Put the onions, chillies, garlic and shrimp paste in a food processor. Process but do not over-chop or the onion will become too wet and spoil the consistency of the meatballs. Dry-fry the coriander and cumin seeds in a preheated pan for about 1 minute, to release the aroma. Do not brown. Grind with a pestle and mortar.

2 Put the meat in a large bowl. Stir in the onion mixture. Add the ground coriander and cumin, soy sauce, seasoning, sugar and lemon juice. Bind with a little beaten egg and shape into small, even-size balls.

3 Chill the meatballs briefly to firm up, if necessary. Fry in shallow oil, turning often, until cooked through and browned. This will take 4–5 minutes, depending on their size.

4 Remove from the pan, drain well on kitchen paper and serve, garnished with coriander sprigs.

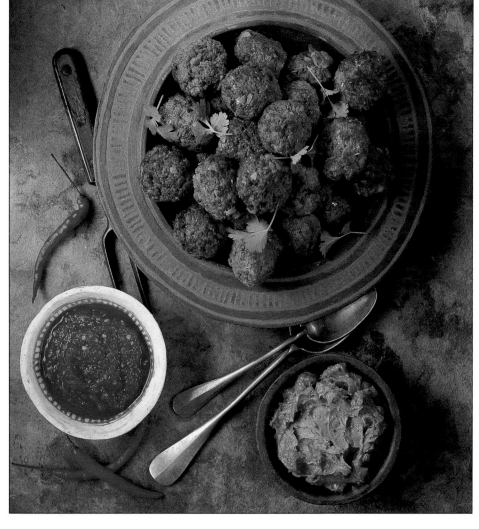

Beef and Aubergine Curry

INGREDIENTS

Serves 6

120ml/4fl oz/½ cup sunflower oil
2 onions, thinly sliced
2.5cm/1in fresh root ginger, sliced and
   cut in matchsticks
1 garlic clove, crushed
2 fresh red chillies, seeded and very
   finely sliced
2.5cm/1in fresh turmeric, peeled and
   crushed, or 5ml/1 tsp
   ground turmeric
1 lemon grass stem, lower part sliced
   finely, top bruised
675g/1½ lb braising steak, cut in even-
   size strips
400ml/14fl oz can coconut milk
300ml/½ pint/1¼ cups water
1 aubergine, sliced and patted dry
5ml/1 tsp tamarind pulp, soaked in
   60ml/4 tbsp warm water
salt and freshly ground black pepper
finely sliced chilli and deep-fried
   onions, to garnish
boiled rice, to serve

1 Heat half the oil and fry the
onions, ginger and garlic until they
give off a rich aroma. Add the chillies,
turmeric and the lower part of the
lemon grass. Push to one side and then
turn up the heat and add the steak,
stirring until the meat changes colour.

COOK'S TIP

If you want to make this curry, *Gulai
Terung Dengan Daging,* ahead, prepare to
the end of step 2 and finish later.

2 Add the coconut milk, water,
lemon grass top and seasoning to
taste. Cover and simmer gently for
1½ hours, or until the meat is tender.

3 Towards the end of the cooking
time heat the remaining oil in a
frying pan. Fry the aubergine slices
until brown on both sides.

4 Add the browned aubergine slices
to the beef curry and cook for a
further 15 minutes. Stir gently from
time to time. Strain the tamarind and
stir the juice into the curry. Taste and
adjust the seasoning. Put into a warm
serving dish. Garnish with the sliced
chilli and deep-fried onions and serve
with boiled rice.

Spicy Fried Chicken

This crispy chicken is superb hot or cold. Served with a salad or vegetables, it makes a delicious lunch and is ideal for picnics or snacks too.

INGREDIENTS

Serves 4–6

4 chicken drumsticks
4 chicken thighs
10ml/2 tsp curry powder
2.5ml/½ tsp garlic granules
2.5ml/½ tsp ground black pepper
2.5ml/½ tsp paprika
about 300ml/½ pint/1¼ cups milk
oil, for deep frying
50g/2oz/4 tbsp plain flour
salt
salad leaves, to serve

1 Place the chicken pieces in a large bowl and sprinkle with the curry powder, garlic granules, black pepper, paprika and salt. Rub the spices well into the chicken, then cover and leave to marinate in a cool place for at least 2 hours, or overnight in the fridge.

2 Preheat the oven to 180°C/350°F/ Gas 4. Pour enough milk into the bowl to cover the chicken and leave to stand for a further 15 minutes.

3 Heat the oil in a large saucepan or deep-fat fryer and tip the flour on to a plate. Shake off excess milk, dip each piece of chicken in flour and fry two or three pieces at a time until golden, but not cooked. Continue until all the chicken pieces are fried.

4 Remove with a slotted spoon, place the chicken pieces on a baking tray, and bake for about 30 minutes. Serve hot or cold with salad.

Spicy Chicken with Coconut

Traditionally, the chicken pieces for this Indonesian dish would be part-cooked by frying, but roasting in the oven is just as successful. This recipe is unusual in that it does not contain any chillies or turmeric, but galangal, lemon grass, coriander and lime leaves add a deliciously spicy flavour.

INGREDIENTS

1.5kg/3−3½lb chicken or 4 chicken
  quarters
4 garlic cloves
1 onion, sliced
4 macadamia nuts or 8 almonds
15ml/1 tbsp coriander seeds, dry-fried,
  or 5ml/1 tsp ground coriander
45ml/3 tbsp oil
2.5cm/1in fresh galangal, peeled
  and bruised
2 lemon grass stems, fleshy part bruised
3 lime leaves
2 bay leaves
5ml/1 tsp sugar
600ml/1 pint/2½ cups coconut milk
salt
boiled rice and deep-fried onions, to
  serve

1 Preheat the oven to 190°C/375°F/ Gas 5. Cut the chicken into four or eight pieces. Season with salt. Put in an oiled roasting tin and cook in the oven for 25−30 minutes. Meanwhile prepare the sauce.

2 Grind the garlic, onion, nuts and coriander to a fine paste in a food processor or with a pestle and mortar. Heat the oil and fry the paste to bring out the flavour. Do not allow it to brown.

3 Add the part-cooked chicken pieces to a wok together with the galangal, lemon grass, lime and bay leaves, sugar, coconut milk and salt to taste. Mix well to coat in the sauce.

4 Bring to the boil and then reduce the heat and simmer gently for 30−40 minutes, uncovered, until the chicken is tender and the coconut sauce is reduced and thickened. Stir the mixture occasionally during cooking.

5 Just before serving, remove the bruised galangal and lemon grass. Serve with boiled rice sprinkled with crisp deep-fried onions.

Crispy and Aromatic Duck

As this dish is often served with pancakes, spring onions, cucumber and duck sauce (a sweet bean paste), many people mistake it for Peking Duck. This recipe, however, uses a different cooking method. The result is just as crispy but the delightful aroma makes this dish particularly distinctive. Plum sauce may be substituted for the duck sauce.

INGREDIENTS

Serves 6–8

1 oven-ready duckling,
  about 2.25kg/5–5¼lb
10ml/2 tsp salt
5–6 whole star anise
15ml/1 tbsp Szechuan peppercorns
5ml/1 tsp cloves
2–3 cinnamon sticks
3–4 spring onions
3–4 slices fresh root ginger, unpeeled
75–90ml/5–6 tbsp Chinese rice wine
  or dry sherry
vegetable oil, for deep-frying
lettuce leaves, to garnish

To serve
Chinese pancakes
duck sauce
spring onions, shredded
cucumber, diced

1 Remove the wings from the duck and split the body in half down the backbone.

2 Rub salt all over the two duck halves, taking care to work it all in thoroughly.

3 Marinate the duck in a dish with the spices, spring onions, fresh ginger and wine or sherry for at least 4–6 hours.

4 Vigorously steam the duck with the marinade for 3–4 hours (or for longer if possible). Carefully remove the steamed duck from the cooking liquid and leave to cool for at least 5–6 hours. The duck must be cold and dry or the skin will not be crisp.

5 Heat the vegetable oil in a wok until it is just smoking, then place the duck pieces in the oil, skin-side down. Deep fry the duck for about 5–6 minutes, or until it becomes crisp and brown. Turn the duck just once at the very last moment.

6 Remove the fried duck, drain it well and place it on a bed of lettuce leaves.

7 To serve, scrape the meat off the bone and wrap a portion in each pancake with a little duck sauce, shredded spring onions and cucumber. Eat with your fingers.

COOK'S TIP

Small pancakes suitable for this dish can be found in most Chinese supermarkets. They can be frozen and will keep for up to 3 months in the freezer.

Barbecued Jerk Chicken

Jerk refers to the blend of herb and spice seasoning rubbed into meat, before it is roasted over charcoal sprinkled with pimiento berries. In Jamaica, jerk seasoning was originally used only for pork, but jerked chicken is equally good.

INGREDIENTS

Serves 4
8 chicken pieces

For the marinade
5ml/1 tsp ground allspice
5ml/1 tsp ground cinnamon
5ml/1 tsp dried thyme
1.5ml/¼ tsp freshly grated nutmeg
10ml/2 tsp demerara sugar
2 garlic cloves, crushed
15ml/1 tbsp finely chopped onion
15ml/1 tbsp chopped spring onion
15ml/1 tbsp vinegar
30ml/2 tbsp oil
15ml/1 tbsp lime juice
1 hot chilli pepper, chopped
salt and freshly ground black pepper
salad leaves, to serve

1 Combine all the marinade ingredients in a small bowl. Using a fork, mash them together well to form a thick paste.

2 Lay the chicken pieces on a plate or board and make several lengthways slits in the flesh. Rub the seasoning all over the chicken and into the slits.

3 Place the chicken pieces in a dish, cover with clear film and marinate overnight in the fridge.

4 Shake off any excess seasoning from the chicken. Brush with oil and either place on a baking sheet or on a barbecue grill if barbecuing. Cook under a preheated grill for 45 minutes, turning often. Or, if barbecuing, light the coals and when ready, cook over the coals for 30 minutes, turning often. Serve hot with salad leaves.

COOK'S TIP

The flavour is best if you marinate the chicken overnight. Sprinkle the charcoal with aromatic herbs such as bay leaves for even more flavour.

Blackened Hot Chicken Breasts

INGREDIENTS

Serves 6
6 skinless boneless chicken breasts
75g/3oz/6 tbsp butter or margarine
5ml/1 tsp garlic powder
10ml/2 tsp onion powder
5ml/1 tsp cayenne pepper
10ml/2 tsp sweet paprika
7.5ml/1½ tsp salt
2.5ml/½ tsp white pepper
5ml/1 tsp ground black pepper
1.5ml/¼ tsp ground cumin
5ml/1 tsp dried thyme

1 Slice each chicken breast piece in half horizontally, making two pieces of about the same thickness. Flatten slightly with the heel of your hand.

2 Melt the butter or margarine in a small saucepan.

4 Heat a large heavy frying pan over a high heat until a drop of water sprinkled on the surface sizzles. This will take 5–8 minutes.

3 Combine all the remaining ingredients in a shallow bowl and stir to blend well. Brush the chicken pieces on both sides with melted butter or margarine, then sprinkle evenly with the seasoning mixture.

5 Drizzle 5ml/1 tsp melted butter on each chicken piece. Place them in the pan in an even layer, two or three at a time. Cook for 2–3 minutes until the underside begins to blacken. Turn and cook the other side for another 2–3 minutes. Serve hot.

Hot Chicken Curry

This curry has a nice thick sauce, and using red and green peppers gives it extra colour. It can be served with either wholemeal chapatis or plain boiled rice.

INGREDIENTS

Serves 4

30ml/2 tbsp corn oil
1.5ml/¼ tsp fenugreek seeds
1.5ml/¼ tsp onion seeds
2 onions, chopped
2.5ml/½ tsp garlic pulp
2.5ml/½ tsp ginger pulp
5ml/1 tsp ground coriander
5ml/1 tsp chilli powder
5ml/1 tsp salt
400g/14oz/1¾ cups canned tomatoes
30ml/2 tbsp lemon juice
350g/12oz/2½ cups chicken, skinned, boned and cubed
30ml/2 tbsp chopped fresh coriander
3 fresh green chillies, chopped
½ red pepper, cut into chunks
½ green pepper, cut into chunks
fresh coriander sprigs

1 In a medium saucepan, heat the oil and fry the fenugreek and onion seeds until they turn a shade darker. Add the chopped onions, garlic and ginger and fry for about 5 minutes until the onions turn golden brown. Turn the heat to very low.

2 Meanwhile, in a separate bowl, mix together the ground coriander, chilli powder, salt, canned tomatoes and lemon juice.

3 Pour this mixture into the saucepan and turn up the heat to medium. Stir-fry for about 3 minutes.

4 Add the chicken pieces and stir-fry for 5–7 minutes.

5 Add the fresh coriander, green chillies and the red and green peppers. Lower the heat, cover the saucepan and let this simmer for about 10 minutes until the chicken is cooked.

6 Serve hot, garnished with fresh coriander sprigs.

COOK'S TIP

For a milder version of this delicious chicken curry, simply omit some of the fresh green chillies.

Spatchcocked Devilled Poussins

English mustard adds a hot touch to the spice paste used in this tasty recipe.

INGREDIENTS

Serves 4

15ml/1 tbsp English mustard powder
15ml/1 tbsp paprika
15ml/1 tbsp ground cumin
20ml/4 tsp tomato ketchup
15ml/1 tbsp lemon juice
65g/2½oz/5 tbsp butter, melted
4 poussins, about 450g/1lb each
salt

1 In a mixing bowl, combine the English mustard, paprika, ground cumin, tomato ketchup, lemon juice and salt. Mix together until smooth, then gradually stir in the melted butter until incorporated.

2 Using game shears or a strong pair of kitchen scissors, split each poussin along one side of the backbone, then cut down the other side of the backbone to remove it.

3 Open out a poussin, skin-side uppermost, then press down firmly with the heel of your hand. Pass a long skewer through one leg and out through the other to secure the bird open and flat. Repeat with the remaining birds.

4 Spread the spicy mustard mixture evenly over the skin of each of the poussins. Cover them loosely and leave in a cool place for at least 2 hours. Preheat the grill.

5 Place the prepared poussins, skin-side uppermost, on a grill rack and grill them for about 12 minutes. Turn the birds over and baste with any juices in the pan. Cook the poussins for a further 7 minutes, until all the juices run clear.

COOK'S TIP

Spatchcocked poussins cook very well on the barbecue. Make sure that the coals are very hot, then cook the birds for about 15–20 minutes, turning and basting them frequently as they cook.

Bon-bon Chicken with Spicy Sesame

In this recipe, the chicken meat is tenderized by being beaten with a stick (called a "bon" in Chinese) – hence the name for this very popular Szechuan dish.

INGREDIENTS

Serves 6–8
1 whole chicken, about 1kg/2¼lb
1.2 litres/2 pints/5 cups water
15ml/1 tbsp sesame oil
shredded cucumber, to garnish

For the sauce
30ml/2 tbsp light soy sauce
5ml/1 tsp sugar
15ml/1 tbsp finely chopped
　spring onions
5ml/1 tsp red chilli oil
2.5ml/½ tsp Szechuan peppercorns
5ml/1 tsp white sesame seeds
30ml/2 tbsp sesame paste, or
　30ml/2 tbsp peanut butter creamed
　with a little sesame oil

1 Clean the chicken well. In a wok or saucepan bring the water to a rolling boil, add the chicken, reduce the heat and cook under cover for 40–45 minutes. Remove the chicken and immerse in cold water to cool.

2 After at least 1 hour, remove the chicken and drain; dry well with kitchen paper and brush with sesame oil. Carve the meat from the legs, wings and breast and pull the meat off the rest of the bones.

3 On a flat surface, pound the meat with a rolling pin, then tear the meat into shreds with your fingers.

4 Place the meat in a dish with the shredded cucumber around the edge. In a bowl, mix together all the sauce ingredients, keeping a few spring onions to garnish. Pour over the chicken and serve.

COOK'S TIP

To make chilli oil, slit and blanch chillies, pack into sterilized jars and fill with oil. Leave for 2 weeks.

Chicken Sauce Piquante

Red chilli peppers add heat to this Cajun recipe. Sauce Piquante is commonly used in lots of recipes to liven up meat and fish and give meals a spicy taste.

Ingredients

Serves 4

4 chicken legs or 2 legs and 2 breasts
75ml/5 tbsp oil
50g/2oz/½ cup plain flour
1 onion, chopped
2 celery sticks, sliced
1 green pepper, seeded and diced
2 garlic cloves, crushed
1 bay leaf
2.5ml/½ tsp dried thyme
2.5ml/½ tsp dried oregano
1–2 red chilli peppers, seeded and
   finely chopped
400g/14oz can tomatoes, chopped,
   with their juice
300ml/½ pint/1¼ cups chicken stock
salt and ground black pepper
watercress, to garnish
boiled potatoes, to serve

COOK'S TIP

If you prefer to err on the side of caution with chilli heat, use just 1 chilli pepper and hot up the seasoning at the end with a dash or two of Tabasco sauce.

---

1 Halve the chicken legs through the joint, or the breasts across the middle, to give eight pieces.

2 In a heavy frying pan, fry the chicken pieces in the oil until brown on all sides, lifting them out and setting them aside as they are done.

3 Strain the oil from the pan into a heavy flameproof casserole. Heat it and stir in the flour. Stir constantly over a low heat until the roux is the colour of peanut butter.

4 As soon as the roux reaches the right stage, tip in the onion, celery and pepper and stir over the heat for 2–3 minutes.

5 Add the garlic, bay leaf, thyme, oregano and chilli pepper(s). Stir for 1 minute, then turn down the heat and stir in the tomatoes with their juice.

6 Return the casserole to the heat and gradually stir in the stock. Add the chicken pieces, cover and leave to simmer for 45 minutes, until the chicken is tender.

7 If there is too much sauce or it is too runny, remove the lid for the last 10–15 minutes of the cooking time and raise the heat a little.

8 Check the seasoning and serve garnished with watercress and accompanied by boiled potatoes, or perhaps rice or pasta, and a green vegetable or salad of your choice.

VARIATION

Any kind of meat, poultry or fish can be served with Sauce Piquante. Just cook the meat or fish first, then serve it with plenty of the sauce.

Tandoori Chicken

Ingredients

Serves 4

4 chicken quarters
175ml/6fl oz/³/₄ cup natural
   low-fat yogurt
5ml/1 tsp garam masala
5ml/1 tsp ginger pulp
5ml/1 tsp garlic pulp
7.5ml/1½ tsp chilli powder
1.5ml/¼ tsp turmeric
5ml/1 tsp ground coriander
15ml/1 tbsp lemon juice
5ml/1 tsp salt
few drops red food colouring
30ml/2 tbsp corn oil
mixed salad leaves, lime wedges and
   1 tomato, quartered, to garnish

1 Skin, rinse and pat dry the chicken quarters. Make two slits into the flesh of each piece, place them in a dish and set aside.

2 Mix together the yogurt, garam masala, ginger, garlic, chilli powder, turmeric, ground coriander, lemon juice, salt, red colouring and oil, and beat so that all the ingredients are well mixed together.

3 Cover the chicken quarters with the spice mixture and leave to marinate for about 3 hours.

4 Preheat the oven to 240°C/475°F/ Gas 9. Transfer the chicken pieces to an ovenproof dish.

5 Bake in the preheated oven for 20–25 minutes, or until the chicken is cooked right through and browned on top.

6 Remove from the oven, transfer to a serving dish and garnish with the salad leaves, lime and tomato.

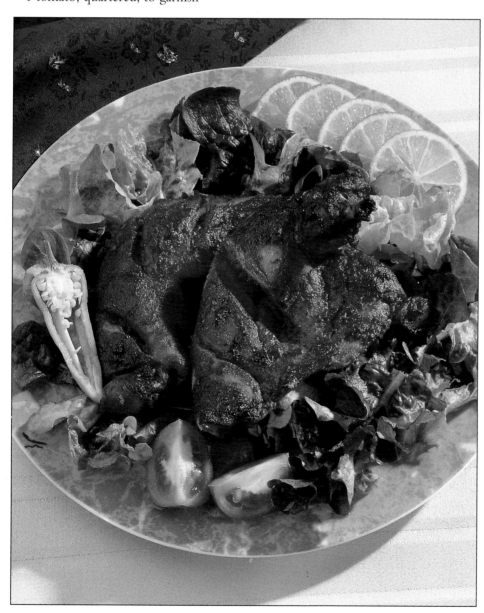

— Cook's Tip —

The red food colouring gives this dish its traditional appearance, but it can be omitted if wished.

Spicy Masala Chicken

These chicken pieces are grilled and have a sweet-and-sour taste. They can be served cold with a salad and rice, or hot with Masala Mashed Potatoes.

INGREDIENTS

Serves 6

12 chicken thighs
90ml/6 tbsp lemon juice
5ml/1 tsp ginger pulp
5ml/1 tsp garlic pulp
5ml/1 tsp crushed dried red chillies
5ml/1 tsp salt
5ml/1 tsp soft brown sugar
30ml/2 tbsp clear honey
30ml/2 tbsp chopped fresh coriander
1 fresh green chilli, finely chopped
30ml/2 tbsp vegetable oil
fresh coriander sprigs, to garnish

— COOK'S TIP —

Masala refers to the blend of spices used in this dish. The amounts can be varied according to taste.

---

1 Prick all the chicken thighs with a fork. Rinse them, pat dry and set aside in a bowl.

2 In a large mixing bowl, mix together the lemon juice, ginger, garlic, crushed dried red chillies, salt, sugar and honey.

3 Transfer the chicken thighs to the spice mixture and coat well. Set aside for about 45 minutes.

4 Preheat the grill to medium. Add the fresh coriander and chopped green chilli to the chicken thighs and place them in a flameproof dish.

5 Pour any remaining marinade over the chicken and baste with the oil, using a pastry brush.

6 Grill the chicken thighs under the preheated grill for 15–20 minutes, turning and basting occasionally, until cooked through and browned.

7 Transfer to a serving dish and garnish with the fresh coriander sprigs.

HOT AND VIBRANT VEGETABLES AND SALADS

Vegetables have a mild flavour which makes them perfect partners for assertive spices and hot chillies. Potatoes will never seem bland again after Potatoes with Red Chillies – this dish is for serious chilli addicts. Have fun with Mexican recipes such as Black Bean Burritos and Frijoles, which is simply cooked beans spiked with serrano chillies.

Szechuan Spicy Tofu

Szechuan pepper adds a spicy,
woody aroma to tofu in this dish.

INGREDIENTS

Serves 4
1 packet tofu
1 leek
115g/4oz minced beef
45ml/3 tbsp vegetable oil
15ml/1 tbsp black bean sauce
15ml/1 tbsp light soy sauce
5ml/1 tsp chilli bean sauce
15ml/1 tbsp Chinese rice wine
 or dry sherry
about 45–60ml/3–4 tbsp water or
 vegetable stock
10ml/2 tsp cornflour paste
ground Szechuan peppercorns, to taste
few drops sesame oil

1 Cut the tofu into 1cm/½in cubes
and blanch them in a pan of
boiling water for about 2–3 minutes
until they harden. Remove and drain.
Cut the leek into short sections.

2 Stir-fry the minced beef in oil until
the colour changes, then add the
chopped leek and black bean sauce.
Add the tofu with the soy sauce, chilli
bean sauce and wine or sherry. Stir
gently for 1 minute.

3 Add the vegetable stock or water,
bring to the boil and braise for
about 2–3 minutes.

4 Thicken the spicy sauce with the
cornflour paste, season with the
ground Szechuan peppercorns and
sprinkle with some drops of sesame oil.
Serve immediately.

Potatoes with Red Chillies

The quantity of red chillies used in this potato dish may be too fiery for some palates. If you would prefer to make a milder version, you could either seed the red chillies, use fewer of them or just substitute them with a roughly chopped red pepper instead.

INGREDIENTS

Serves 4

12–14 baby new potatoes, halved
30ml/2 tbsp vegetable oil
2.5ml/½ tsp crushed dried red chillies
2.5ml/½ tsp white cumin seeds
2.5ml/½ tsp fennel seeds
2.5ml/½ tsp crushed coriander seeds
15ml/1 tbsp salt
1 onion, sliced
1–4 fresh red chillies,
   halved lengthways
15ml/1 tbsp chopped fresh coriander

COOK'S TIP

Serve this dish with plenty of cooling yogurt or raita, and some naan or chapatis.

---

1 Boil the halved baby potatoes in a saucepan of salted water until they are soft but still firm to the touch. Remove them from the heat and drain off the water.

2 In a deep frying pan, heat the oil, then turn down the heat to medium. Add the crushed chillies, cumin, fennel and coriander seeds and salt and fry for 30–40 seconds.

3 Add the sliced onion and fry until it is golden brown. Then add the potatoes, fresh red chillies and chopped fresh coriander.

4 Cover and cook for 5–7 minutes over a very low heat. Serve hot.

Green Chilli Dhal

This dhal (Tarka Dhal) is probably the most popular of lentil dishes and is found in most Indian and Pakistani restaurants.

INGREDIENTS

Serves 4

115g/4oz/½ cup masoor dhal (split red lentils)
50g/2oz/¼ cup moong dhal (small split yellow lentils)
600ml/1 pint/2½ cups water
5ml/1 tsp ginger pulp
5ml/1 tsp garlic pulp
1.5ml/¼ tsp turmeric
2 fresh green chillies, chopped
7.5ml/1½ tsp salt

For the tarka

30ml/2 tbsp oil
1 onion, sliced
1.5ml/¼ tsp mixed mustard and onion seeds
4 dried red chillies
1 tomato, sliced

To garnish

15ml/1 tbsp chopped fresh coriander
1–2 fresh green chillies, seeded and sliced
15ml/1 tbsp chopped fresh mint

1 Pick over the lentils for any stones before washing them.

2 Boil the lentils in the water with the ginger, garlic, turmeric and chopped green chillies for about 15–20 minutes until soft.

3 Mash the lentil mixture down. The consistency of the mashed lentils should be similar to that of a creamy chicken soup.

4 If the mixture looks too dry, just add some more water. Season with the salt.

5 To prepare the tarka, heat the oil and fry the onion with the mustard and onion seeds, dried red chillies and sliced tomato for 2 minutes.

6 Pour the tarka over the dhal and garnish with fresh coriander, green chillies and mint.

COOK'S TIP

Dried red chillies are available in many different sizes. If the ones you have are large, or if you want a less spicy flavour, reduce the quantity specified to 1–2.

Frijoles

Ingredients

Serves 6–8

350g/12oz/1¼–1½ cups dried red
   kidney, pinto or black haricot beans,
   picked over and rinsed
2 onions, finely chopped
2 garlic cloves, chopped
1 bay leaf
1 or more *serrano* chillies (small fresh
   green chillies)
30ml/2 tbsp corn oil
2 tomatoes, peeled, seeded and
   chopped
salt
sprigs of fresh bay leaves, to garnish

Cook's Tip

In Yucatan black haricot beans are cooked
with the Mexican herb *epazote*.

---

1 Put the beans into a pan and add
cold water to cover by 2.5cm/1in.

2 Add half the onion, half the garlic,
the bay leaf and the chilli(es). Bring
to the boil and boil vigorously for
about 10 minutes. Put the beans and
liquid into an earthenware pot or large
saucepan, cover and cook over a low
heat for 30 minutes. Add boiling water
if the mixture starts to become dry.

3 When the beans begin to wrinkle,
add 15ml/1 tbsp of the corn oil
and cook for a further 30 minutes or
until the beans are tender. Add salt to
taste and cook for 30 minutes more,
but do not add any more water.

4 Remove the beans from the heat.
Heat the remaining oil in a small
frying pan and sauté the remaining
onion and garlic until the onion is soft.
Add the tomatoes and cook for a few
minutes more.

5 Spoon 45ml/3 tbsp of the beans
out of the pot or pan and add
them to the tomato mixture. Mash to a
paste. Stir this into the beans to thicken
the liquid. Cook for just long enough
to heat through, if necessary. Serve the
beans in small bowls and garnish with
sprigs of fresh bay leaves.

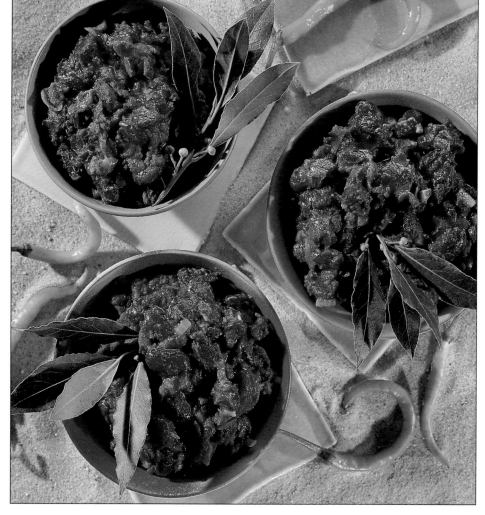

Black Bean Burritos

INGREDIENTS

Serves 4

175g/6oz/1 cup dried black beans,
  soaked overnight and drained
1 bay leaf
45ml/3 tbsp sea salt
1 small red onion, chopped
225g/8oz/2 cups grated cheese
45ml/3 tbsp chopped pickled jalapeños
15ml/1 tbsp chopped fresh coriander
750ml/1¼ pints/3 cups tomato salsa
8 flour tortillas
diced avocado, to serve

1 Place the beans in a large pan. Add cold water to cover and the bay leaf. Bring to the boil, then cover, and simmer for 30 minutes. Add the salt and continue simmering for about 30 minutes until tender. Drain and cool slightly. Discard the bay leaf.

2 Preheat the oven to 180°C/350°F/ Gas 4. Grease a rectangular baking dish well.

3 In a mixing bowl, combine the beans, onion, half the cheese, the jalapeños, coriander and one-third of the salsa. Stir to blend, then season.

4 Place one tortilla on a clean work surface. Spread a large spoonful of the filling down the middle, then roll it up to enclose the filling completely. Place the burrito in the prepared dish, seam-side down. Repeat this process with the remaining tortillas until the dish is full.

5 Sprinkle the remaining cheese over the burritos, in an even line right down the middle. Bake in the oven for about 15 minutes, or until the cheese melts completely.

6 Serve the bean burritos immediately, with diced avocado and the remaining salsa.

Chilli Courgettes

Calabacitas is an extremely easy recipe to make. If the cooking time seems unduly long, this is because the acid present in the tomatoes slows down the cooking of the courgettes. Use young tender courgettes.

INGREDIENTS

Serves 4
30ml/2 tbsp corn oil
450g/1lb young courgettes, sliced
1 onion, finely chopped
2 garlic cloves, chopped
450g/1lb tomatoes, peeled, seeded and chopped
2 drained canned *jalapeño* chillies, rinsed, seeded and chopped
15ml/1 tbsp chopped fresh coriander
salt
fresh coriander, to garnish

1 Heat the oil in a flameproof casserole and add all the remaining ingredients, except the salt.

2 Bring to simmering point, cover and cook over a low heat for about 30 minutes until the courgettes are tender, checking from time to time that the dish is not drying out. If it is, add a little tomato juice, stock or water.

3 Season with salt and serve the Mexican way as a separate course. Alternatively, serve accompanied by any plainly cooked meat or poultry. Garnish with fresh coriander.

Refried Beans (Frijoles Refritos)

There is much disagreement about the translation of the term *refrito*. It means, literally, twice fried. Some cooks say this implies that the beans must be really well fried, others that it means twice cooked. However named, *Frijoles Refritos* are delicious.

INGREDIENTS

Serves 6–8
90–120ml/6–8 tbsp lard or corn oil
1 onion, finely chopped
1 quantity Frijoles (cooked beans)

To garnish
freshly grated Parmesan cheese or crumbled cottage cheese
crisp fried corn tortillas, cut into quarters

1 Heat 30ml/2 tbsp of the lard in a large heavy-based frying pan and sauté the onion until it is soft. Add about 225ml/8fl oz/1 cup of the Frijoles (cooked beans).

— COOK'S TIP —

Lard is the traditional (and best tasting) fat for the beans but many people prefer to use corn oil. Avoid using olive oil, which is too strongly flavoured and distinctive.

2 Mash the beans with the back of a wooden spoon or potato masher, adding more beans and melted lard or oil until all the ingredients are used up and the beans have formed a heavy paste. Use extra lard or oil if necessary.

3 Tip out on to a warmed platter, piling the mixture up in a roll. Garnish with the cheese. Spike with the tortilla triangles, placing them at intervals along the length of the roll. Serve as a side dish.

Spicy Carrots

Adding spices to the carrots before leaving them to cool infuses them with flavour – an ideal dish to serve cold the next day (or up to a week later, if you keep them in the fridge).

Ingredients

Serves 4
450g/1lb carrots
475ml/16fl oz/2 cups water
2.5ml/½ tsp salt
5ml/1 tsp cumin seeds
½–1 red chilli (to taste)
1 large garlic clove, crushed
30ml/2 tbsp olive oil
5ml/1 tsp paprika
juice of 1 lemon
flat leaf parsley, to garnish

1 Cut the carrots into slices about 5mm/¼in thick. Bring the water to the boil and add the salt and carrot slices. Simmer for about 8 minutes or until the carrots are just tender, without allowing them to get too soft. Drain the carrots, put them into a bowl and set aside.

2 Grind or crush the cumin to a powder. Remove the seeds from the chilli and chop the chilli finely. Take care when handling as they can irritate the skin and eyes.

3 Gently heat the oil in a pan and toss in the garlic and the chilli. Stir over medium heat for about a minute, without allowing the garlic to brown. Stir in the paprika and the lemon juice.

4 Pour the warm mixture over the carrots, tossing them well so they are coated with the spices. Spoon into a serving dish and garnish with a sprig of flat leaf parsley.

Kenyan Mung Bean Stew

The Kenyan name for this simple and tasty stew is *Dengu*.

INGREDIENTS

Serves 4

225g/8oz/1¼ cups mung beans, soaked
    overnight
25g/1oz/2 tbsp ghee or butter
2 garlic cloves, crushed
1 red onion, chopped
30ml/2 tbsp tomato purée
½ green pepper, seeded and cut into
    small cubes
½ red pepper, seeded and cut into
    small cubes
1 green chilli, seeded and finely chopped
300ml/½ pint/1¼ cups water

1 Put the mung beans in a large saucepan, cover with water and boil until the beans are soft and the water has evaporated. Remove from the heat and mash roughly with a fork or potato masher.

2 Heat the ghee or butter in a separate saucepan, add the garlic and onion and fry for 4–5 minutes until golden brown, then add the tomato purée and cook for a further 2–3 minutes, stirring all the time.

3 Stir in the mashed beans, then the green and red peppers and chilli.

4 Add the water, stirring well to mix all the ingredients together.

5 Pour back into a clean saucepan and simmer for about 10 minutes, then spoon into a serving dish and serve at once.

--- COOK'S TIP ---

If you prefer a more traditional, smoother texture, cook the mung beans until very soft, then mash them thoroughly until smooth.

Broad Beans in Hot Sauce

A tasty dish of lima beans with a tomato and chilli sauce.

INGREDIENTS

Serves 4

450g/1lb green lima or broad beans,
  thawed if frozen
30ml/2 tbsp olive oil
1 onion, finely chopped
2 garlic cloves, chopped
350g/12oz tomatoes, peeled, seeded
  and chopped
1 or 2 drained canned *jalapeño* chillies,
  seeded and chopped
salt
chopped fresh coriander sprigs,
  to garnish

1 Cook the beans in a saucepan of boiling water for 15–20 minutes until tender. Drain and keep hot, to one side, in the covered saucepan.

2 Heat the olive oil in a frying pan and sauté the onion and garlic until the onion is soft but not brown. Add the tomatoes and cook until the mixture is thick and flavoursome.

3 Add the *jalapeños* and cook for 1–2 minutes. Season with salt.

4 Pour the mixture over the reserved beans and check that they are hot. If not, return everything to the frying pan and cook over low heat for just long enough to heat through. Put into a warm serving dish, garnish with the coriander and serve.

Broad Bean and Cauliflower Curry

This is a hot and spicy vegetable curry, ideal when served with cooked rice (especially a brown basmati variety), small poppadums and maybe a cooling cucumber raita as well.

INGREDIENTS

Serves 4

2 garlic cloves, chopped
2.5cm/1in cube fresh root ginger
1 fresh green chilli, seeded
  and chopped
15ml/1 tbsp oil
1 onion, sliced
1 large potato, chopped
30ml/2 tbsp ghee or softened butter
15ml/1 tbsp curry powder, mild or hot
1 cauliflower, cut into small florets
600ml/1 pint/2½ cups stock
30ml/2 tbsp creamed coconut
275g/10oz can broad beans, and liquor
juice of ½ lemon (optional)
salt and ground black pepper
fresh coriander, chopped, to garnish

1 Blend the garlic, ginger, chilli and oil in a food processor or blender until they form a smooth paste.

2 In a large saucepan, fry the onion and potato in the ghee or butter for 5 minutes, then stir in the spice paste and curry powder. Cook for 1 minute.

3 Add the cauliflower florets and stir well into the spicy mixture, then pour in the stock. Bring to the boil and mix in the creamed coconut, stirring until it melts.

4 Season well, then cover and simmer for 10 minutes. Add the beans and their liquor and cook, uncovered, for a further 10 minutes.

5 Check the seasoning and add a good squeeze of lemon juice, if liked. Serve hot, garnished with the chopped coriander.

Masala Mashed Potatoes

These potatoes are very versatile and will perk up any meal.

INGREDIENTS

Serves 4

3 potatoes
15ml/1 tbsp chopped fresh mint and coriander, mixed
5ml/1 tsp mango powder
5ml/1 tsp salt
5ml/1 tsp crushed black peppercorns
1 fresh red chilli, chopped
1 fresh green chilli, chopped
50g/2oz/4 tbsp margarine

1 Boil the potatoes until soft enough to be mashed. Mash them down using a masher.

2 Blend together the chopped herbs, mango powder, salt, pepper, chillies and margarine to form a paste.

3 Stir the mixture into the mashed potatoes and mix together thoroughly with a fork. Serve warm as an accompaniment.

VARIATION

Instead of potatoes, try sweet potatoes. Cook them until tender, mash and continue from step 2.

Spicy Cabbage

An excellent vegetable accompaniment, this is a very versatile spicy dish that can also be served as a warm side salad. It's so quick to make that it can be a handy last minute addition to any meal.

INGREDIENTS

Serves 4

50g/2oz/4 tbsp margarine
2.5ml/½ tsp white cumin seeds
3–8 dried red chillies, to taste
1 small onion, sliced
225g/8oz/2½ cups cabbage, shredded
2 carrots, grated
2.5ml/½ tsp salt
30ml/2 tbsp lemon juice

1 Melt the margarine in a saucepan and fry the white cumin seeds and dried red chillies for about 30 seconds.

2 Add the sliced onion and fry for about 2 minutes. Add the cabbage and carrots and stir-fry for a further 5 minutes until the cabbage is soft.

3 Finally, stir in the salt and lemon juice and serve.

Vinegared Chilli Cabbage

A hot cabbage dish that will certainly add a bit of spice to every meal. The addition of vinegar at the end gives this dish its distinct flavour.

Ingredients

Serves 4–6
1 fresh red chilli, halved, seeded and shredded
25g/1oz/2 tbsp lard or butter
2 garlic cloves, crushed (optional)
1 white cabbage, cored and shredded
10ml/2 tsp cider vinegar
5ml/1 tsp cayenne pepper
salt

─────── Cook's Tip ───────

A wok with a domed lid is good for this part-frying, part-steaming method of cooking cabbage.

1 Put the chilli with the lard or butter into a large pan and cook over a medium heat until the chilli sizzles and curls at the edges.

2 Add the garlic and cabbage and stir, over the heat, until the cabbage is coated and warm. Add salt to taste and 75ml/5 tbsp water. Bring to the boil, cover and lower the heat.

3 Cook, shaking the pan regularly, for 3–4 minutes until the cabbage wilts. Remove the lid, raise the heat and cook off the liquid. Check the seasoning and sprinkle with vinegar and cayenne pepper.

Coleslaw in Triple-hot Dressing

The triple hotness in this coleslaw is supplied by mustard, horseradish and Tabasco.

Ingredients

Serves 6
½ white cabbage, cored and shredded
2 celery sticks, finely sliced
1 green pepper, seeded and finely sliced
4 spring onions, shredded
30ml/2 tbsp chopped fresh dill
cayenne pepper

For the dressing
15ml/1 tbsp Dijon mustard
10ml/2 tsp creamed horseradish
5ml/1 tsp Tabasco sauce
30ml/2 tbsp red wine vinegar
75ml/5 tbsp olive oil
salt and ground black pepper

1 Mix the cabbage, celery, pepper and spring onions in a salad bowl.

2 Mix the mustard, horseradish and Tabasco sauce, then gradually stir in the vinegar with a fork and finally beat in the oil and seasoning. Toss the salad in the dressing and leave to stand, if possible, for at least 1 hour, turning it once or twice.

3 Immediately before serving, season the salad if necessary, toss again and sprinkle with dill and cayenne.

─────── Cook's Tip ───────

This is a good salad for a buffet table or picnic as it improves after standing in its dressing (it could be left overnight in the fridge) and travels well in a covered plastic bowl or box.

Vegetables in Peanut and Chilli Sauce

INGREDIENTS

Serves 4

15ml/1 tbsp palm or vegetable oil
1 onion, chopped
2 garlic cloves, crushed
400g/14oz can tomatoes, puréed
45ml/3 tbsp smooth peanut butter,
  preferably unsalted
750ml/1¼ pint/3⅔ cups water
5ml/1 tsp dried thyme
1 green chilli, seeded and chopped
1 vegetable stock cube
2.5ml/½ tsp ground allspice
2 carrots
115g/4oz white cabbage
175g/6oz okra
½ red pepper
150ml/¼ pint/⅔ cup vegetable stock
salt

1 Heat the oil in a large saucepan and fry the onion and garlic over a moderate heat for 5 minutes, stirring frequently. Add the tomatoes and peanut butter and stir well.

2 Stir in the water, thyme, chilli, stock cube, allspice and a little salt. Bring to the boil and then simmer gently, uncovered for about 35 minutes.

3 Cut the carrots into sticks, slice the cabbage, top and tail the okra and seed and slice the red pepper.

4 Place the vegetables in a saucepan with the stock, bring to the boil and cook until tender but still with a little "bite".

5 Drain the vegetables and place in a warmed serving dish. Pour the sauce over the top and serve.

Marinated Vegetables on Skewers

These kebabs are a delightful main dish for vegetarians, or serve them as a vegetable side dish.

INGREDIENTS

Serves 4
115g/4oz pumpkin
1 red onion
1 small courgette
1 ripe plantain
1 aubergine
½ red pepper, seeded
½ green pepper, seeded
12 button mushrooms
60ml/4 tbsp lemon juice
60ml/4 tbsp olive or sunflower oil
45–60ml/3–4 tbsp soy sauce
150ml/¼ pint/⅔ cup tomato juice
1 green chilli, seeded and chopped
½ onion, grated
3 garlic cloves, crushed
7.5ml/1½ tsp dried tarragon, crushed
4ml/¾ tsp dried basil
4ml/¾ tsp dried thyme
4ml/¾ tsp ground cinnamon
25g/1oz/2 tbsp butter or margarine
300ml/½ pint/1¼ cups vegetable stock
freshly ground black pepper
fresh parsley sprigs, to garnish

1 Peel and cube the pumpkin, place in a small bowl and cover with boiling water. Blanch for 2–3 minutes, then drain and refresh under cold water.

2 Cut the onion into wedges, slice the courgette and plantain and cut the aubergine and red and green peppers into chunks. Trim the mushrooms. Place the vegetables, including the pumpkin in a large bowl.

3 Mix together the lemon juice, oil, soy sauce, tomato juice, chilli, grated onion, garlic, herbs, cinnamon and black pepper and pour over the vegetables. Toss together and then set aside in a cool place to marinate for a few hours.

4 Thread the vegetables on to eight skewers, using a variety of vegetables on each to make a colourful display. Preheat the grill.

5 Grill the vegetables under a low heat, for about 15 minutes, turning frequently, until golden brown, basting with the marinade to keep the vegetables moist.

6 Place the remaining marinade, butter or margarine and stock in a pan and simmer for 10 minutes to cook the onion and reduce the sauce.

7 Pour the sauce into a serving jug and arrange the vegetable skewers on a plate. Garnish with parsley and serve with a rice dish or salad.

— COOK'S TIP —

You can use any vegetable that you prefer. Just first parboil any that may require longer cooking.

Black-eyed Bean Stew with Spicy Pumpkin

INGREDIENTS

Serves 3–4

225g/8oz/1¼ cups black-eyed beans,
  soaked for 4 hours or overnight
1 onion, chopped
1 green or red pepper, seeded and
  chopped
2 garlic cloves, chopped
1 vegetable stock cube
1 thyme sprig or 5ml/1 tsp dried thyme
5ml/1 tsp paprika
2.5ml/½ tsp mixed spice
2 carrots, sliced
15–30ml/1–2 tbsp palm oil
salt and hot pepper sauce

For the spicy pumpkin

675g/1½ lb pumpkin
1 onion
25g/1oz/2 tbsp butter or margarine
2 garlic cloves, crushed
3 tomatoes, peeled and chopped
2.5ml/½ tsp ground cinnamon
10ml/2 tsp curry powder
pinch of grated nutmeg
300ml/½ pint/⅔ cup water
salt, hot pepper sauce and freshly
  ground black pepper

1 Drain the beans, place in a pan and cover generously with water. Bring the beans to the boil.

2 Add the onion, green or red pepper, garlic, stock cube, herbs and spices. Simmer for 45 minutes or until the beans are just tender. Season to taste with the salt and a little hot pepper sauce.

3 Add the carrots and palm oil and continue cooking for about 10–12 minutes until the carrots are cooked, adding a little more water if necessary. Remove from the heat and set aside.

4 To make the spicy pumpkin, cut the pumpkin into cubes and finely chop the onion.

5 Melt the butter or margarine in a frying pan or saucepan, and add the pumpkin, onion, garlic, tomatoes, spices and water. Stir well to combine and simmer until the pumpkin is soft. Season with salt, hot pepper sauce and black pepper, to taste. Serve with the black-eyed beans.

Red Bean Chilli

This vegetarian chilli can be adapted to accommodate meat eaters by adding either minced beef or lamb in place of the lentils. Add the meat once the onions are soft and fry until nicely browned before adding the tomatoes.

INGREDIENTS

Serves 4

30ml/2 tbsp vegetable oil
1 onion, chopped
400g/14oz can chopped tomatoes
2 garlic cloves, crushed
300ml/½ pint/1¼ cups white wine
about 300ml/½ pint/1¼ cups
    vegetable stock
115g/4oz red lentils
2 thyme sprigs or 5ml/1 tsp dried
    thyme
10ml/2 tsp ground cumin
45ml/3 tbsp dark soy sauce
½ hot chilli pepper, finely chopped
5ml/1 tsp mixed spice
15ml/1 tbsp oyster sauce (optional)
225g/8oz can red kidney beans,
    drained
10ml/2 tsp sugar
salt

1 Heat the oil in a large saucepan and fry the onion over a moderate heat for a few minutes until slightly softened.

2 Add the tomatoes and garlic, cook for 10 minutes, then stir in the wine and stock.

3 Add the lentils, thyme, cumin, soy sauce, hot pepper, mixed spice and oyster sauce, if using.

4 Cover and simmer for 40 minutes or until the lentils are cooked, stirring occasionally and adding more water if the lentils begin to dry out.

5 Stir in the kidney beans and sugar and continue cooking for 10 minutes, adding a little extra stock or water if necessary. Season to taste with salt and serve hot with boiled rice and sweetcorn.

COOK'S TIP

Fiery chillies can irritate the skin, so always wash your hands well after handling them and take care not to touch your eyes. If you like really hot, spicy food, then add the seeds from the chilli, too.

Chiles Rellenos

INGREDIENTS

Serves 4

8 large green peppers or fresh green
   chillies such as poblano
15–30ml/1–2 tbsp vegetable oil, plus
   extra for frying
450g/1lb/4 cups grated cheese
4 eggs, separated
75g/3oz/²⁄₃ cup flour

For the sauce

15ml/1 tbsp vegetable oil
1 small onion, chopped
1.5ml/¼ tsp salt
5–10ml/1–2 tsp red pepper flakes
2.5ml/½ tsp ground cumin
250ml/8fl oz/1 cup beef stock
750ml/1¼pints/3 cups canned tomatoes

COOK'S TIP

If necessary, work in batches, but do not coat
the peppers until you are ready to fry them.

---

1 For the sauce, heat the oil in a
frying pan. Add the onion and
cook over a low heat for 8 minutes
until just soft. Stir in the salt, pepper
flakes, cumin, stock and tomatoes.
Cover and simmer gently for about
5 minutes, stirring occasionally.

2 Transfer the mixture to a food
processor or blender and process
until smooth. Strain into a clean
saucepan. Taste for seasoning, and set
aside. Preheat the grill.

3 Brush the peppers lightly with oil.
Lay them on a baking sheet. Grill
as close to the heat as possible for 5–8
minutes until blackened all over. Cover
with a dish towel and set aside.

4 When cool enough to handle,
remove the charred skin. Carefully
slit the peppers or chillies and scoop
out the seeds.

5 With your hands, form the cheese
into eight cylinders that are slightly
shorter than the peppers. Place the cheese
cylinders inside the peppers. Secure the
slits with cocktail sticks. Set aside.

6 Beat the egg whites until just stiff.
Add the egg yolks, one at a time,
beating on low speed to incorporate
them. Beat in 15ml/1 tbsp flour.

7 Put a 2.5cm/1in layer of oil in a
frying pan. Heat until hot but not
smoking (to test, drop a little batter in
the oil: if the oil sizzles, it is hot
enough for frying).

8 Coat the peppers lightly in flour all
over, shaking off any excess. Dip
into the egg batter, then place in the
hot oil. Fry for about 2 minutes until
brown on one side. Turn carefully and
brown the other side.

9 Reheat the sauce and serve with
the *Chiles Rellenos*.

VARIATION

If using peppers instead of green chillies,
mix the grated cheese with 15ml/1 tbsp
hot chilli powder for a more authentic
Southwest taste.

Stir-fried Chilli Greens

This attractive dish is spiced with ginger and red chillies, and given added zest by the addition of oyster sauce.

INGREDIENTS

Serves 4

2 bunches spinach or chard or 1 head
  Chinese leaves or 450g/1lb curly kale
3 garlic cloves, crushed
5cm/2in fresh root ginger, peeled and
  cut in matchsticks
45–60ml/3–4 tbsp groundnut oil
115g/4oz boneless, skinless chicken
  breast, or pork fillet, or a mixture of
  both, very finely sliced
12 quail's eggs, hard-boiled and shelled
1 fresh red chilli, seeded and shredded
30–45ml/2–3 tbsp oyster sauce
15ml/1 tbsp brown sugar
10ml/2 tsp cornflour, mixed with
  50ml/2fl oz/¼ cup cold water
salt

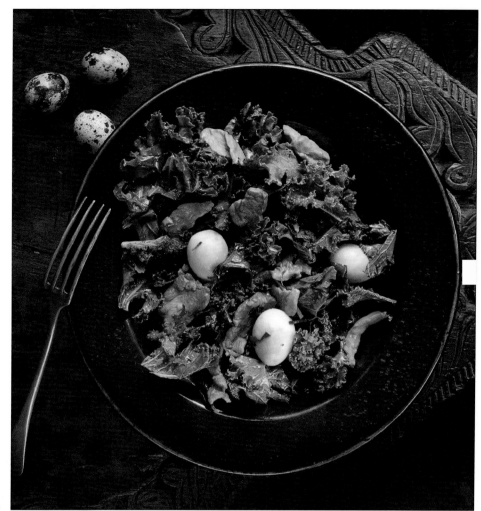

> ——————— COOK'S TIP ———————
>
> As with all stir-fries, don't start cooking until you have prepared all the ingredients and arranged them to hand. Cut everything into small, even-size pieces so the food can be cooked very quickly and all the colours and flavours preserved.

1 Wash the chosen leaves well and shake them dry. Strip the tender leaves from the stems and tear them into pieces. Discard the lower, tougher part of the stems and slice the remainder evenly.

2 Fry the garlic and ginger in the hot oil, without browning, for a minute. Add the chicken and/or pork and keep stirring it in the wok until the meat changes colour. When the meat looks cooked, add the sliced stems first and cook them quickly; then add the torn leaves, quail's eggs and chilli. Spoon in the oyster sauce and a little boiling water, if necessary. Cover and cook for 1–2 minutes only.

3 Remove the cover, stir and add sugar and salt to taste. Stir in the cornflour and water mixture and toss thoroughly. Cook until the mixture is well coated in a glossy sauce.

4 Serve immediately, while still very hot and the colours are bright and positively jewel-like.

Green Bean and Chilli Pepper Salad

Ingredients

Serves 4

350g/12oz cooked green beans, quartered

2 red peppers, seeded and chopped

2 spring onions (white and green parts), chopped

1 or more drained pickled *serrano* chillies, well rinsed and then seeded and chopped

1 iceberg lettuce, coarsely shredded, or mixed salad leaves

olives, to garnish

For the dressing

45ml/3 tbsp red wine vinegar

135ml/9 tbsp olive oil

salt and freshly ground black pepper

1 Combine the cooked green beans, chopped peppers, chopped spring onions and chillies in a salad bowl.

2 Make the salad dressing. Pour the red wine vinegar into a bowl or jug. Add salt and freshly ground black pepper to taste, then gradually whisk in the olive oil until well combined.

3 Pour the salad dressing over the prepared vegetables and toss lightly together to mix and coat thoroughly.

4 Line a large platter with the shredded lettuce leaves and arrange the salad attractively on top. Garnish with the olives and serve.

Mushrooms with Chipotle Chillies

INGREDIENTS

Serves 6
450g/1lb/4 cups button mushrooms
60ml/4 tbsp olive oil
1 onion, finely chopped
2 garlic cloves, chopped
2 drained canned *chipotle* chillies,
  rinsed and sliced
salt
chopped fresh coriander, to garnish

> ——— COOK'S TIP ———
>
> Never wash mushrooms as they quickly
> absorb water. Wipe them with kitchen
> paper or a clean, damp cloth.

1 Wipe the mushrooms gently and carefully with kitchen paper. Heat the olive oil in a large frying pan and add the mushrooms, finely chopped onion, chopped garlic, and sliced chillies. Stir to coat in oil.

2 Fry the mixture over a moderate heat for 6–8 minutes, stirring from time to time, until the onions and mushrooms are tender. Season to taste with salt and serve on small individual plates, sprinkled with a little chopped fresh coriander.

Jalapeño and Prawn Salad

Pickled jalapeño chilli gives a distinctive spicy flavour to this delicious salad. In Mexico, it is quite usual to serve such a hearty salad as a separate course.

INGREDIENTS

Serves 4
1 iceberg lettuce or 2 Little Gem
  lettuces, separated into leaves, or
  assorted lettuce leaves
60ml/4 tbsp mayonnaise
60ml/4 tbsp soured cream
350g/12oz cooked prawns, thawed if
  frozen, chopped
75g/3oz/½ cup cooked green
  beans, chopped
75g/3oz/½ cup cooked carrots,
  chopped
½ cucumber, about 115g/4oz chopped
2 hard-boiled eggs, coarsely chopped
1 drained pickled *jalapeño* chilli, seeded
  and chopped
salt

1 Line a large salad bowl or platter with the lettuce leaves. Mix the mayonnaise and soured cream together in a small bowl and put aside.

2 Combine the prawns, beans, carrot, cucumber, eggs and chilli in a separate bowl. Season with salt.

3 Add the mayonnaise and soured cream mixture to the prawns, folding it in very gently so that all the ingredients are well mixed and coated with the dressing. Pile the mixture into the lined salad bowl or arrange attractively on the platter and serve.

Spicy Potato Salad

This tasty salad is quick to prepare, and makes a satisfying accompaniment to grilled or barbecued meat or fish.

INGREDIENTS

Serves 6

900g/2lb potatoes, peeled
2 red peppers
2 celery sticks
1 shallot
2 or 3 spring onions
1 green chilli, finely chopped
1 garlic clove, crushed
10ml/2 tsp finely snipped
  fresh chives
10ml/2 tsp finely chopped fresh basil
15ml/1 tbsp finely chopped fresh
  parsley
15ml/1 tbsp single cream
30ml/2 tbsp salad cream
15ml/1 tbsp mayonnaise
5ml/1 tsp mild mustard
7.5ml/½ tbsp sugar
snipped fresh chives, to garnish

1 Boil the potatoes until tender but still firm. Drain and cool, then cut into 2.5cm/1in cubes and place in a large salad bowl.

2 Halve the peppers, cut away and discard the core and seeds and cut into small pieces. Finely chop the celery, shallot, and spring onions and slice the chilli very thinly, discarding the seeds. Add the vegetables to the potatoes together with the garlic and chopped herbs.

3 Blend the cream, salad cream, mayonnaise, mustard and sugar in a small bowl, stirring until the mixture is well combined.

4 Pour the dressing over the potato and vegetable salad and stir gently to coat evenly. Serve, garnished with the snipped chives.

Peppery Bean Salad

This pretty salad uses canned beans for speed and convenience.

INGREDIENTS

Serves 4–6

425g/15oz can kidney beans, drained
425g/15oz can black-eyed beans, drained
425g/15oz can chick-peas, drained
¼ red pepper
¼ green pepper
6 radishes
15ml/1 tbsp chopped spring onion
5ml/1 tsp ground cumin
15ml/1 tbsp tomato ketchup
30ml/2 tbsp olive oil
15ml/1 tbsp white wine vinegar
1 garlic clove, crushed
½ tsp hot pepper sauce
salt
sliced spring onion, to garnish

1 Drain the canned beans and chick-peas and rinse under cold running water. Shake off the excess water and tip them into a large salad bowl.

2 Core, seed and chop the peppers. Trim the radishes and slice thinly. Add to the beans with the pepper and spring onion.

3 Mix together the cumin, ketchup, oil, vinegar and garlic in a small bowl. Add a little salt and hot pepper sauce to taste and stir again thoroughly.

4 Pour the dressing over the salad and mix. Chill for at least 1 hour before serving, garnished with spring onion.

COOK'S TIP

For an even tastier salad, allow the ingredients to marinate for a few hours.

Balti Potatoes

Balti is a traditional way of cooking Indian curries in a karahi cooking pan.

INGREDIENTS

Serves 4
75ml/3 tbsp corn oil
2.5ml/½ tsp white cumin seeds
3 curry leaves
5ml/1 tsp crushed dried red chillies
2.5ml/½ tsp mixed onion, mustard and fenugreek seeds
2.5ml/½ tsp fennel seeds
3 garlic cloves
2.5ml/½ tsp shredded ginger
2 onions, sliced
6 new potatoes, sliced thinly
15ml/1 tbsp chopped fresh coriander
1 fresh red chilli, seeded and sliced
1 fresh green chilli, seeded and sliced

1 Heat the oil in a deep round-bottomed frying pan or a karahi. Lower the heat slightly and add the cumin seeds, curry leaves, dried red chillies, mixed onion, mustard and fenugreek seeds, fennel seeds, garlic cloves and ginger. Fry for 1 minute, then add the onions and fry for a further 5 minutes, or until the onions are golden brown.

2 Add the potatoes, fresh coriander and fresh red and green chillies and mix well. Cover the pan tightly with a lid or foil, making sure the foil does not touch the food. Cook over a very low heat for about 7 minutes, or until the potatoes are tender.

3 Remove the pan from the heat, take off the foil and serve hot.

Okra with Green Mango and Lentils

If you like okra, you'll love this spicy tangy dish.

INGREDIENTS

Serves 4
115g/4oz/½ cup yellow lentils (toor dhal)
45ml/3 tbsp corn oil
2.5ml/½ tsp onion seeds
2 onions, sliced
2.5ml/½ tsp ground fenugreek
5ml/1 tsp ginger pulp
5ml/1 tsp garlic pulp
7.5ml/1½ tsp chilli powder
1.5ml/¼ tsp turmeric
5ml/1 tsp ground coriander
1 green mango, peeled and sliced
450g/1lb okra, cut into 1cm/½in pieces
7.5ml/1½ tsp salt
2 fresh red chillies, seeded and sliced
30ml/2 tbsp chopped fresh coriander
1 tomato, sliced

1 Wash the lentils thoroughly and put in a saucepan with enough water to cover. Bring to the boil and cook until soft but not mushy. Drain and set to one side.

2 Heat the oil in a deep round-bottomed frying pan or a karahi and fry the onion seeds until they begin to pop. Add the onions and fry until golden brown. Lower the heat and add the ground fenugreek, ginger, garlic, chilli powder, turmeric and ground coriander.

3 Throw in the mango slices and the okra. Stir well and add the salt, red chillies and fresh coriander. Stir-fry for about 3 minutes, or until the okra is well cooked.

4 Finally, add the cooked lentils and sliced tomato and cook for a further 3 minutes. Serve hot.

Spicy Vegetables with Almonds

INGREDIENTS

Serves 4

30ml/2 tbsp vegetable oil
2 onions, sliced
5cm/2in fresh root ginger, shredded
5ml/1 tsp crushed black peppercorns
1 bay leaf
1.5ml/¼ tsp turmeric
5ml/1 tsp ground coriander
5ml/1 tsp salt
2.5ml/½ tsp garam masala
175g/6oz/2½ cups mushrooms, sliced
1 courgette, thickly sliced
50g/2oz French beans, sliced into
   2.5cm/1in pieces
15ml/1 tbsp chopped fresh mint
150ml/¼ pint/⅔ cup water
30ml/2 tbsp natural low-fat yogurt
25g/1oz/¼ cup flaked almonds

1 In a medium deep frying pan, heat the vegetable oil and fry the sliced onions with the shredded fresh ginger, crushed black peppercorns and the bay leaf for 3–5 minutes.

2 Lower the heat and add the turmeric, ground coriander, salt and garam masala, stirring occasionally. Gradually add the mushrooms, courgette, French beans and the mint. Stir gently so that the vegetables retain their shape.

3 Pour in the water and bring to a simmer, then lower the heat and cook until most of the water has evaporated.

4 Beat the natural low-fat yogurt well with a fork, then pour it on to the vegetables in the pan and mix together well.

5 Cook the spicy vegetables for a further 2–3 minutes, stirring occasionally. Sprinkle with flaked almonds and serve.

--- COOK'S TIP ---

For an extra creamy dish, add soured cream instead of the natural yogurt.

Masala Beans with Fenugreek

"Masala" means spice and this vegetarian dish is spicy, though not necessarily hot. You can adapt the spiciness of the dish by using smaller or larger quantities of the spices, as you wish. Serve it as an accompaniment to a meat dish with freshly cooked basmati rice for a wonderful Indian meal.

INGREDIENTS

Serves 4

1 onion
5ml/1 tsp ground cumin
5ml/1 tsp ground coriander
5ml/1 tsp sesame seeds
5ml/1 tsp chilli powder
2.5ml/½ tsp garlic pulp
1.5ml/¼ tsp turmeric
5ml/1 tsp salt
30ml/2 tbsp vegetable oil
1 tomato, quartered
225g/8oz French beans
1 bunch fresh fenugreek leaves, stems discarded
60ml/4 tbsp chopped fresh coriander
15ml/1 tbsp lemon juice

1 Roughly chop the onion. In a mixing bowl, combine the ground cumin and coriander, sesame seeds, chilli powder, garlic pulp, turmeric and salt. Mix well.

2 Place all of these ingredients, including the onion, in a food processor or blender and process for 30–45 seconds.

3 In a medium saucepan, heat the vegetable oil and fry the spice mixture for about 5 minutes, stirring it occasionally as it cooks.

4 Add the quartered tomato, French beans, fresh fenugreek and fresh chopped coriander.

5 Stir-fry the mixture for about 5 minutes, then sprinkle over the lemon juice, pour into a serving dish and serve immediately.

----- COOK'S TIP -----

If you can't find fenugreek leaves, use 5ml/1 tsp fenugreek seeds instead.

FLAME-FILLED RICE AND NOODLES

Rice and noodles are the cornerstones of many cuisines and their unassertive taste lends itself to flavouring with mild or hot spices, or a mixture of both. Many of the classic rice dishes appear: Nasi Goreng, Chicken Jambalaya and Sushi, seasoned with the breathtaking wasabi paste. Noodle dishes are justly popular in Thailand and China where they are combined with chillies, limes, sesame oil, coriander and many other emphatic ingredients to produce such delights as Spicy Szechuan Noodles and Thai Fried Noodles.

Yogurt Chicken and Rice

This is flavoured with *zereshk*, small dried berries available from Middle Eastern stores.

INGREDIENTS

Serves 6
40g/1½ oz/3 tbsp butter
1.5kg/3–3½ lb chicken pieces
1 large onion, chopped
250ml/8fl oz/1 cup chicken stock
2 eggs
475ml/16fl oz/2 cups natural yogurt
2–3 saffron strands, dissolved in 15ml/
   1 tbsp boiling water
5ml/1 tsp ground cinnamon
450g/1lb/generous 2¼ cups basmati
   rice, soaked in salted water
   for 2 hours
75g/3oz *zereshk*
salt and ground black pepper
herb salad, to serve

1 Melt two-thirds of the butter in a casserole and fry the chicken and onion for 4–5 minutes, until the onion is softened and the chicken browned.

2 Add the stock and salt and pepper, bring to the boil and then simmer for 45 minutes, or until the chicken is cooked and the stock reduced by half.

3 Skin and bone the chicken. Cut the flesh into large pieces and place in a large bowl. Reserve the stock.

4 Beat the eggs and blend with the yogurt. Add the saffron water and cinnamon and season with salt and pepper. Pour over the chicken and leave to marinate on one side for up to 2 hours.

5 Drain the rice and then boil in salted water for 5 minutes, reduce the heat and simmer very gently for 10 minutes, until half cooked. Drain and rinse in warm water.

6 Transfer the chicken from the yogurt mixture to a dish and mix half the rice into the yogurt.

7 Preheat the oven to 160°C/325°F/ Gas 3 and grease a large 10cm/4in deep ovenproof dish.

8 Place the rice and yogurt mixture in the bottom of the dish, arrange the chicken pieces in a layer on top and then add the plain rice. Warm the *zereshk* thoroughly, then sprinkle over.

9 Mix the remaining butter with the chicken stock and pour over the rice. Cover tightly with foil and cook in the oven for 35–45 minutes.

10 Leave the dish to cool for a few minutes. Place on a cold, damp dish towel which will help lift the rice from the base of the dish, then run a knife around the inside edge of the dish. Place a large flat plate over the dish and turn out. You should have a rice "cake" which can be cut into wedges. Serve hot with a herb salad.

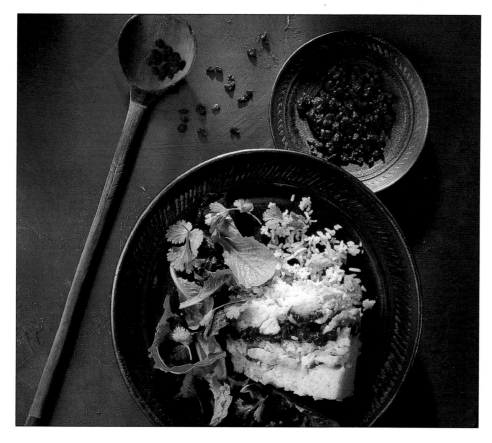

Louisiana Rice

Aubergine and pork combine with herbs and spices to make a highly flavoursome dish.

INGREDIENTS

Serves 4
60ml/4 tbsp vegetable oil
1 small aubergine, diced
225g/8oz minced pork
1 green pepper, seeded and chopped
2 sticks celery, chopped
1 onion, chopped
1 garlic clove, crushed
5ml/1 tsp cayenne pepper
5ml/1 tsp paprika
5ml/1 tsp black pepper
2.5ml/½ tsp salt
5ml/1 tsp dried thyme
2.5ml/½ tsp dried oregano
475ml/16fl oz/2 cups chicken stock
225g/8oz chicken livers, minced
150g/5oz/scant ⅔ cup long grain rice
1 bay leaf
45ml/3 tbsp chopped fresh parsley
celery leaves, to garnish

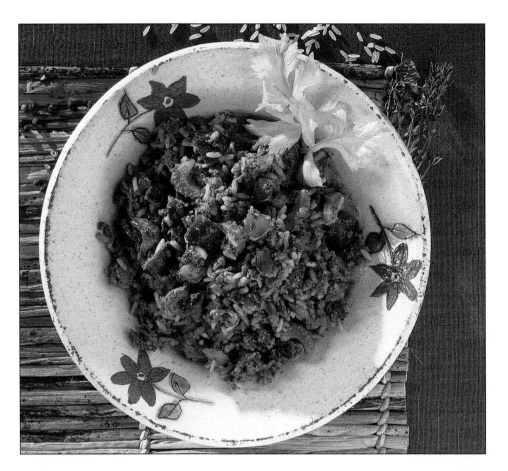

1 Heat the oil in a frying pan until piping hot, then add the aubergine and stir-fry for about 5 minutes.

2 Add the pork and cook for 6–8 minutes until browned, using a wooden spoon to break up any lumps.

3 Add the green pepper, celery, onion, garlic and all the spices and herbs. Cover and cook over a high heat for 5–6 minutes, stirring frequently from the base of the pan to scrape up and distribute the crispy brown bits.

4 Pour in the chicken stock and stir to remove any sediment from the base of the pan. Cover and cook for 6 minutes over a moderate heat. Stir in the chicken livers, cook for 2 minutes, then stir in the rice and add the bay leaf.

5 Reduce the heat, cover and simmer for 6–7 minutes. Turn off the heat and leave to stand for a further 10–15 minutes until the rice is tender. Remove the bay leaf and stir in the chopped parsley. Serve the rice hot, garnished with the celery leaves.

Spicy Fish and Rice

This Arabic fish dish, *Sayadich* is especially popular in Lebanon.

INGREDIENTS

Serves 4–6
juice of 1 lemon
45ml/3 tbsp oil
900g/2lb cod steaks
4 large onions, chopped
5ml/1 tsp ground cumin
2–3 saffron strands
1 litre/1³⁄₄ pints/4 cups fish stock
450g/1lb/generous 2¼ cups basmati or
   long grain rice
50g/2oz/¼ cup pine nuts,
   lightly toasted
salt and ground black pepper
fresh parsley, to garnish

1 Blend the lemon juice and 15ml/ 1 tbsp of oil in a shallow dish. Add the fish, turn to coat thoroughly, then cover and marinate for 30 minutes.

2 Heat the remaining oil in a large saucepan and fry the onions for 5–6 minutes, stirring occasionally.

3 Drain the fish, reserving the marinade, and add to the pan. Fry for 1–2 minutes each side until lightly golden, then add the cumin, saffron strands and a little salt and pepper.

4 Pour in the fish stock and the reserved marinade, bring to the boil and then simmer for 5–10 minutes or until the fish is nearly done.

5 Transfer the fish to a plate and add the rice to the stock. Bring to the boil, reduce the heat and simmer gently for 15 minutes until nearly all the stock has been absorbed.

6 Arrange the fish on top of the rice and cover the pan. Steam over a low heat for 15–20 minutes.

7 Transfer the fish to a plate, then spoon the rice onto a large flat dish and arrange the fish on top. Sprinkle with toasted pine nuts and garnish with fresh parsley.

Masala Prawns and Rice

INGREDIENTS

Serves 4–6
2 large onions, sliced and deep fried
300ml/½ pint/1¼ cups natural yogurt
30ml/2 tbsp tomato purée
60ml/4 tbsp green masala paste
30ml/2 tbsp lemon juice
salt, to taste
5ml/1 tsp black cumin seeds
5cm/2in cinnamon stick
4 green cardamom pods
450g/1lb fresh king prawns, peeled
   and de-veined
225g/8oz/3 cups button mushrooms
225g/8oz/2 cups frozen peas, thawed
450g/1lb/generous 2¼ cups basmati
   rice soaked for 5 minutes in boiled
   water and drained
300ml/½ pint/1¼ cups water
1 sachet saffron powder mixed in
   90ml/6 tbsp milk
30ml/2 tbsp ghee or unsalted butter

1 Mix the first 9 ingredients together in a large bowl. Mix the prawns, mushrooms and peas into the marinade and leave for about 2 hours.

2 Grease the base of a heavy pan and add the prawns, vegetables and any marinade juices. Cover with the drained rice and smooth the surface gently until you have an even layer.

3 Pour the water all over the surface of the rice. Make random holes through the rice with the handle of a spoon and pour in the saffron milk.

4 Place a few knobs of ghee or butter on the surface and place a circular piece of foil directly on top of the rice. Cover and steam over a low heat for 45–50 minutes, until the rice is cooked Gently toss the rice, prawns and vegetables together and serve hot.

Spiced Trout Pilaff

Smoked trout might seem an unusual partner for rice, but this is a winning combination.

INGREDIENTS

Serves 4
225g/8oz/generous 1 cup basmati rice
40g/1½oz/3 tbsp butter
2 onions, sliced into rings
1 garlic clove, crushed
2 bay leaves
2 whole cloves
2 green cardamom pods
2.5cm/2in cinnamon sticks
5ml/1 tsp cumin seeds
4 hot-smoked trout fillets, skinned
50g/2oz/½ cup slivered
    almonds, toasted
50g/2oz/scant ½ cup seedless raisins
30ml/2 tbsp chopped fresh parsley
mango chutney and poppadums,
    to serve

1 Wash the rice thoroughly in several changes of water and drain well. Set aside. Melt the butter in a large frying pan and fry the onions until well browned, stirring frequently.

2 Add the garlic, bay leaves, cloves, cardamom pods, cinnamon and cumin seeds and stir-fry for 1 minute.

3 Stir in the rice, then add 600ml/ 1 pint/2½ cups boiling water. Bring to the boil. Cover the pan tightly, reduce the heat and cook very gently for 20–25 minutes, until the water has been absorbed and the rice is tender.

4 Flake the smoked trout and add to the pan with the almonds and raisins. Fork through gently. Cover the pan and allow the smoked trout to warm in the rice for a few minutes. Scatter over the parsley and serve with mango chutney and poppadums.

Nasi Goreng

One of the most popular and well-known Indonesian dishes, this is a marvellous way to use up leftover rice, chicken and meats such as pork.

INGREDIENTS

Serves 4–6

350g/12oz/scant 1½ cups dry weight basmati rice, cooked and cooled
2 eggs
30ml/2 tbsp water
105ml/7 tbsp oil
225g/8oz pork fillet or fillet of beef
2–3 fresh red chillies, seeded and sliced
1cm/½in cube terasi
2 garlic cloves, crushed
1 onion, sliced
115g/4oz/1 cup cooked, peeled prawns
225g/8oz/1½ cups cooked chicken, chopped
30ml/2 tbsp dark soy sauce or 45–60ml/3–4 tbsp tomato ketchup
salt and ground black pepper
celery leaves, deep-fried onions and coriander sprigs, to garnish

1 Separate the grains of the cooked and cooled rice with a fork. Cover and set aside until needed.

2 Beat the eggs with the water and season lightly. Make two or three thin omelettes in a frying pan, with a minimum of oil and leave to cool. When cold, roll up each omelette and cut into strips. Set aside.

3 Cut the pork or beef fillet into neat strips. Finely shred one of the chillies and set aside.

4 Put the terasi, with the remaining chilli, the garlic and onion, in a food processor, or use a pestle and mortar, and grind to a fine paste.

5 Heat the remaining oil in a wok and fry the paste, without browning, until it gives off a rich, spicy aroma. Add the pork or beef, tossing the meat all the time, to seal in the juices. Cook for 2 minutes, stirring constantly. Add the prawns, cook for 2 minutes and then stir in the chicken, cold rice, dark soy sauce or ketchup and season to taste. Stir all the time to keep the rice light and fluffy and prevent it from sticking.

6 Turn onto a hot serving plate and garnish with the omelette strips, celery leaves, onions, reserved shredded chilli and the coriander sprigs.

Seafood and Rice

INGREDIENTS

Serves 4

30ml/2 tbsp oil
115g/4oz smoked bacon, rind
   removed, diced
1 onion, chopped
2 sticks celery, chopped
2 large garlic cloves, chopped
10ml/2 tsp cayenne pepper
2 bay leaves
5ml/1 tsp dried oregano
2.5ml/¹/₂ tsp dried thyme
4 tomatoes, peeled and chopped
150ml/¹/₄ pint/²/₃ cup tomato sauce
350g/12oz/scant 1 cup long grain rice
475ml/16fl oz/2 cups fish stock
175g/6oz cod, or haddock, skinned,
   boned and cubed
115g/4oz/1 cup cooked,
   peeled prawns
salt and ground black pepper
2 spring onions, chopped, to garnish

1 Preheat the oven to 180°C/350°F/
Gas 4. Heat the oil in a large
saucepan and fry the bacon until crisp.
Add the onion and celery and stir until
beginning to stick to the pan.

2 Add the garlic, cayenne pepper,
herbs, tomatoes and seasoning and
mix well. Stir in the tomato sauce, rice
and stock and bring to the boil.

3 Gently stir in the fish and transfer
to an ovenproof dish. Cover tightly
with foil and bake for 20–30 minutes,
until the rice is just tender. Stir in the
prawns and heat through. Serve
sprinkled with the spring onions.

Chicken Jambalaya

INGREDIENTS

Serves 10

2 x 1.5kg/3–3¹/₂lb chickens
450g/1lb raw smoked gammon
50g/2oz/4 tbsp lard or bacon fat
50g/2oz/¹/₂ cup plain flour
3 onions, finely sliced
2 green peppers, seeded and sliced
675g/1¹/₂lb tomatoes, chopped
2–3 garlic cloves, crushed
10ml/2 tsp chopped fresh thyme or
   5ml/1 tsp dried thyme
24 Mediterranean prawns, peeled
500g/1¹/₄lb/scant 3 cups long
   grain rice
2–3 dashes Tabasco sauce
6 spring onions, finely chopped
45ml/3 tbsp fresh parsley, chopped
salt and ground black pepper

1 Cut each chicken into 10 pieces
and season. Dice the gammon,
discarding the rind and fat.

2 In a large casserole, melt the lard or
bacon fat and brown the chicken
pieces all over, lifting them out and
setting them aside as they are done.

3 Turn the heat down, sprinkle the
flour onto the fat in the pan and
stir until the roux turns golden brown.

4 Return the chicken pieces to the
pan, add the diced gammon,
onions, green peppers, tomatoes, garlic
and thyme and cook, stirring regularly,
for 10 minutes, then stir in the prawns.

5 Stir the rice into the pan with one-
and-a-half times the rice's volume
in cold water. Season with salt, pepper
and Tabasco sauce. Bring to the boil
and cook over a gentle heat until the
rice is tender and the liquid absorbed.
Add a little extra boiling water if the
rice dries out before it is cooked.

6 Mix the spring onions and parsley
into the finished dish, reserving a
little of the mixture to scatter over the
jambalaya. Serve hot.

Spicy Rice Cakes

INGREDIENTS

Makes 16 cakes

1 garlic clove, crushed
1cm/½in piece fresh root ginger,
    peeled and finely chopped
1.5ml/¼ tsp ground turmeric
5ml/1 tsp sugar
2.5ml/½ tsp salt
5ml/1 tsp chilli sauce
10ml/2 tsp fish or soy sauce
30ml/2 tbsp chopped fresh coriander
juice of ½ lime
115g/4oz/generous ½ cup dry weight
    long grain rice, cooked
peanuts, chopped
150ml/¼ pint/⅔ cup vegetable oil, for
    deep-frying
coriander sprigs, to garnish

1 In a food processor, process the garlic, ginger and turmeric. Add the sugar, salt, chilli and fish or soy sauce, coriander and lime juice.

2 Add three-quarters of the cooked rice and process until smooth and sticky. Transfer to a mixing bowl and stir in the remainder of the rice. Wet your hands and shape into thumb-size balls.

3 Roll the balls in chopped peanuts to coat evenly. Then set aside until ready to cook and serve.

4 Heat the vegetable oil in a deep frying pan. Prepare a tray lined with kitchen paper to drain the rice cakes. Deep-fry three cakes at a time until crisp and golden, remove with a slotted spoon, then drain on the kitchen paper before serving hot.

Red Rice Rissoles

INGREDIENTS

Serves 6

1 large red onion, chopped
1 red pepper, chopped
2 garlic cloves, crushed
1 red chilli, finely chopped
30ml/2 tbsp olive oil
25g/1oz/2 tbsp butter
225g/8oz/generous 1 cup risotto rice
1 litre/1¾ pints/4 cups stock
4 sun-dried tomatoes, chopped
30ml/2 tbsp tomato purée
10ml/2 tsp dried oregano
45ml/3 tbsp chopped fresh parsley
150g/6oz cheese, e.g. red Leicester or
    smoked Cheddar
1 egg, beaten
115g/4oz/1 cup dried breadcrumbs
oil, for deep frying
salt and ground black pepper

1 Fry the onion, pepper, garlic and chilli in the oil and butter for 5 minutes. Stir in the rice and fry for a further 2 minutes.

2 Pour in the stock and add the sun-dried tomatoes, purée, oregano and seasoning. Bring to the boil, stirring occasionally, then cover and simmer for 20 minutes.

3 Stir in the parsley then turn into a shallow dish and chill until firm. When cold, divide into 12 and shape into equally-sized balls.

4 Cut the cheese into 12 pieces and press a nugget into the centre of each rice rissole.

5 Put the beaten egg in one bowl and the breadcrumbs into another. Dip the rissoles first into the egg, then into the breadcrumbs, coating each of them evenly.

6 Place the rissoles on a plate and chill again for 30 minutes. Fill a deep frying pan one-third full of oil and heat until a cube of day-old bread browns in under a minute.

7 Fry the rissoles in batches for about 3–4 minutes, reheating the oil in-between. Drain on kitchen paper and keep warm, uncovered. Serve with a side salad.

Persian Rice with a Tahdeeg

Persian or Iranian cuisine is exotic and delicious, and the flavours are intense. A *tahdeeg* is the glorious, golden rice crust or "dig" that forms on the base of the saucepan.

INGREDIENTS

Serves 8

450g/1lb/generous 2¼ cups basmati
   rice, rinsed thoroughly and soaked
2 garlic cloves, crushed
2 onions, 1 chopped, 1 thinly sliced
150ml/¼ pint/⅔ cup sunflower oil
150g/5oz/⅔ cup green lentils, soaked
600ml/1 pint/2½ cups stock
50g/2oz/½ cup raisins
10ml/2 tsp ground coriander
45ml/3 tbsp tomato purée
a few saffron strands
1 egg yolk, beaten
10ml/2 tsp natural yogurt
75g/3oz/6 tbsp butter, melted
   and strained
extra oil, for frying
salt and ground black pepper

1 Drain the soaked rice, then cook it in plenty of boiling salted water for 3 minutes. Drain again.

2 In a large saucepan, fry the garlic and chopped onion in 30ml/2 tbsp oil for 5 minutes, then add the lentils, stock, raisins, coriander, tomato purée and seasoning. Bring to the boil, then cover and simmer for 20 minutes.

3 Soak the saffron strands in a little hot water. Remove about 120ml/8 tbsp of the cooked rice and mix with the egg yolk and yogurt. Season well.

4 In a large saucepan, heat about two-thirds of the remaining oil and scatter the egg and yogurt rice evenly over the base.

5 Scatter the remaining rice into the pan, alternating it with the lentil mixture. Build up in a pyramid shape away from the sides of the pan, finishing with plain rice on top.

6 With a long wooden spoon handle, make three holes down to the base of the pan and drizzle over the butter. Bring to a high heat, then wrap the pan lid in a clean, wet dish towel and place firmly on top. When a good head of steam appears, turn the heat down to low. Cook for about 30 minutes.

7 Meanwhile, fry the sliced onion in the remaining oil until browned and crisp. Drain well and set aside.

8 Remove the rice pan from the heat, still covered, and stand it briefly in a sink of cold water for a minute or two to loosen the base. Remove the lid and mix a few spoons of the white rice with the saffron water.

9 Toss the rice and lentils together in the pan and spoon out onto a serving dish in a mound. Scatter the saffron rice on top. Break up the rice crust on the pan base and place pieces of it around the mound. Scatter over the crispy fried onions and serve.

Festive Rice

This Thai dish is traditionally served shaped into a cone and surrounded by a variety of accompaniments.

INGREDIENTS

Serves 8

450g/1lb/generous 2¼ cups Thai fragrant rice
60ml/4 tbsp oil
2 garlic cloves, crushed
2 onions, finely sliced
5cm/2in fresh turmeric, peeled and crushed
750ml/1¼ pints/3 cups water
400ml/14fl oz can coconut milk
1–2 lemon grass stems, bruised

For the accompaniments

omelette strips
2 fresh red chillies, shredded
cucumber chunks
tomato wedges
deep-fried onions
prawn crackers

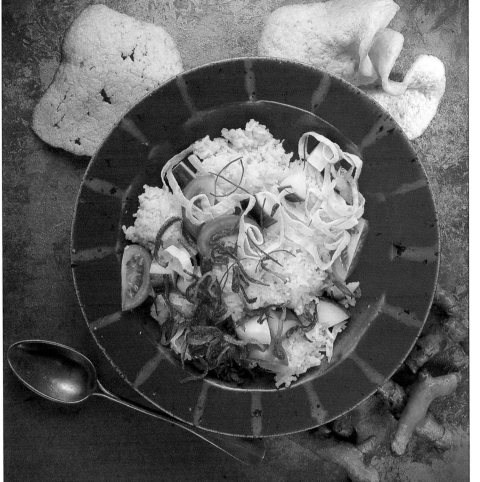

1 Wash the rice in several changes of water. Drain well.

2 Heat the oil in a wok and gently fry the garlic, onions and turmeric for a few minutes, until they are softened but not browned.

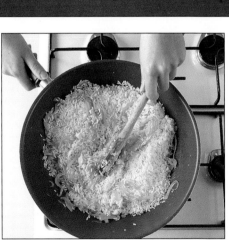

3 Add the rice and stir well so that each grain is thoroughly coated. Pour in the water and coconut milk and add the lemon grass.

4 Bring to the boil, stirring well. Cover the pan and cook gently for 15–20 minutes, or until all of the liquid has been completely absorbed.

5 Remove the pan from the heat. Cover with a clean dish towel, put on the lid and leave to stand in a warm place for 15 minutes.

6 Remove the lemon grass, turn out on to a serving platter and garnish the dish with the accompaniments.

Indian Pilau Rice

INGREDIENTS

Serves 4

225g/8oz/generous 1 cup basmati
  rice, rinsed well
30ml/2 tbsp vegetable oil
1 small onion, finely chopped
1 garlic clove, crushed
5ml/1 tsp fennel seeds
15ml/1 tbsp sesame seeds
2.5ml/½ tsp ground turmeric
5ml/1 tsp ground cumin
1.5ml/½ tsp salt
2 whole cloves
4 green cardamom pods,
  lightly crushed
5 black peppercorns
450ml/¾ pint/1⅞ cups vegetable stock
15ml/1 tbsp ground almonds
coriander sprigs, to garnish

1 Soak the rice in water for 30 minutes. Heat the oil in a saucepan, add the onion and garlic, and fry gently for 5–6 minutes, until softened.

2 Stir in the fennel and sesame seeds, the turmeric, cumin, salt, cloves, cardamom pods and peppercorns and fry for about 1 minute. Drain the rice well, add it to the pan and stir-fry for a further 3 minutes.

3 Pour in the vegetable stock. Bring to the boil, then cover, reduce the heat to very low and simmer gently for 20 minutes, without removing the lid, until all the liquid has been absorbed.

4 Remove from the heat and leave to stand for 2–3 minutes. Fork up the rice and stir in the ground almonds. Garnish the rice with coriander sprigs.

Okra Fried Rice

Sliced okra provides a wonderful creamy texture to this delicious, simple dish.

INGREDIENTS

Serves 3–4

30ml/2 tbsp vegetable oil
15ml/1 tbsp butter or margarine
1 garlic clove, crushed
½ red onion, finely chopped
115g/4oz okra, topped and tailed
30ml/2 tbsp diced green and
  red peppers
2.5ml/½ tsp dried thyme
2 green chillies, finely chopped
2.5ml/½ tsp five-spice powder
1 vegetable stock cube
30ml/2 tbsp soy sauce
15ml/1 tbsp chopped fresh coriander
225g/8oz/3 cups cooked rice
salt and ground black pepper
coriander sprigs, to garnish

1 Heat the oil and the butter or margarine in a frying pan, add the garlic and onion and cook on a medium heat for 5 minutes until soft.

2 Thinly slice the okra, add to the frying pan and stir-fry gently for a further 6–7 minutes.

3 Add the green and red peppers, thyme, chillies and five-spice powder and cook for 3 minutes, then crumble in the stock cube.

4 Add the soy sauce, coriander and rice and heat through, stirring. Season with salt and pepper. Serve hot, garnished with coriander sprigs.

Pistachio Pilaff

Saffron and ginger are traditional rice spices and delicious when mixed with fresh pistachios.

Ingredients

Serves 4

3 onions
60ml/4 tbsp olive oil
2 garlic cloves, crushed
2.5cm/1in piece fresh root
 ginger, grated
1 green chilli, chopped
2 carrots, coarsely grated
225g/8oz/generous 1 cup basmati
 rice, rinsed
1.5ml/¼ tsp saffron strands, crushed
450ml/¾ pint/1⅞ cups stock
5cm/2in cinnamon stick
5ml/1 tsp ground coriander
salt and ground black pepper
75g/3oz/¼ cup fresh pistachios
450g/1lb fresh leaf spinach
5ml/1 tsp garam masala
tomato salad, to serve

1 Roughly chop two of the onions. Heat half the oil in a large saucepan and fry the onion with half the garlic, the ginger and the chilli for 5 minutes until softened.

2 Mix in the carrots and rice, cook for 1 more minute and then add the saffron, stock, cinnamon and coriander. Season well. Bring to the boil, then cover and simmer gently for 10 minutes without lifting the lid.

3 Remove from the heat and leave to stand, uncovered, for 5 minutes. Add the pistachios, mixing them in with a fork. Remove the cinnamon stick and keep the rice warm.

4 Thinly slice the third onion and fry in the remaining oil for about 3 minutes. Stir in the spinach. Cover and cook for another 2 minutes.

5 Add the garam masala powder. Cook until just tender, then drain and roughly chop the spinach.

6 Spoon the spinach round the edge of a round serving dish and pile the pilaff in the centre. Serve immediately with a tomato salad.

Basmati and Nut Pilaff

Use whatever nuts are your favourite in this dish – even unsalted peanuts are good, although almonds, cashew nuts or pistachios are more exotic.

INGREDIENTS

Serves 4–6

225g/8oz/generous 1 cup basmati rice
1 onion, chopped
1 garlic clove, crushed
1 large carrot, coarsely grated
15–30ml/1–2 tbsp sunflower oil
5ml/1 tsp cumin seeds
10ml/2 tsp ground coriander
10ml/2 tsp black mustard seeds
   (optional)
4 green cardamom pods
450ml/³/₄ pint/1⁷/₈ cups stock or water
1 bay leaf
75g/3oz/¹/₂ cup unsalted nuts
salt and ground black pepper
fresh chopped parsley or coriander,
   to garnish

1 Wash the rice in a sieve under cold running water. If there is time, soak the rice for 30 minutes, then drain it well in a sieve.

3 Stir in the rice and spices and cook for a further 1–2 minutes so that the grains are coated in oil.

6 If the rice is cooked, there will be small steam holes in the centre of the pan. Discard the bay leaf and the cardamom pods.

2 In a large shallow frying pan, gently fry the onion, garlic and carrot in the oil for 3–4 minutes.

4 Pour in the stock or water, add the bay leaf and season well. Bring to the boil, cover and simmer very gently.

5 Remove from the heat without lifting the lid. Leave to stand on one side for about 5 minutes.

7 Stir in the nuts and check the seasoning. Scatter over the chopped parsley or coriander.

Coconut Rice

This is a very popular way of cooking rice throughout the whole of south-east Asia. *Nasi Uduk* makes a wonderful accompaniment to any dish, and goes particularly well with fish, chicken and pork.

INGREDIENTS

Serves 4–6
350g/12oz Thai fragrant rice
400ml/14fl oz can coconut milk
300ml/½ pint/1¼ cups water
2.5ml/½ tsp ground coriander
1 cinnamon stick
1 lemon grass stem, bruised
1 *pandan* or bay leaf (optional)
salt
Deep-fried Onions, to garnish

1 Wash the rice in several changes of water and then put in a pan with the coconut milk, water, coriander, cinnamon stick, lemon grass and *pandan* or bay leaf, if using, and salt. Bring to the boil, stirring to prevent the rice from settling on the base of the pan. Cover and cook over a very low heat for 12–15 minutes, or until all the coconut milk has been absorbed.

2 Fork the rice through carefully and remove the cinnamon stick, lemon grass and *pandan* or bay leaf. Cover the pan with a tight-fitting lid and then cook over the lowest possible heat for a further 3–5 minutes.

3 Pile the rice on to a warm serving dish and serve garnished with the crisp Deep-fried Onions.

Spicy Rice with Chicken

This is a dish that is popular all over the East, in countries such as Indonesia. It is often served as sustaining breakfast fare. Hearty eaters tuck into a feast of spicy rice with chicken, and add prawns, deep-fried onions, garlic and strips of fresh red and green chilli. This is topped with a lightly fried egg and garnished with celery leaves.

INGREDIENTS

Serves 6
1kg/2¼ lb chicken, cut in 4 pieces or
  4 chicken quarters
1.75 litres/3 pints/7½ cups water
1 large onion, quartered
2.5cm/1in fresh root ginger, peeled,
  halved and bruised
350g/12oz Thai fragrant rice, rinsed
salt and freshly ground black pepper

1 Place the chicken pieces in a large pan with the water, onion quarters and ginger. Add seasoning, bring to the boil and then simmer for 45–50 minutes, until the chicken is tender. Remove from the heat. Lift out the chicken, remove the meat and discard the skin and bones. Cut the chicken into bite-size pieces. Reserve the stock.

2 Strain the chicken stock into a clean pan and make it up to 1.75 litres/3 pints/7½ cups with water.

3 Add the rinsed rice to the chicken stock and stir continuously until it comes to the boil, to prevent the rice from settling on the base of the pan. Simmer gently for 20 minutes, without a lid. Stir, cover and cook for a further 20 minutes, stirring from time to time until the rice is soft and rather like a creamy risotto.

4 Stir the chicken pieces into the porridge and heat through for 5 minutes. Serve as it is, or with any of the garnishes and accompaniments suggested in the introduction.

Sushi

INGREDIENTS

Makes 8–10

Tuna sushi

3 sheets nori (paper-thin seaweed)
150g/5oz fresh tuna fillet, cut
   into fingers
5ml/1 tsp wasabi (Japanese horseradish)
6 young carrots, blanched
450g/1lb/6 cups cooked Japanese rice

Salmon sushi

2 eggs
2.5ml/¹/₂ tsp salt
10ml/2 tsp sugar
5 sheets nori
450g/1lb/6 cups cooked Japanese rice
150g/5oz fresh salmon fillet, cut
   into fingers
5ml/1 tsp wasabi paste
¹/₂ small cucumber, cut into strips

1 To make the tuna sushi, spread half a sheet of nori on to a bamboo mat, lay strips of tuna across the full length and season with the thinned wasabi. Place a line of blanched carrot next to the tuna and roll tightly. Moisten the edge with water and seal.

2 Place a square of damp wax paper on to the bamboo mat, then spread evenly with sushi rice. Place the non-wrapped tuna along the centre and wrap tightly, enclosing the nori completely. Remove the paper and cut into neat rounds with a wet knife.

3 To make the salmon sushi, make a simple flat omelette by beating together the eggs, salt and sugar. Heat a large non-stick pan, pour in the egg mixture, stir briefly and allow to set. Transfer to a clean dish towel and cool.

4 Place the nori on to a bamboo mat, cover with the omelette, and trim to size. Spread a layer of rice over the omelette, then lay strips of salmon across the width. Season the salmon with the thinned wasabi, then place a strip of cucumber next to the salmon. Fold the bamboo mat in half. Cut into neat rounds with a wet knife.

French Beans, Rice and Beef

INGREDIENTS

Serves 4

25g/1oz/2 tbsp butter or margarine
1 large onion, chopped
450g/1lb stewing beef, cubed
2 garlic cloves, crushed
5ml/1 tsp ground cinnamon
5ml/1 tsp ground cumin
5ml/1 tsp ground turmeric
450g/1lb tomatoes, chopped
30ml/2 tbsp tomato purée
350ml/12fl oz/1½ cups water
350g/12oz/2½ cups French
   beans, trimmed and halved
salt and ground black pepper

For the rice

275g/10oz/scant 1½ cups basmati rice,
   soaked in salted water for 2 hours
1.75 litres/3 pints/7½ cups water
45ml/3 tbsp melted butter
2–3 saffron strands, soaked in
   15ml/1 tbsp boiling water
pinch of salt

1 Melt the butter or margarine in a large saucepan or flameproof casserole and fry the onion until golden. Add the beef and fry until evenly browned, then add the garlic, spices, tomatoes, tomato purée and water. Season with salt and pepper. Bring to the boil, then simmer over a low heat for about 30 minutes.

2 Add the French beans and continue cooking for a further 15 minutes until the meat is tender and most of the meat juices have evaporated.

3 Meanwhile, prepare the rice. Drain, then boil it in salted water for about 5 minutes. Reduce the heat and simmer very gently for 10 minutes or until it is half-cooked. Drain, and rinse the rice in warm water. Wash and dry the saucepan.

4 Heat 15ml/1 tbsp of the melted butter in the pan and stir in about a third of the rice. Spoon half of the meat mixture over the rice, add a layer of rice, then the remaining meat and finish with another layer of rice.

5 Pour the remaining melted butter over the rice and cover the pan with a clean dish towel. Secure with the lid and then steam the rice for 30–45 minutes over a low heat.

6 Take 45ml/3 tbsp of cooked rice from the pan and mix with the saffron water. Serve the cooked rice and beef on a large dish and sprinkle the saffron rice on top.

Sweet and Sour Rice

Zereshk Polo is flavoured with fruit and spices and is commonly served with chicken dishes.

INGREDIENTS

Serves 4

50g/2oz *zereshk*
45ml/3 tbsp melted butter
50g/2oz/⅓ cup raisins
30ml/2 tbsp sugar
5ml/1 tsp ground cinnamon
5ml/1 tsp ground cumin
350g/12oz/scant 2 cups basmati rice, soaked in salted water for 2 hours
2–3 saffron strands, soaked in 15ml/ 1 tbsp boiling water
salt

1 Thoroughly wash the *zereshk* in cold water at least 4–5 times to rinse off any bits of grit.

2 Heat 15ml/1 tbsp of the butter in a small frying pan and stir fry the raisins for 1–2 minutes.

3 Add the *zereshk*, fry for a few seconds and then add the sugar, and half of the cinnamon and cumin. Cook briefly and then set aside.

4 Drain the rice and then boil in salted water for 5 minutes, reduce the heat and simmer for 10 minutes until half cooked.

5 Drain and rinse in lukewarm water and wash and dry the pan. Heat half of the remaining butter in the pan, add 15ml/1 tbsp water and stir in half of the rice.

6 Sprinkle with half of the raisin and *zereshk* mixture and top with all but 45ml/3 tbsp of the rice. Sprinkle over the remaining raisin mixture.

7 Blend the reserved rice with the remaining cinnamon and cumin and scatter over the top of the rice mixture. Dribble the remaining butter over and then cover the pan with a clean dish towel and secure with a tightly fitting lid, lifting the corners of the cloth back over the lid. Steam the rice over a very low heat for about 30–40 minutes.

8 Just before serving, mix 45ml/ 3 tbsp of the rice with the saffron water. Spoon the rice on to a large flat serving dish and scatter the saffron rice over the top to decorate.

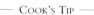
COOK'S TIP

Zereshk are very small dried berries that are delicious mixed with rice. They are available from most Persian and Middle Eastern food stores.

Bamie Goreng

This fried noodle dish is wonderfully accommodating. To the basic recipe you can add other vegetables, such as mushrooms, tiny pieces of chayote, broccoli, leeks or beansprouts, if you prefer. As with fried rice, you can use whatever you have to hand, bearing in mind the need to achieve a balance of colours, flavours and textures.

INGREDIENTS

Serves 6–8

450g/1lb dried egg noodles
1 boneless, skinless chicken breast
115g/4oz pork fillet
115g/4oz calves' liver (optional)
2 eggs, beaten
90ml/6 tbsp oil
25g/1oz butter or margarine
2 garlic cloves, crushed
115g/4oz cooked, peeled prawns
115g/4oz spinach or Chinese leaves
2 celery sticks, finely sliced
4 spring onions, shredded
about 60ml/4 tbsp chicken stock
dark soy sauce and light soy sauce
salt and ground black pepper
deep-fried onions and celery leaves, to
 garnish

2 Finely slice the chicken, pork fillet and calves' liver, if using.

3 Season the eggs. Heat 5ml/1 tsp oil with the butter or margarine in a small pan until melted and then stir in the eggs and keep stirring until scrambled. Set aside.

4 Heat the remaining oil in a wok and fry the garlic with the chicken, pork and liver for 2–3 minutes, until they have changed colour. Add the prawns, spinach or Chinese leaves, celery and spring onions, tossing well.

5 Add the cooked and drained noodles and toss well again so that all the ingredients are well mixed. Add enough stock just to moisten and dark and light soy sauce to taste. Finally, stir in the scrambled eggs.

6 Serve, garnished with deep-fried onions and celery leaves.

1 Cook the noodles in salted, boiling water for 3–4 minutes. Drain, rinse with cold water and drain again. Set aside until required.

Rice with Dill and Spicy Beans

This spiced rice dish is a favourite in Iran, where it is known as *Baghali Polo*.

INGREDIENTS

Serves 4

275g/10oz/scant 1½ cups basmati rice, soaked in salted water for 3 hours
45ml/3 tbsp melted butter
175g/6oz/1½ cups broad beans, fresh or frozen
90ml/6 tbsp finely chopped fresh dill
5ml/1 tsp ground cinnamon
5ml/1 tsp ground cumin
2–3 saffron strands, soaked in 15ml/ 1 tbsp boiling water
salt

1 Drain the rice and then boil it in fresh salted water for 5 minutes. Reduce the heat and simmer very gently for 10 minutes, until half-cooked. Drain and rinse in warm water.

2 Put 15ml/1 tbsp of the butter in a non-stick saucepan and add enough rice to cover the base. Add a quarter of the beans and a little dill.

3 Add another layer of rice, then a layer of beans and dill and continue layering until all the beans and dill are used up, finishing with a layer of rice. Cook over a gentle heat for 10 minutes.

4 Pour the remaining melted butter over the rice. Sprinkle with the cinnamon and cumin. Cover the pan with a clean dish towel and secure with a tight-fitting lid, lifting the corners of the cloth back over the lid. Steam over a low heat for 30–45 minutes.

5 Mix 45ml/3 tbsp of the rice with the saffron water. Spoon the remaining rice onto a large serving plate and scatter on the saffron-flavoured rice to decorate. Serve with either a lamb or chicken dish.

— COOK'S TIP —

Saffron may seem expensive, however you only need a little to add flavour and colour to a variety of savoury and sweet dishes. And, as long as it is kept dry and dark, it never goes off.

Mexican-style Rice

INGREDIENTS

Serves 6

350g/12oz/1¾ cups long grain
   white rice
1 onion, chopped
2 garlic cloves, chopped
450g/1lb tomatoes, peeled, seeded and
   coarsely chopped
60ml/4 tbsp corn or peanut oil
900ml/1½ pints/3¾ cups chicken stock
4 – 6 small red chillies
175g/6oz/1 cup cooked green peas
salt and freshly ground black pepper
fresh coriander sprigs, to garnish

1 Soak the rice in a bowl of hot
water for 15 minutes. Drain, rinse
well under cold running water, drain
again and set aside.

2 Combine the onion, garlic and
tomatoes in a food processor and
process to a purée.

3 Heat the oil in a large frying pan.
Add the drained rice and sauté
until it is golden brown. Using a slotted
spoon, transfer the rice to a saucepan.

4 Reheat the oil remaining in the
pan and cook the tomato purée for
2–3 minutes. Tip it into the saucepan
and pour in the stock. Season to taste.
Bring to the boil, reduce the heat to
the lowest possible setting, cover the
pan and cook for 15–20 minutes until
almost all the liquid has been absorbed.
Slice the red chillies from tip to stem
end into four or five sections. Place in
a bowl of iced water until they curl
back to form flowers, then drain.

5 Stir the peas into the rice mixture
and cook, without a lid, until all
the liquid has been absorbed and the
rice is tender. Stir the mixture from
time to time.

6 Transfer the rice to a serving dish
and garnish with the drained chilli
flowers and sprigs of coriander. Warn
the diners that these elaborate chilli
"flowers" are hot and should be
approached with caution.

Tossed Noodles with Seafood

INGREDIENTS

Serves 4–6

350g/12oz thick egg noodles
60ml/4 tbsp vegetable oil
3 slices fresh root ginger, grated
2 garlic cloves, finely chopped
225g/8oz mussels or clams
225g/8oz raw prawns, peeled
225g/8oz squid, cut into rings
115g/4oz oriental fried fish cake, sliced
1 red pepper, seeded and cut into rings
50g/2oz sugar snap peas, topped
    and tailed
30ml/2 tbsp soy sauce
2.5ml/½ tsp sugar
120ml/4fl oz/½ cup stock or water
15ml/1 tbsp cornflour
5–10ml/1–2 tsp sesame oil
salt and freshly ground black pepper
2 spring onions, chopped, and 2 red
    chillies, seeded and chopped,
    to garnish

1 Cook the noodles in a large saucepan of boiling water until just tender. Drain, rinse under cold water and drain well.

2 Heat the oil in a wok or large frying pan. Fry the ginger and garlic for 30 seconds. Add the mussels or clams, prawns and squid and stir-fry for about 4–5 minutes until the seafood changes colour. Add the fish cake slices, red pepper rings and sugar snap peas and stir well.

3 In a bowl, mix the soy sauce, sugar, stock or water and cornflour. Stir into the seafood and bring to the boil. Add the noodles and cook until they are heated through.

4 Add the sesame oil to the wok or pan and season with salt and pepper to taste. Serve at once, garnished with the spring onions and red chillies.

Noodles with Spicy Meat Sauce

INGREDIENTS

Serves 4–6

30ml/2 tbsp vegetable oil
2 dried red chillies, chopped
5ml/1 tsp grated fresh root ginger
2 garlic cloves, finely chopped
15ml/1 tbsp chilli bean paste
450g/1lb minced pork or beef
450g/1lb broad flat egg noodles
15ml/1 tbsp sesame oil
2 spring onions, chopped, to garnish

For the sauce
1.25ml/¼ tsp salt
5ml/1 tsp sugar
15ml/1 tbsp soy sauce
5ml/1 tsp mushroom ketchup
15ml/1 tbsp cornflour
250ml/8fl oz/1 cup chicken stock
5ml/1 tsp shaohsing wine or
    dry sherry

1 Heat the vegetable oil in a large saucepan. Add the dried chillies, ginger and garlic. Fry until the garlic starts to colour, then gradually stir in the chilli bean paste.

2 Add the minced pork or beef, breaking it up with a spatula or wooden spoon. Cook over a high heat until the minced meat changes colour and any liquid has evaporated.

3 Mix all the sauce ingredients in a jug. Make a well in the centre of the pork mixture. Pour in the sauce mixture and stir together. Simmer for 10–15 minutes until tender.

4 Meanwhile, cook the noodles in a large saucepan of boiling water for 5–7 minutes until just tender. Drain well and toss with the sesame oil. Serve, topped with the meat sauce and garnished with the spring onions.

Tomato Noodles with Fried Egg

INGREDIENTS

Serves 4

350g/12oz medium-thick
    dried noodles
60ml/4 tbsp vegetable oil
2 garlic cloves, very
    finely chopped
4 shallots, chopped
2.5ml/½ tsp chilli powder
5ml/1 tsp paprika
2 carrots, finely diced
115g/4oz button mushrooms,
    quartered
50g/2oz peas
15ml/1 tbsp tomato ketchup
10ml/2 tsp tomato purée
salt and freshly ground black pepper
butter for frying
4 eggs

1 Cook the noodles in a saucepan of boiling water until just tender. Drain, rinse under cold running water and drain well.

2 Heat the oil in a wok or large frying pan. Add the garlic, shallots, chilli powder and paprika. Stir-fry for about 1 minute, then add the carrots, mushrooms and peas. Continue to stir-fry until the vegetables are cooked.

3 Stir the tomato ketchup and purée into the vegetable mixture. Add the noodles and cook over a medium heat until the noodles are heated through and have taken on the reddish tinge of the paprika and tomato.

4 Meanwhile melt the butter in a frying pan and fry the eggs. Season the noodle mixture, divide it among four serving plates and top each portion with a fried egg.

Curry Fried Noodles

On its own bean curd (tofu) has a fairly bland flavour, but it takes on the flavour of the curry spices wonderfully.

INGREDIENTS

Serves 4

60ml/4 tbsp vegetable oil
30–45ml/2–3 tbsp curry paste
225g/8oz smoked bean curd, cut into
    2.5cm/1in cubes
225g/8oz green beans, cut into
    2.5cm/1in lengths
1 red pepper, seeded and cut into
    fine strips
350g/12oz rice vermicelli, soaked in
    warm water until soft
15ml/1 tbsp soy sauce
salt and freshly ground black pepper
2 spring onions, finely sliced, 2 red
    chillies, seeded and chopped, and
    1 lime, cut into wedges, to garnish

1 Heat half the oil in a wok or large frying pan. Add the curry paste and stir-fry for a few minutes, then add the bean curd and continue to fry until golden brown. Using a slotted spoon remove the cubes from the pan and set aside until required.

2 Add the remaining oil to the wok or pan. When hot, add the green beans and red pepper. Stir-fry until the vegetables are cooked. You may need to moisten them with a little water.

3 Drain the noodles and add them to the wok or frying pan. Continue to stir-fry until the noodles are heated through, then return the curried bean curd to the wok. Season with soy sauce, salt and pepper.

4 Transfer the mixture to a serving dish. Sprinkle with the spring onions and chillies and serve the lime wedges on the side.

Penne with Chilli and Broccoli

INGREDIENTS

Serves 4

450g/1lb/3 cups penne
450g/1lb small broccoli florets
30ml/2 tbsp stock
1 garlic clove, crushed
1 small red chilli pepper, sliced, or
  2.5ml/½ tsp chilli sauce
60ml/4 tbsp natural yogurt
30ml/2 tbsp toasted pine nuts
  or cashews
salt and ground black pepper

—— VARIATION ——

Green chillies can be used instead of red
chillies and toasted almonds make a good
substitute for pine nuts.

1 Add the pasta to a large pan of
lightly salted boiling water and
return to the boil. Place the broccoli in
a steamer basket over the top. Cover
and cook for 8–10 minutes until both
are just tender. Drain.

2 Heat the stock and add the crushed
garlic and chilli or chilli sauce. Stir
over a low heat for 2–3 minutes.

3 Stir in the broccoli, pasta and
yogurt. Adjust the seasoning,
sprinkle with nuts and serve hot.

Crispy Fried Rice Vermicelli – Mee Krob

Mee Krob is usually served at celebration meals. It is a crisp tangle of fried rice vermicelli, which is tossed in a piquant garlic, sweet and sour sauce.

INGREDIENTS

Serves 4–6

oil for frying
175g/6oz rice vermicelli
15ml/1 tbsp chopped garlic
4–6 dried chillies, seeded and chopped
30ml/2 tbsp chopped shallot
15ml/1 tbsp dried shrimps, rinsed
115g/4oz minced pork
115g/4oz uncooked shelled prawns, chopped
30ml/2 tbsp brown bean sauce
30ml/2 tbsp rice wine vinegar
45ml/3 tbsp fish sauce
75g/3 tbsp palm sugar
30ml/2 tbsp tamarind or lime juice
115g/4oz beansprouts

For the garnish

2 spring onions, shredded
30ml/2 tbsp fresh coriander leaves
2 heads pickled garlic (optional)
2-egg omelette, rolled and sliced
2 red chillies, chopped

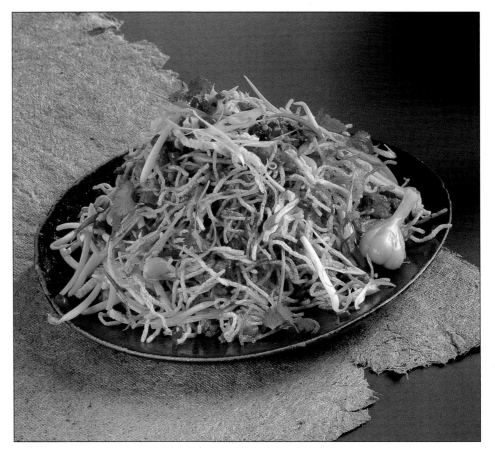

3 Add the minced pork and stir-fry until it is no longer pink, about 3–4 minutes. Add the prawns and fry for a further 2 minutes. Remove the mixture and set aside.

4 To the same wok, add the brown bean sauce, vinegar, fish sauce and palm sugar. Bring to a gentle boil, stir to dissolve the sugar and cook until thick and syrupy.

6 Reduce the heat. Add the pork and prawn mixture, and beansprouts to the sauce, stir to mix.

1 Heat the oil in a wok. Break the rice vermicelli apart into small handfuls about 7.5cm/3in long. Deep fry in the hot oil until they puff up. Remove and drain on kitchen paper.

2 Leave 30ml/2 tbsp of the hot oil in the wok, add the garlic, chillies, shallots and shrimps. Fry until fragrant.

5 Add the tamarind or lime juice and adjust the seasoning. It should be sweet, sour and salty.

7 Add the rice noodles and toss gently to coat them with the sauce without breaking the noodles too much. Transfer the noodles to a platter. Garnish with spring onions, coriander leaves, pickled garlic, omelette strips and red chillies.

Vegetarian Fried Noodles

When making this dish for non-vegetarians, or for vegetarians who eat fish, add a piece of *blacan* (compressed shrimp paste). A small chunk about the size of a stock cube, mashed with the chilli paste, will add a deliciously rich, aromatic flavour.

INGREDIENTS

Serves 4

2 eggs
5ml/1 tsp chilli powder
5ml/1 tsp turmeric
60ml/4 tbsp vegetable oil
1 large onion, finely sliced
2 red chillies, seeded and
   finely sliced
15ml/1 tbsp soy sauce
2 large cooked potatoes, cut into
   small cubes
6 pieces fried bean curd, sliced
225g/8oz beansprouts
115g/4oz green beans, blanched
350g/12oz fresh thick egg noodles
salt and freshly ground black pepper
sliced spring onions, to garnish

1 Beat the eggs lightly, then strain them into a bowl. Heat a lightly greased omelette pan. Pour in half of the egg to cover the bottom of the pan thinly. When the egg is just set, turn the omelette over and fry the other side briefly. Slide on to a plate, blot with kitchen paper, roll up and cut into narrow strips. Make a second omelette in the same way and slice. Set the omelette strips aside for the garnish.

—— COOK'S TIP ——

Always be very careful when handling chillies. Keep your hands away from your eyes as chillies will sting them. Wash your hands thoroughly after touching chillies.

2 In a cup, mix together the chilli powder and turmeric. Form a paste by stirring in a little water.

3 Heat the oil in a wok or large frying pan. Fry the onion until soft. Reduce the heat and add the chilli paste, sliced chillies and soy sauce. Fry for 2–3 minutes.

4 Add the potatoes and fry for about 2 minutes, mixing well with the chillies. Add the bean curd, then the beansprouts, green beans and noodles.

5 Gently stir-fry until the noodles are evenly coated and heated through. Take care not to break up the potatoes or the bean curd. Season with salt and pepper. Serve hot, garnished with the reserved omelette strips and spring onion slices.

Thai Fried Noodles

Phat Thai has a fascinating flavour and texture. It is made with rice noodles and is considered one of the national dishes of Thailand.

INGREDIENTS

Serves 4–6
350g/12oz rice noodles
45ml/3 tbsp vegetable oil
15ml/1 tbsp chopped garlic
16 uncooked king prawns, shelled, tails
   left intact and deveined
2 eggs, lightly beaten
15ml/1 tbsp dried shrimps, rinsed
30ml/2 tbsp pickled white radish
50g/2oz fried bean curd, cut into
   small slivers
2.5ml/½ tsp dried chilli flakes
115g/4oz garlic chives, cut into
   5cm/2in lengths
225g/8oz beansprouts
50g/2oz roasted peanuts, coarsely
   ground
5ml/1 tsp granulated sugar
15ml/1 tbsp dark soy sauce
30ml/2 tbsp fish sauce
30ml/2 tbsp tamarind juice
30ml/2 tbsp coriander leaves,
   to garnish
1 kaffir lime, to garnish

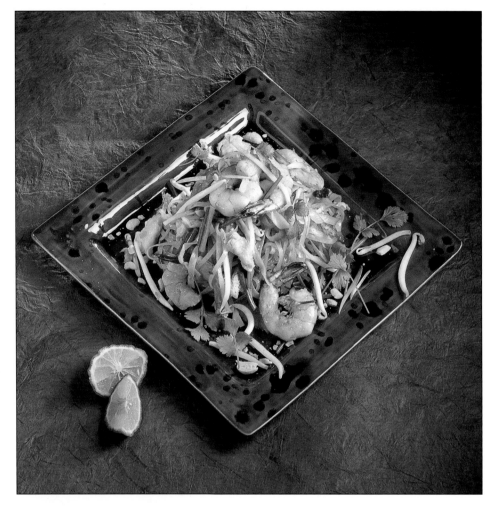

1 Soak the noodles in warm water for 20–30 minutes, then drain.

2 Heat 15ml/1 tbsp of the oil in a wok or large frying pan. Add the garlic and fry until golden. Stir in the prawns and cook for about 1–2 minutes until pink, tossing from time to time. Remove and set aside.

3 Heat another 15ml/1 tbsp of oil in the wok. Add the eggs and tilt the wok to spread them into a thin sheet. Stir to scramble and break the egg into small pieces. Remove from the wok and set aside with the prawns.

4 Heat the remaining oil in the same wok. Add the dried shrimps, pickled radish, bean curd and dried chillies. Stir briefly. Add the soaked noodles and stir-fry for 5 minutes.

5 Add the garlic chives, half the beansprouts and half the peanuts. Season with the granulated sugar, soy sauce, fish sauce and tamarind juice. Mix well and cook until the noodles are heated through.

6 Return the prawn and egg mixture to the wok and mix with the noodles. Serve garnished with the rest of the beansprouts, peanuts, coriander leaves and lime wedges.

Spicy Szechuan Noodles

INGREDIENTS

Serves 4
350g/12oz thick noodles
175g/6oz cooked chicken,
    shredded
50g/2oz roasted cashew nuts

For the dressing
4 spring onions, chopped
30ml/2 tbsp chopped coriander
2 garlic cloves, chopped
30ml/2 tbsp smooth peanut butter
30ml/2 tbsp sweet chilli sauce
15ml/1 tbsp soy sauce
15ml/1 tbsp sherry vinegar
15ml/1 tbsp sesame oil
30ml/2 tbsp olive oil
30ml/2 tbsp chicken stock
    or water
10 toasted Szechuan peppercorns,
    ground

1 Cook the noodles in a saucepan of boiling water until just tender, following the directions on the packet. Drain, rinse under cold running water and drain well.

2 While the noodles are cooking combine all the ingredients for the dressing in a large bowl and whisk together well.

3 Add the noodles, shredded chicken and cashew nuts to the dressing, toss gently to coat and adjust the seasoning to taste. Serve at once.

— COOK'S TIP —

You could substitute cooked turkey or pork for the chicken for a change.

Sesame Noodles with Spring Onions

This simple but very tasty warm salad can be prepared and cooked in just a few minutes.

INGREDIENTS

Serves 4
2 garlic cloves, roughly chopped
30ml/2 tbsp Chinese sesame paste
15ml/1 tbsp dark sesame oil
30ml/2 tbsp soy sauce
30ml/2 tbsp rice wine
15ml/1 tbsp honey
pinch of five-spice powder
350g/12oz soba or
    buckwheat noodles
4 spring onions, finely
    sliced diagonally
50g/2oz beansprouts
7.5cm/3in piece of cucumber, cut
    into matchsticks
toasted sesame seeds
salt and freshly ground black pepper

1 Process the garlic, sesame paste, oil, soy sauce, rice wine, honey and five-spice powder with a pinch each of salt and pepper in a blender or food processor until smooth.

2 Cook the noodles in a saucepan of boiling water until just tender, following the directions on the packet. Drain the noodles immediately and tip them into a bowl.

3 Toss the hot noodles with the dressing and the spring onions. Top with the beansprouts, cucumber and sesame seeds and serve.

— COOK'S TIP —

If you can't find Chinese sesame paste, then use either tahini paste or smooth peanut butter instead.

SEARING-HOT SIDE DISHES, SALSAS AND RELISHES

Grilled meat, poultry or fish are delicious when spiced up with a red-hot salsa, chutney, relish or pickle. The selection varies from Coconut Chilli Relish, which is pleasantly hot, to scorchingly hot Double Chilli Salsa. Tomato and Onion Salad with red chilli is surprisingly refreshing, and Pickled Cucumbers are good with cold meats or cheese.

Tomato and Onion Salad

A refreshing salad, *Atjar Ketimun,* which can be made ahead; it improves if well chilled before serving. Use firm, slightly under-ripe tomatoes so the flesh does not collapse when cut into dice.

INGREDIENTS

Serves 6

1 cucumber
45ml/3 tbsp good-quality rice or white wine vinegar
10ml/2 tsp sugar
1 tomato, skinned, seeded and diced
1 small onion, finely sliced
1 fresh red chilli, seeded and chopped
salt

1 Trim the ends from the cucumber. Peel it lengthways but leave some of the skin on, to make the salad look more attractive. Cut it in thin slices and lay them out on a large plate. Sprinkle with a little salt and leave for 15 minutes. Rinse well and dry.

2 Mix the vinegar, sugar and a pinch of salt together. Arrange all the vegetables in a bowl and pour over the vinegar, sugar and salt mixture. Cover the salad and chill before serving.

Coconut and Peanut Relish

The aroma of toasted coconut is wonderful and immediately will have you dreaming of warmer climes! *Serudeng* is served as an accompaniment to many Indonesian dishes; any leftovers can be stored in an airtight tin.

INGREDIENTS

Serves 6–8

115g/4oz fresh coconut, grated, or desiccated coconut
175g/6oz salted peanuts
5mm/¼in cube *terasi*
1 small onion, quartered
2–3 garlic cloves, crushed
45ml/3 tbsp oil
2.5ml/½ tsp tamarind pulp, soaked in 30ml/2 tbsp warm water
5ml/1 tsp coriander seeds, dry-fried and ground
2.5ml/½ tsp cumin seeds, dry-fried and ground
5ml/1 tsp dark brown sugar

1 Dry-fry the coconut in a wok or large frying pan over a medium heat, turning *all the time,* until crisp and a rich, golden colour. Allow to cool and add half to the peanuts. Toss together to mix.

2 Grind the *terasi*, with the onion and garlic, to a paste in a food processor or with a pestle and mortar. Fry in hot oil, without browning. Strain the tamarind and reserve the juice. Add the coriander, cumin, tamarind juice and brown sugar to the fried paste. Stir all the time and cook for 2–3 minutes.

3 Stir in the remaining toasted coconut and leave to cool. When quite cold, mix with the peanut and coconut mixture.

Fiery Citrus Salsa

This very unusual salsa makes a fantastic marinade for all kinds of shellfish and it is also delicious when drizzled over freshly barbecued meat.

Ingredients

Serves 4

1 orange
1 green apple
2 fresh red chillies, halved and seeded
1 garlic clove
8 fresh mint leaves
juice of 1 lemon
salt and ground black pepper

1 Slice the bottom off the orange so that it stands firmly on a chopping board. Using a large sharp knife, remove the peel by slicing from the top to the bottom of the orange.

2 Hold the orange in one hand over a bowl. Slice towards the middle of the fruit, to one side of a segment, and then gently twist the knife to ease the segment away from the membrane and out of the orange. Repeat to remove all the segments. Squeeze any juice from the remaining membrane.

3 Peel the apple, slice it into wedges and remove the core.

4 Place the chillies in a blender or food processor with the orange segments and juice, apple wedges, garlic and mint.

5 Process until smooth, then, with the motor running, pour in the lemon juice.

6 Season, pour into a bowl or small jug and serve immediately.

Variation

If you're feeling really fiery, don't seed the chillies! They will make the salsa particularly hot and fierce.

Salsa Verde

There are many versions of this classic green salsa. Serve this one with creamy mashed potatoes or drizzled over the top of char-grilled squid.

INGREDIENTS

Serves 4
2–4 green chillies
8 spring onions
2 garlic cloves
50g/2oz salted capers
fresh tarragon sprig
1 bunch of fresh parsley
grated rind and juice of 1 lime
juice of 1 lemon
90ml/6 tbsp olive oil
about 15ml/1 tbsp green Tabasco, or
   to taste
ground black pepper

1 Halve the green chillies and remove their seeds. Trim the spring onions and halve the garlic, then place in a food processor or blender. Pulse the power briefly until the ingredients are roughly chopped.

2 Use your fingertips to rub the excess salt off the capers but do not rinse them. Add the capers, tarragon and parsley to the food processor or blender and pulse again until they are fairly finely chopped.

3 Transfer the mixture to a small bowl. Stir in the lime rind and juice, lemon juice and olive oil. Stir the mixture lightly so the citrus juice and oil do not emulsify.

4 Add green Tabasco and black pepper to taste. Chill until ready to serve but do not prepare more than 8 hours in advance.

--- VARIATION ---

If you can find only capers pickled in vinegar, they can be used for this salsa but they must be rinsed well in cold water first.

Berry Salsa

INGREDIENTS

Makes 3 cups
1 fresh jalapeño pepper
½ red onion, chopped
2 spring onions, chopped
1 tomato, finely diced
1 small yellow pepper, seeded
  and chopped
60ml/4 tbsp chopped fresh coriander
1.5ml/¼ tsp salt
15ml/1 tbsp raspberry vinegar
15ml/1 tbsp fresh orange juice
5ml/1 tsp honey
15ml/1 tbsp olive oil
150g/5oz/1 cup strawberries, hulled
115g/4oz/1 cup blueberries or
  blackberries
175g/6oz/1 cup raspberries

1 Wearing rubber gloves, finely mince the jalapeño pepper. Discard the seeds and membrane if a less hot flavour is desired. Place the pepper in a bowl.

2 Add the red onion, spring onions, tomato, pepper and coriander, and stir to blend.

3 In a small mixing bowl, whisk together the salt, raspberry vinegar, orange juice, honey and olive oil. Pour this over the jalapeño mixture and stir well to combine.

4 Coarsely chop the strawberries. Add them to the jalapeño mixture with the blueberries or blackberries and the raspberries. Stir to blend together. Leave to stand at room temperature for about 3 hours.

5 Serve the salsa at room temperature, with grilled fish or poultry.

Mixed Vegetable Pickle

If you can obtain fresh turmeric, it makes such a difference to the colour and appearance of *Acar Campur*. You can use almost any vegetable, bearing in mind that you need a balance of textures, flavours and colours.

INGREDIENTS

Makes 2–3 x 300g/11oz jars
1 fresh red chilli, seeded and sliced
1 onion, quartered
2 garlic cloves, crushed
1cm/½ in cube *terasi*
4 macadamia nuts or 8 almonds
2.5cm/1in fresh turmeric, peeled and
    sliced, or 5ml/1 tsp ground turmeric
50ml/2fl oz/¼ cup sunflower oil
475ml/16fl oz/2 cups white vinegar
250ml/8fl oz/1 cup water
25–50g/1–2oz granulated sugar
3 carrots
225g/8oz green beans
1 small cauliflower
1 cucumber
225g/8oz white cabbage
115g/4oz dry-roasted peanuts,
    roughly crushed
salt

1 Place the chilli, onion, garlic, *terasi*, nuts and turmeric in a food processor and blend to a paste, or pound in a mortar with a pestle.

2 Heat the oil and stir-fry the paste to release the aroma. Add the vinegar, water, sugar and salt. Bring to the boil. Simmer for 10 minutes.

3 Cut the carrots into flower shapes. Cut the green beans into short, neat lengths. Separate the cauliflower into neat, bite-size florets. Peel and seed the cucumber and cut the flesh in neat, bite-size pieces. Cut the cabbage in neat, bite-size pieces.

4 Blanch each vegetable separately, in a large pan of boiling water, for 1 minute. Transfer to a colander and rinse with cold water, to halt the cooking. Drain well.

COOK'S TIP

This pickle is even better if you make it a few days ahead.

---

5 Add the vegetables to the sauce. Slowly bring to the boil and allow to cook for 5–10 minutes. Do not overcook – the vegetables should still be crunchy.

6 Add the peanuts and cool. Spoon into clean jars with lids.

Apricot Chutney

Chutneys can add zest to most meals, and in Pakistan you will usually find a selection of different kinds served in tiny bowls for people to choose from. Dried apricots are readily available from supermarkets or health food shops.

INGREDIENTS

Makes about 450g/1lb
450g/1lb/3 cups dried apricots, finely chopped
5ml/1 tsp garam masala
275g/10oz/1¼ cups soft light brown sugar
450ml/16fl oz/scant 2 cups malt vinegar
5ml/1 tsp ginger pulp
5ml/1 tsp salt
75g/3oz/½ cup sultanas
450ml/16fl oz/scant 2 cups water

1 Put all of the ingredients into a medium saucepan and mix them together thoroughly.

VARIATION

For a change, you could try dried peaches instead of the apricots. If wished, you can add heat with green chillies.

2 Bring the mixture to the boil, then turn down the heat and simmer for about 30–35 minutes, stirring occasionally as it cooks.

3 When the chutney has thickened to a fairly stiff consistency, transfer it to 2–3 clean jam jars and leave to cool thoroughly. This chutney should be covered tightly with a lid and stored in the fridge.

Tasty Toasts

These crunchy toasts have a wonderful spicy flavour. They make an ideal snack or part of a weekend brunch. They are especially delicious when served with freshly grilled tomatoes and baked beans.

INGREDIENTS

Serves 4
4 eggs
300ml/½ pint/1¼ cups milk
2 fresh green chillies, finely chopped
30ml/2 tbsp chopped fresh coriander
75g/3oz/¾ cup Cheddar or mozzarella cheese, grated
2.5ml/½ tsp salt
1.5ml/¼ tsp ground black pepper
4 slices bread
corn oil, for frying

1 Break the eggs into a medium bowl and whisk together. Slowly add the milk and whisk again. Add the green chillies, fresh coriander, grated cheese and salt and pepper to taste.

2 Cut the bread slices in half diagonally, and soak them, one at a time, in the egg mixture.

3 Heat the corn oil in a medium frying pan and fry the soaked bread slices over a medium heat, turning them once or twice, until they are golden brown.

4 Drain off any excess oil as you remove the toasts from the pan and serve them immediately.

Double Chilli Salsa

Only the very brave should sample this scorchingly hot salsa! Spread it sparingly on to cooked meats and burgers.

INGREDIENTS

Serves 4–6

6 habanero chillies or Scotch bonnets
2 ripe tomatoes
4 standard green jalapeño chillies
30ml/2 tbsp chopped fresh parsley
30ml/2 tbsp olive oil
15ml/1 tbsp balsamic or sherry vinegar
salt

— COOK'S TIP —

Habanero chillies, or Scotch bonnets, are among the hottest fresh chillies available. You may prefer to tone down the heat of this salsa by using a milder variety.

---

1 Skewer an habanero chilli on a metal fork and hold it in a gas flame for 2–3 minutes, turning until the skin blackens and blisters. Repeat with all the chillies, then set aside.

2 Skewer and blister the tomatoes in the flame for 1–2 minutes, until the skin splits and wrinkles. Slip off the skins, halve the tomatoes, then use a teaspoon to scoop out and discard the seeds. Chop the flesh very finely.

3 Use a clean dish towel to rub the skins off the chillies.

4 Try not to touch the chillies with your bare hands: use a fork to hold them and slice them open with a sharp knife. Scrape out and discard the seeds, then finely chop the flesh.

5 Halve the jalapeño chillies, then remove their seeds and slice them finely widthways into tiny strips. Mix together both types of chilli, the tomatoes and the parsley.

6 Mix the olive oil, vinegar and a little salt, pour this over the salsa and cover the dish. The salsa will keep in the fridge for up to 3 days.

Piquant Pineapple Relish

This fruity sweet and sour relish is really excellent when it is served with grilled chicken or bacon rashers.

INGREDIENTS

Serves 4
400g/14oz can crushed pineapple in natural juice
30ml/2 tbsp light muscovado sugar
30ml/2 tbsp wine vinegar
1 garlic clove
4 spring onions
2 red chillies
10 fresh basil leaves
salt and ground black pepper

1 Drain the crushed pineapple pieces thoroughly and reserve about 60ml/4 tbsp of the juice.

2 Place the juice in a small saucepan with the muscovado sugar and wine vinegar, then heat gently, stirring, until the sugar dissolves. Remove the pan from the heat and add salt and pepper to taste.

3 Finely chop the garlic and spring onions. Halve the chillies, remove the seeds and finely chop them. Finely shred the basil.

4 Place the pineapple, garlic, spring onions and chillies in a bowl. Mix well and pour in the sauce. Allow to cool for 5 minutes, then stir in the basil.

--- COOK'S TIP ---

This relish tastes extra special when made with fresh pineapple – substitute the juice of a freshly squeezed orange for the canned juice.

Pickled Cucumbers

Often served with salt beef, these gherkins or cucumbers are simple to prepare but take a couple of days for the flavour to develop.

INGREDIENTS

Serves 6–8
6 small pickling cucumbers
75ml/5 tbsp white wine vinegar
475ml/16fl oz/2 cups cold water
15ml/1 tbsp salt
10ml/2 tsp sugar
10 black peppercorns
1 garlic clove
1 bunch fresh dill (optional)

1 You will need a large lidded jar or an oblong non-metallic container with a tightly fitting lid. Cut each cucumber lengthways into six spears.

2 Mix together the wine vinegar, water, salt and sugar. Crush a few of the peppercorns and leave the rest whole. Add them to the liquid. Cut the garlic clove in half.

3 Arrange the cucumber spears in the jar or container, pour over the pickling liquid and add the garlic. Put in a few sprigs of dill if using. Make sure they are completely submerged.

4 Leave the cucumbers, covered, in the fridge for at least two days. To serve, lift them out and discard the garlic, dill and peppercorns. Store any uneaten cucumbers in their pickling liquid in the fridge.

Spicy Fried Dumplins

Spicy Fried Dumplins are very easy to make. In the Caribbean, they are often served with saltfish or fried fish, but they can be eaten quite simply with butter and jam or cheese.

INGREDIENTS

Makes about 10

450g/1lb/4 cups self-raising flour
10ml/2 tsp sugar
2.5ml/½ tsp ground cinnamon
pinch of ground nutmeg
2.5ml/½ tsp salt
300ml/½ pint/1¼ cups milk
oil for frying

1 Sift the dry ingredients together into a large bowl, add the milk and mix and knead until smooth.

2 Divide the dough into ten balls, kneading each ball with floured hands. Press the balls gently to flatten into 7.5cm/3in rounds.

3 Heat a little oil in a non-stick frying pan until moderately hot. Place half the dumplins in the pan, reduce the heat to low and fry for about 15 minutes until they are golden brown, turning once.

4 Stand them on their sides for a few minutes to brown the edges, before removing them and draining on kitchen paper. Serve warm.

Kachumbali Salad

Katchumbali is a peppery relish from Tanzania, where it is served with grilled meat or fish dishes, together with rice – this salad uses the same combination of vegetables and flavours.

INGREDIENTS

Serves 4–6
2 red onions
4 tomatoes
1 green chilli
½ cucumber
1 carrot
juice of 1 lemon
salt and freshly ground black pepper

1 Slice the onions and tomatoes very thinly and place in a bowl.

2 Slice the chilli lengthways, discard the seeds, then chop very finely. Peel and slice the cucumber and carrot and add to the onions and tomatoes.

3 Squeeze the lemon juice over the salad. Season with salt and freshly ground black pepper and toss together to mix. Serve as an accompaniment, salad or relish.

--- COOK'S TIP ---

Traditional *Katchumbali* is made by very finely chopping the onions, tomatoes, cucumber and carrot. This produces a very moist, sauce-like mixture, which is good served inside chapatis, and eaten as a snack.

Coconut Chilli Relish

This simple but delicious relish is widely made in Tanzania. Only the white part of the coconut flesh is used – either shred it fairly coarsely, or grate it finely for a moister result.

INGREDIENTS

Makes about 50g/2oz
50g/2oz fresh or desiccated coconut
10ml/2 tsp lemon juice
1.5ml/¼ tsp salt
10ml/2 tsp water
1.5ml/¼ tsp finely chopped red chilli

1 Grate the coconut and place in a mixing bowl. If using desiccated coconut, add just enough water to moisten.

2 Add the lemon juice, salt, water and chilli. Stir thoroughly and serve as a relish with meats or as an accompaniment to a main dish.

Chilli Bean Dip

This creamy and spicy dip made from kidney beans is best served warm with triangles of golden brown grilled pitta bread or a generous helping of crunchy tortilla chips.

INGREDIENTS

Serves 4
2 garlic cloves
1 onion
2 fresh green chillies
30ml/2 tbsp vegetable oil
5–10ml/1–2 tsp hot chilli powder
400g/14oz can kidney beans
75g/3oz mature Cheddar
   cheese, grated
1 red chilli, seeded
salt and ground black pepper

1 Finely chop the garlic and onion. Seed and finely chop the fresh green chillies.

2 Heat the oil in a frying pan and add the garlic, onion, green chillies and chilli powder. Cook gently for 5 minutes, stirring regularly, until the onions are softened.

3 Drain the can of kidney beans, reserving the liquor. Blend all but 30ml/2 tbsp of the beans to a purée in a food processor or blender.

4 Add the puréed beans to the pan with 30–45ml/2–3 tbsp of the reserved liquor. Heat gently, stirring to mix well.

5 Stir in the whole kidney beans and the grated Cheddar cheese. Cook gently for about 2–3 minutes, stirring until all the cheese melts. Add salt and plenty of freshly ground black pepper to taste.

6 Cut the fresh red chilli into tiny strips. Spoon the dip into four individual serving bowls and scatter the chilli strips over the top of each one. Serve warm.

COOK'S TIP

For a dip with a coarser texture, do not purée the kidney beans in a food processor or blender; instead, mash them with a potato masher.

Chilli Relish

This spicy tomato and red pepper relish will keep for at least a week in the fridge. Serve it with bangers and burgers in fresh white baps with a crisp salad.

INGREDIENTS

Serves 8

6 tomatoes
1 onion
1 red pepper, seeded
2 garlic cloves
30ml/2 tbsp olive oil
5ml/1 tsp ground cinnamon
5ml/1 tsp chilli flakes
5ml/1 tsp ground ginger
5ml/1 tsp salt
2.5ml/½ tsp ground black pepper
75g/3oz/⅓ cup light muscovado sugar
75ml/5 tbsp cider vinegar
1 handful of fresh basil leaves

COOK'S TIP

This relish thickens slightly on cooling so don't worry if the mixture seems a little wet at the end of step 5.

1 Skewer each of the tomatoes in turn on a metal fork and hold in a gas flame for 1–2 minutes, turning until the skin splits and wrinkles. Slip off the skins, then roughly chop the tomatoes.

2 Roughly chop the onion, red pepper and garlic. Heat the oil in a saucepan. Add the onion, red pepper and garlic.

3 Cook gently for 5–8 minutes, until the pepper is softened. Add the chopped tomatoes, cover and cook for 5 minutes, until the tomatoes release their juices.

4 Stir in the cinnamon, chilli flakes, ginger, salt, pepper, sugar and vinegar. Bring gently to the boil, stirring until the sugar dissolves.

5 Simmer, uncovered, for about 20 minutes, or until the mixture is pulpy. Stir in the basil leaves and check the seasoning.

6 Allow the relish to cool completely, then transfer it to a glass jam jar or a plastic container with a tightly fitting lid. Store, covered, in the fridge.

Spiced Carrot Dip

This is a delicious low-fat dip with a sweet and spicy flavour. Serve wheat crackers or fiery tortilla chips as accompaniments for dipping.

INGREDIENTS

Serves 4

1 onion
3 carrots
grated rind and juice of 2 oranges
15ml/1 tbsp hot curry paste
150ml/¼ pint/²⁄₃ cup low-fat
   natural yogurt
1 handful of fresh basil leaves
15–30ml/1–2 tbsp fresh lemon juice,
   to taste
red Tabasco, to taste
salt and ground black pepper

1 Using a sharp vegetable knife, finely chop the onion. Peel and grate the carrots. Place the onion, carrots, orange rind and juice and hot curry paste in a small saucepan. Bring the mixture to the boil, cover with a lid and simmer for about 10 minutes, or until tender.

2 Process the mixture in a blender or food processor until smooth. Leave to cool completely.

3 Stir in the yogurt, then tear the basil leaves into small pieces and stir them into the carrot mixture.

4 Add lemon juice, Tabasco, salt and pepper to taste and serve.

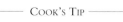

— COOK'S TIP —

Use Greek-style yogurt or soured cream instead of natural yogurt for a creamier dip.

Red Onion Raita

Raita is a traditional Indian accompaniment for most hot curries. It is also delicious when served with a pile of spicy poppadums as a dip.

INGREDIENTS

Serves 4

5ml/1 tsp cumin seeds
1 small garlic clove
1 small green chilli, seeded
1 large red onion
150ml/¼ pint/⅔ cup natural yogurt
30ml/2 tbsp chopped fresh coriander, plus extra to garnish
2.5ml/½ tsp sugar
salt

1 Heat a small frying pan and dry fry the cumin seeds for 1–2 minutes, until they release their aroma and begin to pop.

2 Lightly crush the cumin seeds in a pestle and mortar, or flatten them with the heel of a heavy-bladed knife until crushed.

3 Finely chop the garlic, green chilli and red onion. Stir into the yogurt with the crushed cumin seeds and chopped coriander.

4 Add sugar and salt to taste. Spoon the raita into a small bowl and chill until ready to serve. Garnish with extra coriander before serving.

COOK'S TIP

For an extra tangy raita, stir in 15ml/1 tbsp lemon juice.

SWEET AND SPICY DESSERTS AND CAKES

Warm spices, such as nutmeg, ginger, cinnamon and cardamom, are added to fresh fruit salads, ice creams, pastries, hot puddings and cakes. The selection ranges from Fresh Pineapple with Ginger to wickedly sweet spicy Baklava, from Cinnamon Rolls to Caribbean Fruit and Rum Cake with an Egyptian version of Spiced Bread Pudding and delicious spicy Caramel Rice Pudding.

Spicy Noodle Pudding

A traditional Jewish recipe, Spicy Noodle Pudding has a warm aromatic flavour and makes a delicious dessert.

INGREDIENTS

Serves 4–6

175g/6oz wide egg noodles
225g/8oz cottage cheese
115g/4oz cream cheese
75g/3oz caster sugar
2 eggs
120ml/4fl oz/½ cup soured cream
5ml/1 tsp vanilla essence
pinch of ground cinnamon
pinch of grated nutmeg
2.5ml/½ tsp grated lemon rind
50g/2oz butter
25g/1oz nibbed almonds
25g/1oz fine dried white breadcrumbs
icing sugar for dusting

1 Preheat the oven to 180°C/350°F/ Gas 4. Grease a shallow baking dish. Cook the noodles in a large saucepan of boiling water until just tender. Drain well.

2 Beat the cottage cheese, cream cheese and sugar together in a bowl. Add the eggs, one at a time, and stir in the soured cream. Stir in the vanilla essence, cinnamon, nutmeg and lemon rind.

3 Fold the noodles into the cheese mixture. Spoon into the prepared baking dish and level the surface.

4 Melt the butter in a frying pan. Add the almonds and fry for about 1 minute. Remove from the heat.

5 Stir in the breadcrumbs, mixing well. Sprinkle the mixture over the pudding. Bake for 30–40 minutes or until the mixture is set. Serve hot, dusted with a little icing sugar.

Avocado Salad in Ginger and Orange Sauce

This is an unusual fruit salad since avocado is more often treated as a vegetable. However, in the Caribbean it is used as a fruit, which of course it is!

INGREDIENTS

Serves 4
2 firm ripe avocados
3 firm ripe bananas, chopped
12 fresh cherries or strawberries
juice of 1 large orange
shredded fresh root ginger

For the ginger syrup
50g/2oz fresh root ginger, chopped
900ml/1½ pints/3¾ cups water
225g/8oz/1 cup demerara sugar
2 cloves

1 First make the ginger syrup; place the ginger, water, sugar and cloves in a saucepan and bring to the boil. Reduce the heat and simmer for about 1 hour, until well reduced and syrupy.

2 Remove the ginger and discard. Leave to cool. Store in a covered, clean container in the fridge.

3 Peel the avocados, cut into cubes and place in a bowl with the bananas and cherries or strawberries.

4 Pour the orange juice over the fruits. Add 60ml/4 tbsp of the ginger syrup and mix gently, using a metal spoon. Chill for 30 minutes and add a little shredded ginger.

Fresh Pineapple with Ginger

This refreshing dessert can also be made with vacuum-packed pineapple. This makes a good substitute, but fresh is best.

INGREDIENTS

Serves 4

1 fresh pineapple, peeled
slivers of fresh coconut
300ml/½ pint/1¼ cups pineapple juice
60ml/4 tbsp coconut liqueur
2.5cm/1in piece stem ginger, plus
   45ml/3 tbsp of the syrup

1 Peel and slice the pineapple, arrange in a serving dish and scatter the coconut slivers on top.

2 Place the pineapple juice and coconut liqueur in a saucepan and heat gently.

3 Thinly slice the stem ginger and add to the pan along with the ginger syrup. Bring just to the boil and then simmer gently until the liquid is slightly reduced and the sauce is fairly thick.

4 Pour the sauce over the pineapple and coconut, leave to cool, then chill before serving.

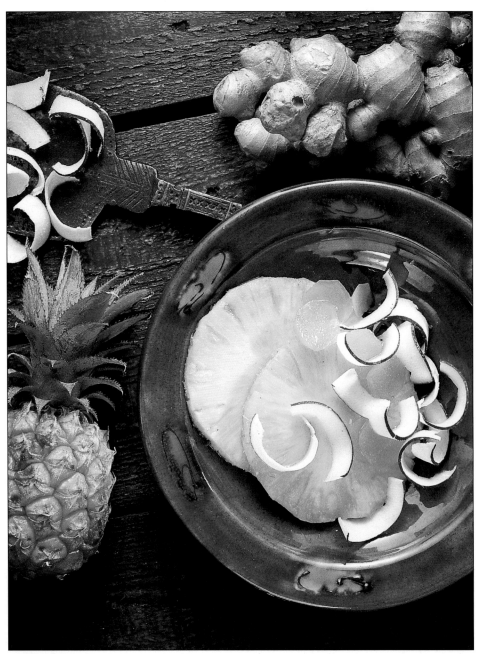

COOK'S TIP

If fresh coconut is not available, then use desiccated coconut instead.

Spiced Nutty Bananas

Cinnamon and nutmeg are spices which perfectly complement bananas in this delectable dessert.

INGREDIENTS

Serves 3

6 ripe, but firm, bananas
30ml/2 tbsp chopped unsalted cashew nuts
30ml/2 tbsp chopped unsalted peanuts
30ml/2 tbsp desiccated coconut
7.5–15ml/½–1 tbsp demerara sugar
5ml/1 tsp ground cinnamon
2.5ml/½ tsp freshly grated nutmeg
150ml/¼ pint/⅔ cup orange juice
60ml/4 tbsp rum
15g/½ oz/1 tbsp butter or margarine
double cream, to serve

1 Preheat the oven to 200°C/400°F/ Gas 6. Slice the bananas and place in a greased, shallow ovenproof dish.

2 Mix together the cashew nuts, peanuts, coconut, sugar, cinnamon and nutmeg in a small bowl.

3 Pour the orange juice and rum over the bananas, then sprinkle with the nut and sugar mixture.

4 Dot the top with butter or margarine, then bake in the oven for 15–20 minutes or until the bananas are golden and the sauce is bubbly. Serve with double cream.

— COOK'S TIP —

Freshly grated nutmeg makes all the difference to this dish. More rum can be added if preferred. Chopped mixed nuts can be used instead of peanuts.

Fruits of the Tropics Salad

INGREDIENTS

Serves 4–6

1 medium pineapple
400g/14oz can guava halves in syrup
2 medium bananas, sliced
1 large mango, peeled, stoned and
   diced
115g/4oz stem ginger and 30ml/2 tbsp
   of the syrup
60ml/4 tbsp thick coconut milk
10ml/2 tsp sugar
2.5ml/½ tsp freshly grated nutmeg
2.5ml/½ tsp ground cinnamon
strips of coconut, to decorate

1 Peel, core and cube the pineapple, and place in a serving bowl. Drain the guavas, reserve the syrup and chop. Add the guavas to the bowl with one of the bananas and the mango.

2 Chop the stem ginger and add to the pineapple mixture.

3 Pour 30ml/2 tbsp of the ginger syrup, and the reserved guava syrup into a blender or food processor and add the other banana, the coconut milk and the sugar. Blend to make a smooth creamy purée.

4 Pour the banana and coconut mixture over the fruit, add a little grated nutmeg and a sprinkling of cinnamon. Serve chilled, decorated with strips of coconut.

Coconut and Nutmeg Ice Cream

An easy-to-make, quite heavenly, ice cream that will be loved by all for its tropical taste.

INGREDIENTS

Serves 8

400g/14oz can evaporated milk
400g/14oz can condensed milk
400g/14oz can coconut milk
freshly grated nutmeg
5ml/1 tsp almond essence
lemon balm sprigs, lime slices and
    shredded coconut, to decorate

1 Mix together the evaporated, condensed and coconut milks in a large freezerproof bowl and stir in the nutmeg and almond essence.

2 Chill in a freezer for an hour or two until the mixture is semi-frozen.

3 Remove from the freezer and whisk the mixture with a hand or electric whisk until it is fluffy and almost doubled in volume.

4 Pour into a freezer container, then cover and freeze. Soften slightly before serving, decorated with lemon balm, lime slices and shredded coconut.

Baklava

This is queen of all pastries with its exotic flavours and is usually served for the Persian New Year on 21st March, celebrating the first day of spring.

INGREDIENTS

Serves 6–8
350g/12oz/3¾ cups ground
   pistachio nuts
150g/5oz/1¼ cups icing sugar
15ml/1 tbsp ground cardamom
150g/5oz/²⁄₃ cup unsalted butter,
   melted
450g/1lb filo pastry

For the syrup
450g/1lb/2 cups granulated
   sugar
300ml/½ pint/1¼ cups water
30ml/2 tbsp rose-water

1 First make the syrup: place the sugar and water in a saucepan, bring to the boil and then simmer for 10 minutes until syrupy. Stir in the rose-water and leave to cool.

2 Mix together the nuts, icing sugar and cardamom. Preheat the oven to 160°C/325°F/Gas 3 and brush a large rectangular baking tin with a little melted butter.

3 Taking one sheet of filo pastry at a time, and keeping the remainder covered with a damp cloth, brush with melted butter and lay on the bottom of the tin. Continue until you have six buttered layers in the tin. Spread half of the nut mixture over, pressing down with a spoon.

4 Take another six sheets of filo pastry, brush with butter and lay over the nut mixture. Sprinkle over the remaining nuts and top with a final layer of six filo sheets brushed again with butter. Cut the pastry diagonally into small lozenge shapes using a sharp knife. Pour the remaining melted butter over the top.

5 Bake for 20 minutes then increase the heat to 200°C/400°F/Gas 6 and bake for 15 minutes until light golden in colour and puffed.

6 Remove from the oven and drizzle about three quarters of the syrup over the pastry, reserving the remainder for serving. Arrange the baklava lozenges on a large glass dish and serve with extra syrup.

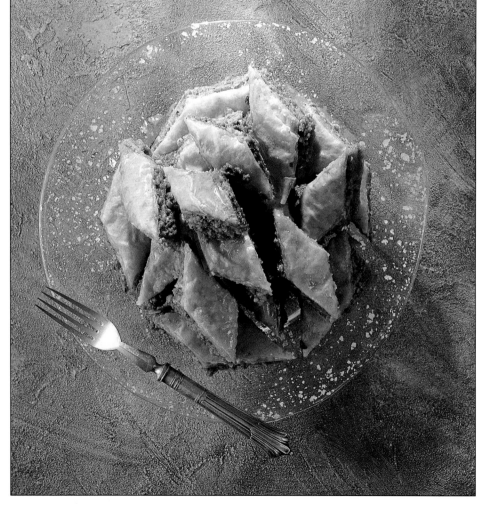

Spiced Bread Pudding

Here's a spicy Egyptian version of bread and butter pudding.

INGREDIENTS

Serves 4

10–12 sheets filo pastry
600ml/1 pint/2½ cups milk
250ml/8fl oz/1 cup double cream
1 egg, beaten
30ml/2 tbsp rose-water
50g/2oz/½ cup each chopped
    pistachio nuts, almonds and hazelnuts
115g/4oz/⅔ cup raisins
15ml/1 tbsp ground cinnamon
single cream, to serve

1 Preheat the oven to 160°C/325°F/ Gas 3. Bake the filo pastry, on a baking sheet, for 15–20 minutes until crisp. Remove from the oven and raise the temperature to 200°C/400°F/Gas 6.

2 Scald the milk and cream by pouring into a pan and heating very gently until hot but not boiling. Slowly add the beaten egg and the rose-water. Cook over a very low heat, until the mixture begins to thicken, stirring all the time.

3 Crumble the pastry using your hands and then spread in layers with the nuts and raisins into the base of a shallow baking dish.

4 Pour the custard mixture over the nut and pastry base and bake in the oven for 20 minutes until golden. Sprinkle with cinnamon and serve with single cream.

Caramel Rice Pudding

This rice pudding is delicious served with crunchy fresh fruit.

INGREDIENTS

Serves 4

50g/2oz/4 tbsp short grain
  pudding rice
75ml/5 tbsp demerara sugar
5ml/1 tsp ground cinnamon
400g/14oz can evaporated milk
  made up to 600ml/1 pint/2½ cups
  with water
knob of butter
1 small fresh pineapple
2 crisp eating apples
10ml/2 tsp lemon juice

1 Preheat the oven to 150°C/300°F/ Gas 2. Put the rice in a sieve and wash thoroughly under cold water. Drain well and put into a lightly greased soufflé dish.

2 Add 30ml/2 tbsp sugar and the cinnamon to the dish. Add the diluted milk and stir gently.

3 Dot the surface of the rice with butter and bake for 2 hours, then leave to cool for 30 minutes.

4 Meanwhile, peel, core and slice the pineapple and apples and then cut the pineapple into chunks. Toss the fruit in lemon juice and set aside.

5 Preheat the grill and sprinkle the remaining sugar over the rice. Grill for 5 minutes or until the sugar has caramelized. Leave the rice to stand for 5 minutes to allow the caramel to harden, then serve with the fresh fruit.

Spiced Rice Pudding

Both Muslim and Hindu communities prepare this pudding, which is traditionally served at mosques and temples.

INGREDIENTS

Serves 4–6

15ml/1 tbsp ghee or melted
  unsalted butter
5cm/2in piece cinnamon stick
225g/8oz/1 cup soft brown sugar
115g/4oz/½ cup ground rice
1.2 litres/2 pints/5 cups milk
5ml/1 tsp ground cardamom seeds
50g/2oz/scant ½ cup sultanas
25g/1oz/¼ cup slivered almonds
2.5ml/½ tsp grated nutmeg, to serve

1 In a heavy pan, heat the ghee or butter and fry the cinnamon and sugar. Keep frying until the sugar begins to caramelize. Reduce the heat immediately when this happens.

2 Add the rice and half of the milk. Bring to the boil, stirring constantly to avoid the milk boiling over. Reduce the heat and simmer until the rice is cooked, stirring regularly.

3 Add the remaining milk, cardamom, sultanas and almonds and leave to simmer, but keep stirring to prevent the rice from sticking to the base of the pan. When the mixture has thickened, serve hot or cold, sprinkled with the grated nutmeg.

Date and Nut Pastries

INGREDIENTS

Makes 35–40

450g/1lb/4 cups plain flour
225g/8oz/1 cup unsalted butter, cut into cubes
45ml/3 tbsp rose-water
60–75ml/4–5 tbsp milk
icing sugar, for sprinkling

For the filling

225g/8oz/1¼ cups dates, stoned and chopped
175g/6oz/1¼ cups walnuts, finely chopped
115g/4oz/¾ cup blanched almonds, chopped
50g/2oz/½ cup pistachio nuts, chopped
120ml/4fl oz/½ cup water
115g/4oz/½ cup sugar
10ml/2 tsp ground cinnamon

1 Preheat the oven to 160°C/325°F/ Gas 3. First make the filling: place the dates, walnuts, almonds, pistachios, water, sugar and cinnamon in a small saucepan and cook over a low heat until the dates are soft and the water has been absorbed.

2 Place the flour in a large bowl and add the butter, working it into the flour with your fingertips.

3 Add the rose-water and milk and knead the dough until it's soft.

4 Take walnut-size lumps of dough. Roll each into a ball and hollow with your thumb. Pinch the sides.

5 Place a spoonful of date mixture in the hollow and then press the dough back over the filling to seal.

6 Arrange the pastries on a large baking tray. Press to flatten them slightly. Make little dents with a fork on the pastry. Bake in the oven for 20 minutes. Do not let them change colour or the pastry will become hard. Cool slightly and then sprinkle with icing sugar and serve.

Cinnamon Balls

Ground almonds or hazelnuts form the basis of most Passover cakes and biscuits. These balls should be soft inside, with a very strong cinnamon flavour. They harden with keeping, so it is a good idea to freeze some and only use them when required.

INGREDIENTS

Makes about 15
175g/6oz/ 1¹/₂ cups ground almonds
75g/3oz/¹/₃ cup caster sugar
15ml/1 tbsp ground cinnamon
2 egg whites
oil, for greasing
icing sugar, for dredging

1 Preheat the oven to 180°C/350°F/ Gas 4. Grease a large baking sheet with oil.

2 Mix together the ground almonds, sugar and cinnamon. Whisk the egg whites until they begin to stiffen and fold enough into the almonds to make a fairly firm mixture.

3 Wet your hands with cold water and roll small spoonfuls of the mixture into balls. Place these at intervals on the baking sheet.

4 Bake for about 15 minutes in the centre of the oven. They should be slightly soft inside – too much cooking will make them hard and tough.

5 Slide a palette knife under the balls to release them from the baking sheet and leave to cool. Sift a few tablespoons of icing sugar on to a plate and when the cinnamon balls are cold slide them on to the plate. Shake gently to completely cover the cinnamon balls in sugar and store in an airtight container or in the freezer.

Apple and Cinnamon Crumble Cake

This scrumptious cake has layers of spicy fruit and crumble and is quite delicious served warm with fresh cream.

INGREDIENTS

Makes 1 cake
3 large cooking apples
2.5ml/½ tsp ground cinnamon
250g/9oz/1 cup butter
250g/9oz/1¼ cups caster sugar
4 eggs
450g/1lb/4 cups self-raising flour

For the crumble topping
175g/6oz/¾ cup demerara sugar
125g/4¼oz/1¼ cups plain flour
5ml/1 tsp ground cinnamon
65g/2½oz/about 4½ tbsp desiccated
   coconut
115g/4oz/½ cup butter

1 Preheat the oven to 180°C/350°F/ Gas 4. Grease a 25cm/10in round cake tin and line the base with greaseproof paper. To make the crumble topping, mix together the sugar, flour, cinnamon and coconut in a bowl, then rub in the butter with your fingertips and set aside.

2 Peel and core the apples, then grate them coarsely. Place them in a bowl, sprinkle with the cinnamon and set aside.

3 Cream the butter and sugar in a bowl with an electric mixer, until light and fluffy. Beat in the eggs, one at a time, beating well after each addition.

4 Sift in half the flour, mix well, then add the remaining flour and stir until smooth.

5 Spread half the cake mixture evenly over the base of the prepared tin. Spoon the apples on top and scatter over half the crumble topping.

6 Spread the remaining cake mixture over the crumble and finally top with the remaining crumble topping.

7 Bake for 1 hour 10 minutes – 1 hour 20 minutes, covering the cake with foil if it browns too quickly. Leave in the tin for about 5 minutes, before turning out on to a wire rack. Once cool, cut into slices to serve.

> ——— COOK'S TIP ———
>
> To make the topping in a food processor, add all the ingredients and process for a few seconds until the mixture resembles bread-crumbs. You can also grate the apples using the grating disc. If you don't have a 25cm/10in round tin you can use a 20cm/8in square cake tin.

Banana Ginger Cake

INGREDIENTS

Makes 1 cake

200g/7oz/1²⁄₃ cups plain flour
10ml/2 tsp bicarbonate of soda
10ml/2 tsp ground ginger
150g/5oz/1¼ cups medium oatmeal
60ml/4 tbsp dark muscovado sugar
75g/3oz/6 tbsp sunflower margarine
150g/5oz/³⁄₄ cup golden syrup
1 egg, beaten
3 ripe bananas, mashed
75g/3oz/³⁄₄ cup icing sugar
stem ginger, to decorate

1 Preheat the oven to 160°C/325°F/ Gas 3. Grease and line an 18 x 28cm/7 x 11in cake tin.

2 Stir together the flour, bicarbonate of soda and ginger, then stir in the oatmeal. Mix the sugar, margarine and golden syrup in a saucepan, then stir into the flour mixture. Beat in the egg and mashed bananas.

3 Spoon into the tin and bake for about 1 hour, or until firm to the touch. Allow to cool in the tin, then turn out and cut into squares.

4 Sift the icing sugar into a bowl and stir in just enough water to make a smooth, runny icing. Drizzle the icing over each square and top with a piece of stem ginger.

COOK'S TIP

This is a nutritious, energy-giving cake that is a really good choice for packed lunches as it doesn't break up too easily.

Spiced Date and Walnut Cake

Mixed spice adds a warm flavour to this low-fat, high-fibre cake. Simply serve it on its own, or spread it with butter and honey for an extra special snack.

INGREDIENTS

Makes 1 cake
300g/11oz/2½ cups wholemeal
   self-raising flour
10ml/2 tsp mixed spice
150g/5oz/scant 1 cup chopped dates
50g/2oz/½ cup chopped walnuts
60ml/4 tbsp sunflower oil
115g/4oz/½ cup dark muscovado sugar
300ml/½ pint/1¼ cups skimmed milk
walnut halves, to decorate

VARIATION

Pecan nuts can be used in place of the walnuts in this cake, if you like.

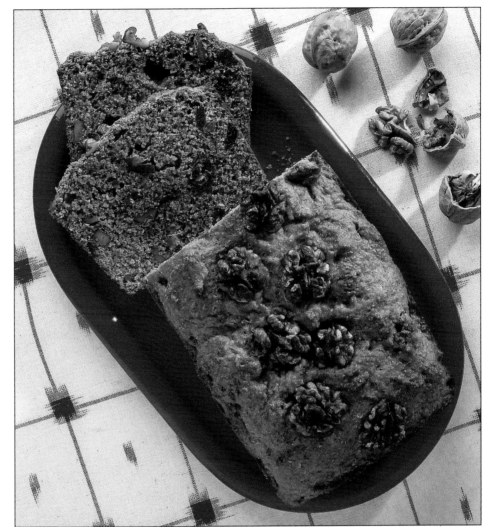

1 Preheat the oven to 180°C/350°F/ Gas 4. Grease and line a 900g/2lb loaf tin with greaseproof paper.

2 Sift together the self-raising flour and mixed spice, adding back any bran from the sieve. Stir in the dates and walnuts.

3 Mix the oil, sugar and milk, then add to the dry ingredients. Mix well then spoon the mixture into the prepared tin.

4 Arrange the walnut halves over the top of the cake mixture. Bake the cake for 45–50 minutes, or until golden brown and firm. Turn out the cake, remove the lining paper and leave to cool on a wire rack.

Cinnamon Rolls

INGREDIENTS

Makes 24 small rolls

For the dough

400g/14oz/1²/₃ cups strong white flour
2.5ml/½ tsp salt
30ml/2 tbsp sugar
5ml/1 tsp quick-acting dried yeast
45ml/3 tbsp oil
1 egg
120ml/4fl oz/½ cup warm milk
120ml/4fl oz/½ cup warm water

For the filling

25g/1oz butter, softened
25g/1oz dark brown sugar
2.5−5ml/½−1 tsp ground cinnamon
15ml/1 tbsp raisins or sultanas

1 Sift the flour, salt and sugar and sprinkle over the yeast. Mix the oil, egg, milk and water and add to the flour. Mix to a dough, then knead until smooth. Leave to rise until doubled in size and then knock it back again.

2 Roll out the dough into a large rectangle and cut in half vertically. Spread over the soft butter, reserving 15ml/1 tbsp for brushing. Mix the sugar and cinnamon and sprinkle over the top. Dot with the raisins.

3 Roll each piece into a long Swiss roll shape, to enclose the filling. Cut into 2.5cm/1in slices, arrange flat on a greased baking sheet and brush with the remaining butter. Leave to prove again for about 30 minutes.

4 Preheat the oven to 200°C/400°F/ Gas 6 and bake the cinnamon rolls for about 20 minutes. Leave to cool on a wire rack. Serve fresh for breakfast or tea, with extra butter if liked.

Peach Kuchen

The joy of this cake is its all-in-one simplicity. It can be served straight from the oven, or cut into squares when cold.

INGREDIENTS

Serves 8

350g/12oz/3 cups self-raising flour
225g/8oz/1 cup caster sugar
175g/6oz/¾ cup unsalted
   butter, softened
2 eggs
120ml/4fl oz/½ cup milk
6 large peeled peaches, sliced or
   450g/1lb plums or cherries, stoned
115g/4oz/½ cup soft brown sugar
2.5ml/½ tsp ground cinnamon
soured cream or crème fraîche,
   to serve (optional)

1 Preheat the oven to 190°C/375°F/ Gas 5. Grease and line a 20 x 25 x 2.5cm/8 x 10 x 1in cake tin.

2 Put the flour, sugar, butter, eggs and milk into a large bowl and beat for a few minutes until you have a smooth batter. Spoon it into the prepared cake tin.

3 Arrange the peaches, plums or cherries over the cake mixture. Mix the brown sugar and cinnamon and sprinkle over the fruit.

───── COOK'S TIP ─────

To skin ripe peaches, cover with boiling water for 20 seconds. The skin will then slip off easily.

4 Bake for about 40 minutes, testing for doneness by inserting a cocktail stick in the centre.

5 Serve the cake warm or cool with the soured cream or crème fraîche, if using.

Caribbean Fruit and Rum Cake

This is a delicious recipe for a cake that is eaten at Christmas, weddings and other special occasions. It is known as Black Cake, because, traditionally, the recipe uses burnt sugar.

INGREDIENTS

Makes 1 cake

450g/1lb/2 cups currants
450g/1lb/3 cups raisins
225g/8oz/1 cup prunes, stoned
115g/4oz/⅔ cup mixed peel
400g/14oz/2¼ cups dark soft brown
  sugar
5ml/1 tsp mixed spice
90ml/6 tbsp rum, plus more if needed
300ml/½ pint/1¼ cups sherry, plus
  more if needed
450g/1lb/2 cups softened butter
10 eggs, beaten
450g/1lb/4 cups self-raising flour
5ml/1 tsp vanilla essence

1 Wash the currants, raisins, prunes and mixed peel, then pat dry. Place in a food processor and process until finely chopped. Transfer to a large, clean jar or bowl, add 115g/4oz of the sugar, the mixed spice, rum and sherry. Mix very well and then cover with a lid and set aside for anything from 2 weeks to 3 months – the longer it is left, the better the flavour will be.

2 Stir the fruit mixture occasionally and keep covered, adding more alcohol, if you like.

3 Preheat the oven to 160°C/325°F/ Gas 3. Grease and line a 25cm/10in round cake tin with a double layer of greaseproof paper.

4 Sift the flour, and set aside. Cream together the butter and remaining sugar and beat in the eggs until the mixture is smooth and creamy.

5 Add the fruit mixture, then gradually stir in the flour and vanilla essence. Mix well, adding 15–30ml/1–2 tbsp sherry if the mixture is too stiff; it should just fall off the back of the spoon, but should not be too runny.

6 Spoon the mixture into the prepared tin, cover loosely with foil and bake for about 2½ hours until the cake is firm and springy. Leave to cool in the tin overnight, then sprinkle with more rum if the cake is not to be used immediately. Wrap the cake in foil to keep it moist.

--- COOK'S TIP ---

Although the dried fruits are chopped in a food processor, they can be marinated whole, if preferred. If you don't have enough time to marinate the fruit, simmer the fruit in the alcohol mixture for about 30 minutes, and leave overnight.

SPICED DRINKS

Spices are added to a wide range of drinks and Sangrita, from Mexico, even uses fresh green chillies! Cocktails such as Bloody Maria are pepped up with Worcestershire and Tabasco sauces, while Caribbean punches, including Caribbean Cream Stout Punch, are enlivened with a sprinkling of spice. Mulled Wine and Spiced Mocha Drink are hot favourites too.

Spiced Mocha Drink

This spicy chocolate milk drink can be served either hot or cold – depending on the weather and your preference.

INGREDIENTS

Serves 4
175g/6oz milk chocolate
120ml/4fl oz/½ cup single cream
750ml/1¼ pints/3 cups hot
   black coffee
2.5ml/½ tsp ground cinnamon
whipped cream or ice, to serve

1 Using a sharp knife, cut the chocolate into small pieces to enable it to melt quickly and evenly.

2 Put the chocolate into a double saucepan or a bowl set over a saucepan of almost simmering water. The base of the bowl should not touch the water.

3 Add the single cream to the chocolate melting in the bowl, then stir well to mix.

4 Continue to heat gently until the chocolate is melted and smooth, stirring occasionally. Remove the bowl from the heat.

5 Add the coffee and cinnamon to the chocolate and whisk until foamy. Divide between four serving glasses, then either serve hot with a spoonful of cream, or cool and chill, and serve over ice.

---- COOK'S TIP ----

If any steam gets into the chocolate while you are melting it, it may turn into a solid mass. If this should happen, stir in about 5ml/1 tsp butter or margarine for each 25g/1oz of chocolate.

Mulled Wine

Cloves, cinnamon and nutmeg add spicy flavour to this delicious mulled wine. It makes a warming drink for a winter party.

INGREDIENTS

Makes 16 x 150ml/¼ pint/⅔ cup glasses
1 orange
60ml/4 tbsp demerara sugar
grated nutmeg
2 cinnamon sticks
few cloves, plus extra for studding
30ml/2 tbsp seedless raisins
75ml/5 tbsp clear honey
2 clementines
1.5 litres/2½ pints/6¼ cups claret
750ml/1¼ pints/3cups medium cider
300ml/½ pint/1¼ cups orange juice

VARIATION

Vary the spices used in this mulled wine – whole allspice can be added instead of cinnamon sticks. If you like, you can also add a selection of sliced citrus fruits.

---

1 With a sharp knife or a rotary peeler, pare off a long strip of orange peel.

2 Place the sugar, nutmeg, cinnamon, cloves, raisins, honey and peel in a large saucepan. Stud the clementines with cloves and add them to the pan. Add the claret and heat gently until the sugar is dissolved. Pour in the cider and continue to gently heat the mulled wine. Do not boil.

3 Add the orange juice to the pan and warm through. Remove the clementines and cinnamon sticks and strain the mulled wine into a warmed punch bowl or other serving bowl. Add the clove-studded clementines and serve hot in warmed glasses, or in glasses containing a small spoon (to prevent the glass breaking).

Sangrita

Ingredients

Serves 8

450g/1lb tomatoes, peeled, seeded
  and chopped
120ml/4fl oz/½ cup orange juice
60ml/4 tbsp freshly squeezed lime juice
1 small onion, chopped
2.5ml/½ tsp granulated sugar
6 small fresh green chillies, seeded
  and chopped
salt
50ml/2oz aged tequila (*Tequila Anejo*)
  per person

--- Cook's Tip ---

Plain white tequila is not suitable for this.
Choose one of the amber aged tequilas
(*Añejos*), which are smoother and more
gentle on the palate.

1 Put the chopped tomatoes, orange
juice, lime juice, chopped onion,
granulated sugar and chopped green
chillies into a food processor.

2 Process the tomato mixture until
very smooth, scraping down the
sides if necessary.

3 Pour the tomato mixture into a jug
and chill well.

4 To serve, pour into small glasses,
allowing about 90ml/6 tbsp per
portion. Pour the tequila into separate
small glasses. Sip the tomato juice and
tequila alternately.

Sangria

This very popular summer drink
was borrowed from Spain. The
Mexican version is slightly less
alcoholic than the original.

Ingredients

Serves 6

ice cubes
1 litre/1¾ pints/4 cups dry red
  table wine
150ml/¼ pint/⅔ cup freshly squeezed
  orange juice
50ml/2fl oz/¼ cup freshly squeezed
  lime juice
115g/4oz/½ cup caster sugar
2 limes or 1 apple, sliced, to serve

1 Half fill a large jug with ice cubes.
Pour in the wine and the orange
and lime juices.

2 Add the sugar and stir well until it
has dissolved. Pour into tumblers
and float the lime or apple slices on
top. Serve at once.

--- Cook's Tip ---

Sugar does not dissolve readily in alcohol. I
prefer to use simple syrup, which is very
easy to make and gives a smoother drink.
Combine 475ml/16fl oz/2 cups granulated
sugar and 450g/1lb water in a jug and set
aside until the sugar has dissolved. Stir from
time to time. 15ml/1 tbsp simple syrup is
the equivalent of 7.5ml/1½ tsp sugar.

Bloody Maria

INGREDIENTS

Serves 2

175ml/6fl oz/³/₄ cup tomato juice
90ml/3fl oz/6 tbsp white tequila
dash each of Worcestershire and
  Tabasco sauces
30ml/2 tbsp lemon juice
salt and freshly ground black pepper
8 ice cubes

— COOK'S TIP —

When drinks are to be served with ice,
make sure all the ingredients are thoroughly chilled ahead of time.

---

1 Combine the tomato juice, tequila, Worcestershire and Tabasco sauces, and lemon juice in a cocktail shaker. Add salt and pepper to taste, and four ice cubes. Shake very vigorously.

2 Place the remaining ice cubes in two heavy-based tumblers and strain the tequila over them.

Margarita

Tequila is made from the sap of a fleshy-leafed plant called the blue agave and gets its name from the town of Tequila, where it has been made for more than 200 years. The Margarita is the most popular and well-known drink made with tequila.

INGREDIENTS

Serves 2

½ lime or lemon
salt
120ml/4fl oz/½ cup white tequila
30ml/2 tbsp Triple Sec or Cointreau
30ml/2 tbsp freshly squeezed lime or
  lemon juice
4 or more ice cubes

— COOK'S TIP —

It really is worth going to the trouble of
buying limes for this recipe. Lemons will
do, but something of the special flavour of
the drink will be lost in the substitution.

---

1 Rub the rims of two cocktail glasses with the lime or lemon. Pour some salt into a saucer and dip in the glasses so that the rims are frosted.

2 Combine the tequila, Triple Sec or Cointreau, and lime and lemon juice in a jug and stir to mix well.

3 Pour the tequila mixture into the prepared glasses. Add the ice cubes and serve at once.

Demerara Rum Punch

The inspiration for this punch came from the rum distillery at Plantation Diamond Estate in Guyana where some of the finest rum in the world is made, and the tantalizing aromas of sugar cane and rum pervade the air.

INGREDIENTS

Serves 4
150ml/¼ pint/⅔ cup orange juice
150ml/¼ pint/⅔ cup pineapple juice
150ml/¼ pint/⅔ cup mango juice
120ml/4fl oz/½ cup water
250ml/8fl oz/1 cup dark rum
a shake of angostura bitters
freshly grated nutmeg
25g/1oz/2 tbsp demerara sugar
1 small banana
1 large orange

1 Pour the orange, pineapple and mango juices into a large punch bowl. Stir in the water.

2 Add the rum, angostura bitters, nutmeg and sugar. Stir gently for a few minutes until the sugar has dissolved.

3 Slice the banana and stir gently into the punch.

4 Slice the orange and add to the punch. Chill and serve with ice.

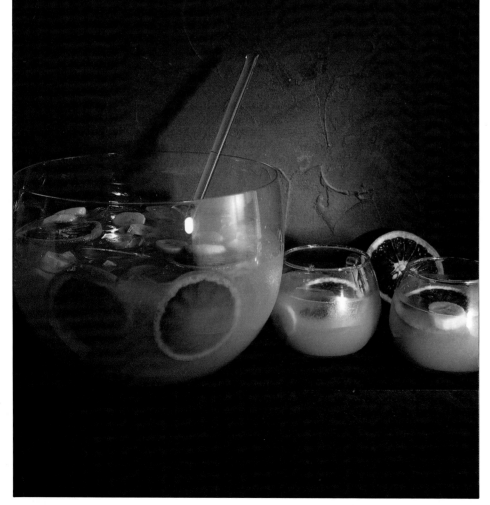

--- COOK'S TIP ---

You can use white rum instead of dark, if you prefer. To make a stronger punch, add more rum.

Caribbean Cream Stout Punch

A well-known "pick-me-up" that is popular all over the Caribbean.

INGREDIENTS

Serves 2

475ml/16fl oz/2 cups stout
300ml/1/2 pint/1 1/4 cups evaporated
 milk
75ml/5 tbsp condensed milk
75ml/5 tbsp sherry
2 or 3 drops vanilla essence
freshly grated nutmeg

1 Mix together the stout, evaporated and condensed milks, sherry and vanilla essence in a blender or food processor, or whisk together in a large mixing bowl, until creamy.

2 Add a little grated nutmeg to the stout mixture and blend or whisk again for a few minutes.

3 Chill for at least 45 minutes until really cold before serving.

Index

almonds: cinnamon balls, 235
   spicy vegetables with
     almonds, 164
apple and cinnamon crumble
   cake, 236
apricot chutney, 210
aubergines: beef and aubergine
   curry, 117
   Louisiana rice, 169
avocados: avocado salad in ginger
   and orange sauce, 225
   guacamole, 48

baklava, 230
Balti potatoes, 162
bamie goreng, 189
bananas: banana ginger
   cake, 238
   spiced nutty bananas, 227
barbecued jerk chicken, 122
barbecued pork spareribs, 98
basmati and nut pilaff, 183
bass: Mexican spicy fish, 76
bean curd see tofu
beansprouts: vegetarian fried
   noodles, 198
beef: beef and aubergine
   curry, 117
   beef and turmeric soup, 24
   beef enchiladas, 102
   beef with cactus pieces, 100
   French beans, rice and
     beef, 187
   spicy kebabs, 58
   spicy meat-filled
     parcels, 54
   spicy meat fritters, 98
   spicy meatballs, 116
   Szechuan spicy tofu, 134
   Tex-Mex baked potatoes with
     chilli, 101
berry salsa, 208
black bean burritos, 139
black-eyed bean stew with spicy
   pumpkin, 152
blackened hot chicken breasts, 123
bloody Maria, 250
bon-bon chicken with spicy
   sesame, 127
bread pudding, spiced, 231
broad beans: broad bean and
   cauliflower curry, 145
   broad beans in hot sauce, 144
   rice with dill and spicy
     beans, 190
broccoli, penne with chilli
   and, 196
burritos, black bean, 139
butterflied prawns in chilli
   chocolate, 38

cabbage: coleslaw in triple-hot
   dressing, 148
   spicy cabbage, 146
   vinegared chilli cabbage, 148
cactus pieces, beef with, 100
Cajun "popcorn", 43

cakes: apple and cinnamon
   crumble cake, 236
   banana ginger cake, 238
   Caribbean fruit and rum
     cake, 242
   peach kuchen, 241
   spiced date and walnut
     cake, 239
caramel rice pudding, 232
Caribbean cream stout punch, 253
Caribbean fruit and rum cake, 242
Caribbean lamb curry, 105
Caribbean spiced fish, 85
carrots: spiced carrot dip, 220
   spicy carrots, 142
catfish: fried catfish fillets with
   piquant sauce, 67
cauliflower: broad bean and
   cauliflower curry, 145
chayotes: prawns with chayote in
   turmeric sauce, 70
cheese: chilli bean dip, 218
   desert nachos, 52
   quesadillas, 44
   red rice rissoles, 176
   tasty toasts, 210
   Welsh rabbit, 55
cheese, soft: cheese fritters, 62
   spicy noodle pudding, 224
chick-peas: hummus, 40
chicken: bamie goreng, 189
   barbecued jerk chicken, 122
   blackened hot chicken
     breasts, 123
   bon-bon chicken with spicy
     sesame, 127
   chicken jambalaya, 174
   chicken mulligatawny, 34
   chicken naan pockets, 56
   chicken sauce piquante, 128
   chicken tikka, 56
   curried noodle and chicken
     soup, 35
   ginger, chicken and coconut
     soup, 28
   hot chicken curry, 124
   mulligatawny soup, 25
   nasi goreng, 173
   San Francisco chicken
     wings, 42
   spicy chicken with
     coconut, 119
   spicy fried chicken, 118
   spicy masala chicken, 131
   spicy rice with chicken, 184
   spicy Szechuan noodles, 200
   tandoori chicken, 130
   yogurt chicken and rice, 168
chiles rellenos, 154
chilli, red bean, 153
chillies: chilli bean dip, 218
   chilli courgettes, 140
   chilli crabs, 84
   chilli relish, 219
   citrus fish with chillies, 77
   double chilli salsa, 212
   fiery citrus salsa, 206

fried dough balls with fiery
   salsa, 60
fried fish in green chilli
   sauce, 82
green bean and chilli pepper
   salad, 157
green chilli dhal, 136
jalapeño and prawn salad, 158
lamb stew, 106
Mexican-style rice, 191
mole poblano de
   Guajolote, 114
mushrooms with chipotle
   chillies, 158
penne with chilli and
   broccoli, 196
pork with chillies and
   pineapple, 113
potatoes with red chillies, 135
salt cod in mild chilli sauce, 73
sangrita, 248
steamed fish with chilli
   sauce, 66
stir-fried chilli greens, 156
tasty toasts, 210
Tex-Mex baked potatoes with
   chilli, 101
vegetables in peanut and chilli
   sauce, 150
vinegar chilli fish, 74
vinegared chilli cabbage, 148
chocolate: spiced mocha
   drink, 246
chutney, apricot, 210
cinnamon balls, 235
cinnamon rolls, 240
citrus fish with chillies, 77
coconut: coconut and peanut
   relish, 204
   coconut chilli relish, 216
coconut milk: coconut and
   nutmeg ice cream, 229
   coconut rice, 184
   curried prawns in coconut
     milk, 94
   festive rice, 179
   ginger, chicken and coconut
     soup, 28
   prawns in spiced coconut
     sauce, 88
   spicy chicken with
     coconut, 119
cod: Caribbean spiced fish, 85
   cod with chilli and mustard
     seeds, 59
   seafood and rice, 174
   spicy fish and rice, 170
   see also salt cod
coffee: spiced mocha
   drink, 246
coleslaw in triple-hot dressing, 148
coriander rice, 106
cornmeal, spicy prawns with, 93
courgettes, chilli, 140
crabs, chilli, 84
crayfish: Cajun "popcorn", 43
cucumbers, pickled, 214

curries: beef and aubergine
   curry, 117
   broad bean and cauliflower
     curry, 145
   Caribbean lamb curry, 105
   curried noodle and chicken
     soup, 35
   curried prawns and saltfish, 88
   curried prawns in coconut
     milk, 94
   curry fried noodles, 194
   hot chicken curry, 124
   khara masala lamb, 110
   king prawns in curry sauce, 82
   pineapple curry with prawns
     and mussels, 94
   yellow curry paste, 94

daikon, 62
dates: date and nut pastries, 234
   spiced date and walnut
     cake, 239
demerara rum punch, 252
desert nachos, 52
devilled kidneys, 51
dips: chilli bean dip, 218
   guacamole, 48
   hummus, 40
   spiced carrot dip, 220
dough balls, fried with fiery
   salsa, 60
dried fruit: Caribbean fruit and
   rum cake, 242
drinks, 244-53
duck, crispy and aromatic, 120
dumplins, spicy fried, 215

eggs: huevos rancheros, 52
   stir-fried chilli greens, 156
   tomato noodles with fried
     egg, 194
enchiladas: beef enchiladas, 102
   red enchiladas, 104

falafel, 40
fenugreek, masala beans with, 165
festive rice, 179
fish and seafood, 64-95
   baked or grilled spiced whole
     fish, 74
   braised fish in chilli and garlic
     sauce, 72
   pickled fish, 68
   steamed fish with chilli
     sauce, 66
   see also individual types of fish
French beans: French beans, rice
   and beef, 187
   masala beans with
     fenugreek, 165
frijoles, 138
   refried beans (frijoles
     refritos), 140
fritters: cheese, 62
   spicy meat, 98
fruit: berry salsa, 208
   caramel rice pudding, 232

see also individual types of fruit

fruit salads: avocado salad in ginger and orange sauce, 225
fruits of the tropics salad, 228

ginger: avocado salad in ginger and orange sauce, 225
banana ginger cake, 238
fresh pineapple with ginger, 226
ginger, chicken and coconut soup, 28
green bean and chilli pepper salad, 157
groundnut soup, spicy, 22
guacamole, 48

halibut: citrus fish with chillies, 77
hot and sour prawn soup with lemon grass, 28
huevos rancheros, 52
hummus, 40

ice cream, coconut and nutmeg, 229
Indian pilau rice, 180
Indonesian spicy fish, 70

jalapeño and prawn salad, 158
jerk chicken, barbecued, 122

kachumbali salad, 216
kebabs: marinated vegetables on skewers, 151
spiced fish kebabs, 86
spicy kebabs, 58
Kenyan mung bean stew, 143
khara masala lamb, 110
kidney beans see red kidney beans
kidneys, devilled, 51

lamb: Caribbean lamb curry, 105
khara masala lamb, 110
lamb stew, 106
lamb tagine with coriander and spices, 109
spiced lamb soup, 30
lemon grass prawns on crisp noodle cake, 90
lentils: green chilli dhal, 136
okra with green mango and lentils, 162
Persian rice with a tahdeeg, 178
Louisiana rice, 169

mackerel: Indonesian spicy fish, 70
vinegar chilli fish, 74
mangoes: okra with green mango and lentils, 162
margarita, 250
marinated vegetables on skewers, 151
masala beans with fenugreek, 165
masala mashed potatoes, 146
masala prawns and rice, 170
meat and poultry, 96-131
see also individual types of meat

meatballs, spicy, 116
mee krob, 197
Mexican spicy fish, 76
Mexican-style rice, 191
mocha drink, spiced, 246
mole poblano de Guajolote, 114
monkfish parcels, chillied, 46
mulled wine, 247
mulligatawny soup, 25
chicken mulligatawny, 34
mung bean stew, Kenyan, 143
mushrooms with chipotle chillies, 158
mussels: pineapple curry with prawns and mussels, 94
tossed noodles with seafood, 192

naan pockets, chicken, 56
nachos, desert, 52
nasi goreng, 173
noodles: bamie goreng, 189
chilled soba noodles with nori, 62
crispy fried rice vermicelli – mee krob, 197
curried noodle and chicken soup, 35
curry fried noodles, 194
lemon grass prawns on crisp noodle cake, 90
noodle soup with pork and Szechuan pickle, 32
noodles with spicy meat sauce, 192
sesame noodles with spring onions, 200
spicy noodle pudding, 224
spicy Szechuan noodles, 200
Thai fried noodles, 199
tomato noodles with fried egg, 194
tossed noodles with seafood, 192
vegetarian fried noodles, 198
nori: chilled soba noodles with nori, 62
sushi, 186
nuts: basmati and nut pilaff, 183
date and nut pastries, 234
spiced nutty bananas, 227

oatmeal: banana ginger cake, 238
okra: okra fried rice, 180
okra with green mango and lentils, 162
spicy prawns with okra, 92
onions: kachumbali salad, 216
red onion raita, 221
tomato and onion salad, 204
orange: avocado salad in ginger and orange sauce, 225
fiery citrus salsa, 206

pastries: baklava, 230
cinnamon rolls, 240
date and nut pastries, 234

samosas, 47
spicy meat-filled parcels, 54
peach kuchen, 241
peanut butter: spicy groundnut soup, 22
vegetables in peanut and chilli sauce, 150
peanuts: coconut and peanut relish, 204
peas: Mexican-style rice, 191
penne with chilli and broccoli, 196
pepper soup, spicy, 31
peppers: chiles rellenos, 154
green bean and chilli pepper salad, 157
peppery bean salad, 161
Persian rice with a tahdeeg, 178
pickled fish, 68
pickles: mixed vegetable pickle, 209
pickled cucumbers, 214
pilaff: basmati and nut, 183
pistachio, 182
spiced trout, 172
pilau rice, Indian, 180
pineapple: fresh pineapple with ginger, 226
pineapple curry with prawns and mussels, 94
piquant pineapple relish, 213
pork with chillies and pineapple, 113
pistachio nuts: baklava, 230
pistachio pilaff, 182
plantain soup with corn and chilli, 22
pomfret: fried fish in green chilli sauce, 82
pork: barbecued pork spareribs, 98
deep-fried spareribs with spicy salt and pepper, 112
Louisiana rice, 169
nasi goreng, 173
noodle soup with pork and Szechuan pickle, 32
noodles with spicy meat sauce, 192
pork with chillies and pineapple, 113
sweet and sour pork, 108
potatoes: Balti potatoes, 162
masala mashed potatoes, 146
potatoes with red chillies, 135
spicy potato salad, 160
spicy potatoes, 39
Tex-Mex baked potatoes with chilli, 101
poultry and meat, 96-131
poussins, spatchcocked devilled, 126
prawns: butterflied prawns in chilli chocolate, 38
curried prawns and saltfish, 88
curried prawns in coconut milk, 94

hot and sour prawn soup with lemon grass, 28
jalapeño and prawn salad, 158
king prawns in curry sauce, 82
lemon grass prawns on crisp noodle cake, 90
masala prawns and rice, 170
pineapple curry with prawns and mussels, 94
prawns in spiced coconut sauce, 88
prawns in spicy tomato sauce, 86
prawns with chayote in turmeric sauce, 70
seafood and rice, 174
seafood wontons with spicy dressing, 50
spicy prawns with cornmeal, 93
spicy prawns with okra, 92
stir-fried prawns with tamarind, 91
tossed noodles with seafood, 192
pumpkin: black-eyed bean stew with spicy pumpkin, 152
pumpkin and chilli soup, 20
punch: Caribbean cream stout punch, 253
demerara rum punch, 252

quail's eggs: stir-fried chilli greens, 156
quesadillas, 44

raita, red onion, 221
red kidney beans: chilli bean dip, 218
frijoles, 138
peppery bean salad, 161
red bean chilli, 153
Tex-Mex baked potatoes with chilli, 101
red mullet: Turkish cold fish, 81
red snapper: red snapper, Veracruz-style, 69
snapper, tomato and tamarind noodle soup, 32
whole fish with sweet and sour sauce, 80
refried beans (frijoles refritos), 140
huevos rancheros, 52
relishes: chilli, 219
coconut and peanut, 204
coconut chilli, 216
kachumbali salad, 216
piquant pineapple, 213
rice: basmati and nut pilaff, 183
caramel rice pudding, 232
chicken jambalaya, 174
coconut rice, 184
coriander rice, 106
festive rice, 179
French beans, rice and beef, 187
Indian pilau rice, 180
Louisiana rice, 169

masala prawns and rice, 170
Mexican-style rice, 191
nasi goreng, 173
okra fried rice, 180
Persian rice with a tahdeeg, 178
pistachio pilaff, 182
red rice rissoles, 176
rice with dill and spicy
    beans, 190
seafood and rice, 174
spiced rice pudding, 232
spiced trout pilaff, 172
spicy fish and rice, 170
spicy rice cakes, 176
spicy rice with chicken, 184
sushi, 186
sweet and sour rice, 188
yogurt chicken and rice, 168
rissoles, red rice, 176
rolls, cinnamon, 240
rum punch, demerara, 252

saffron fish, 78
salads: green bean and chilli
        pepper, 157
    jalapeño and prawn, 158
    peppery bean, 161
    spicy potato, 160
    tomato and onion, 204
    see also fruit salads
salmon: sushi, 186
salmon trout: saffron fish, 78
salsa: berry salsa, 208
    double chilli salsa, 212
    fiery citrus salsa, 206
    fried dough balls with fiery
        salsa, 60
    salsa verde, 207
    tomato salsa, 48
salt cod in mild chilli sauce, 73
saltfish, curried prawns and, 88
samosas, 47
San Francisco chicken wings, 42
sangria, 248
sangrita, 248
sardines, pan-fried spicy, 78
seafood and fish, 64-95
    hot and spicy seafood soup, 27
    seafood and rice, 174
    seafood wontons with spicy
        dressing, 50
    tossed noodles with
        seafood, 192
seaweed: chilled soba noodles with
        nori, 62
    sushi, 186
sesame noodles with spring
        onions, 200
shrimp paste, 20, 27
smoked trout: spiced trout
        pilaff, 172
snapper see red snapper
soups, 16-35
    beef and turmeric, 24
    chicken mulligatawny, 34
    curried noodle and
        chicken, 35

ginger, chicken and
        coconut, 28
hot and sour prawn with lemon
        grass, 28
hot and spicy seafood, 27
mulligatawny, 25
noodle soup with pork and
        Szechuan pickle, 32
plantain with corn and
        chilli, 22
pumpkin and chilli, 20
snapper, tomato and tamarind
        noodle, 32
spiced lamb, 30
spicy groundnut, 22
spicy pepper, 31
spicy vegetable, 21
spicy yogurt, 26
tamarind with peanuts and
        vegetables, 19
tortilla, 18
spareribs see pork
spatchcocked devilled
        poussins, 126
spicy fried dumplins, 215
spicy potatoes, 39
spinach: stir-fried chilli greens, 156
spring onions, sesame noodles
        with, 200
squid: tossed noodles with
        seafood, 192
stout punch, Caribbean cream, 253
sushi, 186
sweet and sour pork, 108
sweet and sour rice, 188
sweet and sour sauce, whole fish
        with, 80
sweetcorn: plantain soup with corn
        and chilli, 22
swordfish: spiced fish kebabs, 86
Szechuan spicy tofu, 134

tagine, lamb, 109
tamarind: stir-fried prawns with
        tamarind, 91
    tamarind soup with peanuts and
        vegetables, 19
tandoori chicken, 130
tequila: bloody Maria, 250
    margarita, 250
Tex-Mex baked potatoes with
        chilli, 101
Thai fried noodles, 199
toasts, tasty, 210
tofu (bean curd): curry fried
        noodles, 194
    Szechuan spicy tofu, 134
tomatoes: bloody Maria, 250
    kachumbali salad, 216
    Mexican-style rice, 191
    prawns in spicy tomato
        sauce, 86
    red snapper, Veracruz-style, 69
    sangrita, 248
    snapper, tomato and tamarind
        noodle soup, 32
    tomato and onion salad, 204

tomato noodles with fried
        egg, 194
    tomato salsa, 48
tortilla chips: desert nachos, 52
tortillas: beef enchiladas, 102
    black bean burritos, 139
    huevos rancheros, 52
    mixed tostadas, 44
    quesadillas, 44
    red enchiladas, 104
    tortilla soup, 18
tostadas, mixed, 44
trout, smoked see smoked trout
tuna: sushi, 186
turkey: mole poblano de
        Guajolote, 114
Turkish cold fish, 81

vegetables, 132-65
    marinated vegetables on
        skewers, 151
    mixed vegetable pickle, 209
    spicy vegetable soup, 21
    spicy vegetables with
        almonds, 164
    tamarind soup with peanuts and
        vegetables, 19
    vegetables in peanut and chilli
        sauce, 150
    see also individual types of
        vegetable
vegetarian fried noodles, 198
vermicelli: crispy fried rice
        vermicelli - mee krob, 197
vinegar chilli fish, 74
vinegared chilli cabbage, 148

walnuts: spiced date and walnut
        cake, 239
Welsh rabbit, 55
white beans: falafel, 40
wine: mulled wine, 247
    sangria, 248
wontons: seafood wontons with
        spicy dressing, 50

yogurt: spicy yogurt soup, 26
    yogurt chicken and rice, 168

zereshk, 188